10/10

# Advance praise for **Multicultural Intelligence**

David Morse **brings us up to date on the cultural shifts taking place in American society.** A must-read for anyone who is trying to understand these cultural shifts and what they mean for marketing.

SANFORD "SANDY" GROSS, *Executive Vice President, NovaMex*

**Morse's observations are eye opening** and sometimes provocative. Whether you agree with him or not, his book is a must read for anyone who hopes to succeed in marketing in an ever changing segmented America.

ROBERTO ORCI, *President, Acento*

*Multicultural Intelligence* **unlocks the historical, sociological, and contextual aspects of Multicultural Marketing**. This timely, comprehensive guide is a must-have for those seeking to more firmly embrace today's diverse population in a relevant manner.

CYNTHIA PERKINS-ROBERTS, *VP Multicultural Marketing and Business Development, Cabletelevision Advertising Bureau*

David Morse is making an important contribution in assembling the cultural diversity of our country in a coherent set and providing important rules for marketers to work with. I strongly recommend this book as a must read for those dealing with multicultural marketing and students of the subject. **I plan to make it required reading for my course** on Multicultural Marketing Communication.

FELIPE KORZENNY, PH.D., *Professor and Director, Center for Hispanic Marketing Communication Florida State University*

*Multicultural Intelligence* is **a refreshing, mind-expanding, provocative and arguably shocking trip down multicultural marketing lane**. Morse dares to take on topics of contention and multicultural taboos directly and passionately such that you really get it and you get it in such a way that you feel exposed and compelled to follow his code for multicultural marketing. If you thought you'd read all you needed to read on multicultural marketing, you're in for quite an eye-opener.

TERRY SOTO, *President, About Marketing Solutions Author of* Marketing to Hispanics: A Strategic Approach to Assessing and Planning Your Initiative

# Practical Books for Smart Marketers from PMP

Now you can equip all your sales and marketing people with **Multicultural Intelligence.** It will help them introduce new solutions to your existing customers and open the doors for new business development. You may also want to distribute the book to potential customers to help them understand the size and purchasing power of these market segments and the implications for their industry.

A customized edition, with "***Compliments of* Your Company Name"** on the cover is available with orders of 200 or more copies.

Call us toll-free at **888-787-8100** for quotes on quantity orders.

For more practical books for smart marketers, go to our website, **www.paramountbooks.com.**

# Multicultural Intelligence

**Eight Make-or-Break Rules
for Marketing to Race, Ethnicity,
and Sexual Orientation**

## DAVID R. MORSE

Paramount Market Publishing, Inc.

Paramount Market Publishing, Inc.
950 Danby Road, Suite 136
Ithaca, NY  14850
www.paramountbooks.com
Telephone: 607-275-8100; 888-787-8100    Facsimile: 607-275-8101

Publisher: James Madden
Editorial Director: Doris Walsh

42.45

This publication is designed to provide accurate and authoritative information in regard to the subject matter covered. It is sold with the understanding that the publisher is not engaged in rendering legal, accounting,
or other professional services. If legal advice or other expert assistance is
required, the services of a competent professional should be sought.

All trademarks are the property of their respective companies.

Cataloging in Publication Data available
ISBN 978-0-9801745-6-4 *hardcover*
ISBN 978-0-9801745-9-5 *paperback*

Dedicated to my parents:
Zee Morse and Myron "Mike" Morse

In loving memory of Ruth Morse

# Contents

# Acknowledgements

Writing this book has been a labor of love. It is the product of having listened to the hundreds of multicultural Americans who have shared with me their stories—in their homes, in focus groups, and over the telephone. It is also the result of all the fantastic people that I have met in my travels, particularly Japan and Mexico. To all those people, especially those that I neglect to mention below, thank you!

First, I would like to thank my fellow co-founders of New American Dimensions, Thomas Tseng, Julio Arreaga, Susana Sanchez, and Susanna Whitmore. Without their vision and hard work, the company would have remained a pipe dream.

My thanks go to Doris Walsh and Jim Madden of Paramount Market Publishing for taking on this book. I'd also like to thank my agent, Claudia Menza, for believing in it when no one else would.

I'd like to give my heartfelt thanks to Larry Buhl who was invaluable in helping me get a cluttered bunch of ideas down on paper. He also helped with the research. If ever there was a talented writer who understands the New Americans it is Larry.

Thank you to Jimmy Chee and Cynthia Simons for all their support. Also, I can't forget Jerame, Tommy Junior, and my sisters, Karen King and Laura Forest.

Thanks to Joan Wai for helping me with the initial phases of this project. The "eight rules" was largely her idea. I thank Antonio Lucio for his brilliant insights. The idea of using Multicultural Intelligence was largely his.

Thanks to the multicultural marketing experts who agreed to be interviewed for this book: Bill Imada, Carl Kravetz, Rochelle Newman-Carrasco, Cynthia Perkins-Roberts, Pepper Miller, Michael Wilke, Gonzalo Perez, Wes Combs, Howard Bragman, Manny Gonzalez, Beatriz Mallory, Giancarlo Pacheco, Chris Lehtonen, and Jaime Gamboa. Also, special thanks to Felipe Korzenny, Terry Soto, Roberto Orci, Bob Tzudiker, Jonathan Weiner and Leon Wynter. For so generously providing the data from Packaged Facts, a.k.a. MarketResearch.com, my thanks go to Tatjana Meerman and Don Montuori.

Finally, to two amazing teachers never to be forgotten, Steve Thomas and Myron Gold, thank you!

# Part I

## Meet the New Americans

# one

## Melting Pots, Multiculturalism, and Marketing to the New America

In 2004, Comedy Central's irreverent *South Park* series aired an episode titled, "Goobacks," a play on the anti-Mexican slur "wetbacks." Instead of a wave of immigration from a country to the south, the cartoon town of South Park must contend with an "invasion" by a time-traveler from the year 3040. We learn that his world (actually Earth) is overpopulated, and the one-way time travel portal will allow him to earn money his family will need more than a thousand years in the future. When he achieves success in shoveling snow for very low pay, more immigrants from the future arrive. A CNN newscast describes them as a "hairless, uniform mix of all races" with the same skin color—a light tan—and their language is also mixed from "all world languages." Working men in the town begin to react with rage. "THEY TOOK OUR JOBS!!" becomes a mantra of the working-class town's men throughout the episode, eventually morphing into a mangled and unintelligible chant of "Dey tuuk ur jerbs!" and devolving to, simply, "Derka DURRRR!" As more immigrants arrive, town residents begin to call them "goobacks," a pejorative term referring to the goo on their bodies, (a side effect of time-traveling, we're told).

Reluctantly, the town accommodates the immigrants, to a point where a future version of "English" is taught in school. Angered that the immigrants are taking their jobs, or "derka durrrr," the working class men hatch a plan to "become gay" in order to stop procreation, and therefore ensure that goobacks, and all future generations, will never exist.

Given the rapidity at which the demographics are changing, the imaginations of *South Park* writers may provide about as much help as the projections of demographers and sociologists when it comes to the future makeup of the United States. Maybe in a thousand years, or a hundred years, we really will be a severely overcrowded nation of barely employed tan-skin ethnic hybrids who speak guttural "world languages."

Peter Salins, an immigration scholar who is provost of the State Universities of New York, expressed a common frustration among those trying to figure out what we are to become: "I do not think that most Americans really understand the historic changes happening before their very eyes. What are we going to become? Who are we? How do the newcomers fit in—and how do the natives handle it—this is the great unknown."

As the scholars and writers weigh in on the question of what is to become of us, we marketers must, at minimum, try to understand the new America of today, and what each new wrinkle in the fabric of society means for products, our brands, our companies. If we get it right, if we are able to crack the code on complex issues like assimilation and ethnic identity, we stand to make a lot of money. If we miss it, we risk becoming as meaningless as the buggy manufacturers of yesteryear who failed to see the emergence of the internal combustion engine.


## Melting Pot or Salad Bowl?

Writing of the Germans in 1751 Pennsylvania, Benjamin Franklin asked why should the "boors be suffered to swarm into our settlements and by herding together establish their language and manners to the exclusion of ours? Why should Pennsylvania, founded by the English, become a colony of aliens, who will shortly be so numerous as to Germanize us instead of our Anglifying them?" In the 1850s, patrician Henry James wrote of the Boston Common: "No sound of English, in a single instance escaped their lips; the greater number spoke a rude form of Italian, the others some outland dialect unknown to me." Sound familiar?

In order to better grasp how to market to today's new immigrants in America, it's important to predict how they might integrate with the mainstream. In the early twentieth century, cities like New York and Chicago swelled with immigrant populations from Poland, Italy, and Germany. In 1910 Chicago, 70 percent of the people were either immigrants or children of immigrants. Woodrow Wilson described the new immigrants as "men out of the ranks where there was neither skill nor energy nor initiative of any quick intelligence" and "sordid and hapless elements." Yet they integrated.

> ⊃ *In order to better grasp how to market to today's new immigrants in America, it's important to predict how they might **integrate** with the mainstream.*

In his 1916 bestseller *The Passing of the Great Race*, Madison Grant blames "the agitation over slavery" for distracting Americans from forging a "national opposition to the intrusion of hordes of immigrants of inferior racial value." Sociologist Herbert J. Gans wrote that the mass migration of "swarthy Jews, 'black' Irish, and Italian 'guineas'" terrified the lighter-skinned native-born Americans, most of whom were of English and German stock.

It took a while for groups like the Irish, Italians, and Jews to find their way into the mainstream. In the 1930s, a generation after the largest wave of immigration in the country's history until now, the children of immigrants were still being vilified as foreigners. During the 1935 World Series, Cubs players and fans went out of control hurling anti-Semitic taunts at Hank Greenberg of the Detroit Tigers, causing umpire George Moriarty to stop the game. (An interesting side note, the baseball commissioner later fined Moriarty $250 for using profanity in demanding that Cubs players stop their bigoted remarks, but did not fine any Cubs players.)

The biggest immigrant group at the start of the 21st century is

Hispanics, (a term I will use interchangeably with Latinos). Millions of today's Hispanic immigrants cross the perilous Mexican-U.S. border with the intention of making money and one day returning home, a hope that is usually shattered when their U.S.-born children don't want to leave the country of their birth. One factor that many argue might preclude the assimilation of Latinos is the sheer magnitude of their immigration in the last 35 years. In the early twentieth century, about 85 percent of immigrants came from one continent, Europe, but they spoke a plethora of languages: Yiddish, Italian, Russian, Polish, German, Hungarian, and English. Over

> ➲ **Over half** of today's immigrants come from a single region, Latin America, and speak one language, Spanish

half of today's immigrants come from a single region, Latin America, and speak one language, Spanish. Of those immigrating from around the world between 2000 and 2006, over one-third came from a single country, Mexico.

In the early twentieth century, ethnic media helped maintain a sense of community, and hundreds of newspapers sprung up in urban areas throughout the Northeast and Midwest. In today's U.S. Hispanic market, one TV network, Univision, has reached behemoth status, on occasion trumping all other networks in English or Spanish. Univision's primetime *telenovelas* reach between 20 and 30 percent of Hispanic households, and into the 40th percentile for those households with their television sets on. Rather than fragmenting ethnic groups like the ethnic press of old, Univision has been a tremendous unifying force. And it has allowed advertisers unprecedented reach to sell products to Latinos around the country.

An important difference between then and now is the current atmosphere of tolerance for diversity in the United States, what some have called the "culture of multiculturalism." San Diego's city council stopped using the term "minority" and other pejorative connotations in official documents in 2001 in favor of more respectful ethnic labels. Today's young Hispanics hear Reggaetón music on mainstream radio stations with DJs who sprinkle their speech with

Spanglish. They are proud of their language and their culture. They are proud of the fact that non-Hispanics are eating their food and listening to their music. Like the immigrants of old, they are making an indelible mark on the mainstream.

Multiculturalism is a double-edged sword, however. On the one hand, it makes it okay for ethnic groups to maintain an identity that is distinct from the mainstream. At the same time, it makes it easier for those immigrants who choose to assimilate to do so.

Clearly there are differences between today's immigrants and those of earlier generations. However, many sociologists have concluded that the differences have been over-hyped and that the melting pot is as real today as it was in the past. In their book *Remaking the American Mainstream*, Richard Alba and Victor Nee argue that the process of assimilation works in much the same way as it always has. What is needed is a reformulation of assimilation; one that accounts not only for the fact that immigrants are changed by the mainstream, but also the reality that the mainstream is, and always has "evolved through incremental inclusion of ethnic and racial groups that formerly were excluded."

> ➲ *Many sociologists have concluded that the differences have been **over-hyped** and that the melting pot is as real today as it was in the past.*

As Alba and Nee point out, assimilation is a two-way street. Immigrants are transformed by America but America is also transformed, even redefined, by immigrants. Let us be reminded that it was not that long ago that pizza, bagels, and apple *strudel*—er, I mean *pie*—were considered foreign foods. And words like graffiti, ballerina, confetti, schmuck, and tuchus were non-comprehensible to most Americans.

Even if the term melting pot applied 100 years ago, it doesn't fit today. Demographers and social historians have adopted a new phrase, the "salad bowl," to describe a united nation of peoples who bump into each other and share the same space (and laws), but retain what makes them "special," and prefer not to blend in, at least not too much.

Now we have our first multicultural President, with a father from Kenya and a mother from Kansas, raised in Hawaii and in Indonesia, with an Asian sister, and who is astoundingly comfortable in his own skin. In his first press conference as President-elect, Barack Obama referred to himself as a "mutt," a self-effacing way of saying that he, like an increasing number of Americans, is the sum of many identities. Putting politics and party and ideology aside, Barack Obama is, at least demographically, much more like the future of the United States than its past.

Is it possible that the nation will fracture into many disconnected communities with no shared commonality or purpose—a salad bar, to extend the food metaphor to ridiculousness? Or will it become something between a salad bar and a salad bowl, a pluralistic society with some core values about capitalism and citizenship, but with minimal interaction among groups? No one can say for sure what our nation will be like fifty years down the road.

## The new multicultural marketing

Multicultural marketing is based on the idea that there are discrete cultures in America, ethnic or otherwise, that have distinct identities that separate them from the mainstream. It assumes that they have unique needs when it comes to the types of brands or products they buy and that they need to be communicated with differently in order to be persuaded to become customers. It is based on the premise that they do not respond to advertising the way the mainstream does, either because they do not speak English or because their culture and history are so different. The chapters in this book will examine what makes the major multicultural groups different from the mainstream and from each other, as well some ideas on how to avoid the most common pitfalls, like stereotyping or assuming that things don't change.

My company, New American Dimensions, conducts market

research for companies or organizations that want to target multicultural people. We call them the new Americans because our country is going through a demographic and cultural overhaul and more and more, they represent the people that we are most likely to live next door to, interact with at the supermarket, or marry. Or be.

If the words of the 19th-century philosopher Auguste Comte, "demography is destiny," still ring true, then it is the destiny of America to be a country of predominately brown people. The convergence of two forces, an aging white population and explosive immigration from Latin America and Asia, is leading to what many have called the "browning of America."

The statistics are impressive. The three biggest hyphenated segments, Hispanic-, Asian-, and African-Americans, make up over 30 percent of the U.S. population—40 percent if you look at just those under 18. Since younger Americans tend to be brown, it is expected that by about the year 2042, white non-Hispanics will drop to less than half the population. Barring any remarkable reversal of current trends, Hispanics will outnumber Anglos sometime in the early 22nd century.

> ➲ *It is expected that by about the year 2042, white non-Hispanics will drop to **less than half** the population.*

In economic terms, these demographic shifts reflect big changes in terms of who has and spends dollars. Multicultural consumers mean big money. In 2007, Hispanics, Asian Americans, and African Americans made up $2.2 trillion in purchasing power. Add openly gay and lesbian adults to the equation (and allowing for some double counting) and the total goes up to $2.9 trillion. That's larger than the gross domestic product (GDP) of every country in the world except China, Japan, India, and of course, the United States.

It's no wonder that both large and small organizations are hiring companies like mine to figure out what all this demographic upheaval means. The economic need to understand and ultimately reach multicultural consumers has spawned an industry of advertisers, strategists, media planners, newspapers, radio stations, television networks, and market researchers. Add to that the many multicultural marketing and diversity departments and the people who work in them and you've got a mega-infrastructure of business-people poised to capitalize on the New America. Welcome to the world of multicultural marketing.

The pioneers of multicultural marketing were the African-American advertising agencies that were created in the 1960s and 1970s, though it has been the immigration explosion since the 1970s that has led to multicultural marketing's precipitous rise. Many clients now feel that because they speak English, African Americans can be reached with mainstream advertising, despite cultural differences. It's a logical conclusion, though I believe, an erroneous one. For the last 25 years, the mantra of Hispanic and Asian American advertising agencies has been "in-language and in-culture messaging." For many of these consumers, in-language has come to mean English.

> *The state of multicultural marketing is in **flux** and possible jeopardy.*

The state of multicultural marketing is in flux and possible jeopardy. At the same time that African-American agencies are losing multicultural corporate budgets to Hispanic agencies, the Hispanic agencies face an even more formidable challenge: assimilation, or its more politically correct cousin, acculturation.

Since 1970, the growth of the Hispanic and Asian-American populations has been driven by immigration. But since then, there has been plenty of time for an entire U.S.-born generation to reach adulthood. In 2007, 85 percent of Hispanics and 76 percent of Asian Americans under the age of nineteen were born in the United States. There is one constant amidst all this change—U.S.-born children speak English. If not by the time they enter school, then certainly by the time they finish the first or second grade. And that means trouble for the zealots who staked their fortunes on equating multicultural marketing with marketing in a language other than English.

That is not good news, for example, to the Spanish-language

television networks and Hispanic advertising agencies that have had a lock on this business for the last 25 years. The reaction of each has fluctuated between denial, defensiveness, and dread at the suggestion that today's younger generation, the source of the Hispanic market's exponential growth, prefers English. Their reaction, however delusional, is not irrational. Should corporate America decide, as many did with African Americans, that they can reach English-speaking Hispanics with their mainstream advertising, the result would be devastating to the agencies—as long as they limit themselves to being "Spanish-language agencies" as many do.

The politics play out on multiple levels. A large swathe of advertising agencies—Hispanic, African American, Asian, general market or otherwise—are owned by large marketing conglomerates like Interpublic Group, WPP Group, or Omnicom Group. If a client switches Hispanic dollars to English, the conglomerate's Hispanic agency might lose that chunk of the business to its general market counterpart. And though it's all in the family, each agency is still responsible for delivering its own return on investment. I've seen the politics rage just as fiercely within the client's own organization. A company's multicultural-marketing department might control the budget for Hispanic marketing dollars in Spanish. Change to English, though, and the dollars move to the general marketing budget. Or they simply disappear. If Hispanics speak English, then they will be reached with a mainstream campaign. At least that's the argument.

The idea of marketing to Hispanics began only a few decades ago when a group of primarily Cuban immigrant pre-revolution advertising executives from Havana found an opportunity for non-English speakers who were not being reached by mainstream advertising. In those days, Hispanic immigration was relatively new, and there were thousands of Hispanics starving for Spanish-language advertising. So when this charismatic group started knocking on the doors of corporate America to sell them on Spanish-language advertising, it was an easy sale. And it's easy to see how the equating of Spanish-language advertising with marketing to Hispanics took hold and exploded with the exploding population.

But the population changed. The immigrants learned English. And more significantly, their children grew up in the United States. Some of them became advertising executives. In the 1990s, a new generation of Hispanics, young, increasingly affluent and comfortable with English, began to emerge (or at least become recognized). They realized that the party line that blindly defended Spanish-language advertising was short sighted. Clearly Hispanics speak both languages and to refuse to acknowledge this would be the kiss of death. Early in the new millennium, the battle lines were drawn between the old guard of Hispanic agencies together with Univision, and the new.

> *In Hispanic marketing circles, it has been **heresy** to say that Latinos prefer English.*

It's no surprise that in Hispanic marketing circles, it has been heresy to say that Latinos, U.S.-born or otherwise, prefer English. But things are changing. One organization, the New Generation Latino Consortium (NGLC), was founded with the stated purpose of "raising the marketing profile of a burgeoning yet underserved segment of the U.S. Hispanic population, known as New Generation Latinos." New Generation Latinos are the ones who prefer English; they are underserved because for too long, corporate America was under the spell of the no-English party line, so until very recently, all marketing directed at U.S. Hispanics was done in Spanish.

In the world of Hispanic marketing, many have ceased to demonize the seven-letter word "English." They realize that America lives up to its reputation for being the graveyard of all other languages. There is an even more sinister word, however, called "assimilation," defined by Alba and Nee as "the attenuation of distinctions based on ethnic origin." If assimilation does occur with today's ethnics, if ethnic distinctions go away, then multicultural marketing becomes extinct.

We should keep in mind when we are talking about assimilation that it is a phenomenon that applies to immigrant populations, and also to Native Americans, but only those that have emerged from reservations after generations of forced isolation. It does not apply to African Americans, who have lived nearly 400 years in what is now the United States, yet who were first enslaved, later segregated, nearly always oppressed. Because of the unnatural separation that occurred between blacks and whites, very distinct cultures emerged that continue to the present day.

Assimilation is an irrelevant term when it comes to African Americans, since it is doubtful given American history that African Americans will lose their racial or cultural distinctiveness any time soon, especially when taking into consideration that blacks have always been exposed to white culture. Rather, the contrary is occurring; more whites than ever are exposed to black culture.

In the case of African Americans, a more relevant term is integration, meaning the bringing together of two discrete cultures. Integration was the goal in the early days of the civil rights movement, and although legal barriers that kept whites and blacks apart have been removed, African Americans and whites continue to inhabit very separate worlds. It is for the future to decide how the immigration and assimilation of largely non-white populations will impact the historic American dichotomy of black and white.

## The long road to visibility

In their book, *Minorities and Media: Diversity and the End of Mass Communication*, (Sage Publications, 1985) Clint C. Wilson II and Felix Gutierrez wrote that advertisers in the U.S. had reflected minorities by "either ignoring them or, when they have been included in advertisements for the mass media audience, by processing and presenting them so as to make them palatable salespersons for the products being advertised." If people of color or gays appeared at all in commercials, they had to be presented in a way that would make people in the mainstream feel good about themselves, not threatened. But because an appearance was so rare, minorities were glad just to see themselves.

The earliest attempts by advertisers to show people of color in mainstream ads were, when seen through the eyes of the 21st century, shocking, consisting of exaggerated images of black slaves to sell products to white consumers. Marilyn Kern-Foxworth describes the portrayal of blacks in the 1940s and beyond in her amazing book, *Aunt Jemima, Uncle Ben and Rastus: Blacks in Advertising, Yesterday, Today and Tomorrow* (Greenwood Press, 1994): "The mouth was opened unusually wide and filled with large and/or carnivorous white teeth encased by exceptionally large, thick, ruby-red protruding lips. The eyes in these advertisements were most often seen bulging uncontrollably with ecstatic fright."

Ads featuring distorted images of blacks were popular through the 1940s, showing up in all the advertising vehicles of the times. It was common to find products bearing the brand name "nigger." There were "Nigger Head" brand canned fruits and vegetables, stove polish, tobacco, and oysters. Black children were often labeled as "pickaninnies" as in Pickaninny brand peanut butter. A typical portrayal of blacks was as African cannibals with a bone through the nose. Soap companies loved to use images of African Americans, claiming that their product was so powerful that it "had the power to cleanse the black skin of Negroes and miraculously change it to white."

> ➲ *Despite the prevalence of African-American images in mainstream advertising, advertisers mostly **ignored** them as consumers until the 1960s.*

Despite the prevalence of African-American images in mainstream advertising, albeit distorted, African Americans were mostly ignored as consumers by advertisers until the 1960s, an astounding fact given that as early as 1920 there were over 11 million African Americans in the United States.

A breakthrough came in 1963, when the *New York Herald Tribune* and other mainstream newspapers ran an ad for the New York Telephone Company featuring a well-dressed, non-stereotypical African-American man. It showed him walking to a phone booth with the caption "A man of action knows—you get action when you telephone." The portrayal was so extraordinary that it made news. The lead from one newspaper read: "What might well be the first use of a Negro model in general circulation publications was published in this and other metropolitan area newspapers yesterday by the New York Telephone Company." Four years later, one of the earliest examples of a multicultural marketing campaign came about. A series of posters in New York showed photographs of a smiling Asian American, African American, and Native American holding a sandwich with the tagline, "You don't have to be Jewish to love Levy's real Jewish Rye."

A *Time* magazine article from 1969, "The Black Man in the Grey Flannel Suit," about the rise of the black middle class and a burgeoning African American market would help precipitate a paradigm shift in the mind of corporate America. Large companies were not just seeing advertising to African Americans as a way to avoid censure from black activists and the government. They were finally beginning to see viable consumers with disposable income to spend on their products. Multicultural marketing was starting to take on wings.

As with early depictions of blacks, Hispanics were portrayed as cartoon-ish, if they were shown at all. Probably the best-known depiction of a Hispanic in an ad campaign was at times human and at times plantain—Chiquita Banana. Developed by the United Fruit Company, later renamed Chiquita, she first hit the radio waves in 1944, singing the now famous jingle, designed to teach Americans how to ripen bananas. She was at first depicted as a banana, but was soon brought to life by actresses and elevated to celebrity status, becoming a ubiquitous presence on commercials, television programs, and the movies. Her form has evolved over the years,

> ➲ As with early depictions of blacks, Hispanics were portrayed as **cartoon-ish**, if they were shown at all.

but a constant has been her fruit-laden hat, ruffled skirt, heels, thick Spanish accent, and rumba dancing. She was never the subject of any serious controversy, but the Carmen Miranda knock-off burned the image of the Latina spitfire firmly into the American consciousness.

An early use of a Latin character in advertising was on a 1940's avocado crate label for "Lazy Peon" brand California avocados. It depicts a man sleeping under a giant sombrero with a cactus and a small village in the background. A large foot and prominent big toe in sandals pokes out from under the sombrero. The whole picture equates the afternoon siesta with laziness.

Frito-Lay debuted the "Frito Bandito" in 1967, an animated sombrero-sporting, mustachioed Mexican who steals Fritos and sings "I am the Frito Bandito" to the tune of the Mexican classic "Cielito Lindo." Voiced with a thick, stereotypical Mexican accent by Mel Blanc, the ad contained the warning "Caution: He loves cronchy Frito corn chips so much he'll stop at nothing to get yours. What's more, he's cunning, clever—and sneaky!" The chip bandit was met with immediate protests by the Mexican Anti-Defamation Committee, which accused Frito-Lay of spreading the image of Mexicans as gun-toting thieves. The company responded by toning down the accent, erasing his gold tooth, and making the character less leering and more cheerful. That wasn't sufficient. Under the threat of a Hispanic boycott, a $610 million lawsuit ($100 for each Mexican American), and pressure from Congress, local television stations, and the press, Frito-Lay reluctantly retired the character in 1971.

The first representations of Asian Americans in the mid-1800s were depictions of Chinese men used to sell rat poison and laundry products to whites. Trade cards (a postcard-like precursor to the in-store sales flyer) for a "Rough On Rats Vermin Exterminator" service depict a "Chinaman" about to place a rat in his mouth, evoking the logic that since Asians eat rats, they make good exterminators. Laundry ads, like Lavine Soap, sported Chinese mascots because an endorsement from a Chinese laundry-man suggested the soap must be effective.

The Chinese laundry stereotype would prove to have remarkable longevity. In 1972, an ad for Calgon water softener featured a Caucasian woman picking up her sparklingly clean clothes at a Chinese laundry. When she asks the proprietor, Mr. Lee, how he does it, he sagely responds with a heavy accent that it is an "ancient Chinese secret." At that point his wife barges out of the backroom to announce, "We need more Calgon!" in unaccented American English. Though many criticized this ad for its stereotyping, others defended it as satirizing the stereotype.

Gays and lesbians, until fairly recently, were the least visible of all groups. The few times they were shown, it was in a way that only wise and aware gays would get it. According to Mike Wilke, founder of the Commercial Closet, gay reference in the early 1900s was a coded affair, with red ties symbolizing homosexuality in New York's gay underworld. A 1917 ad for Ivory soap, illustrated by gay artist J.C. Leyendecker, shows a group of handsome, naked young men in the shower, exchanging admiring glances. In a 1923 ad for Standard Plumbing fixtures, a man in a red bathrobe with the bathtub behind him gets a light for his cigarette from another man, apparently his "roommate." A print ad for Smirnoff vodka in a 1958 edition of *Esquire* magazine features two men in business suits with drinks in their hands. The tag line reads "Mixed or straight—it leaves you breathless!" It features two dandyish men, one with his arm behind the other, staring at him daintily.

> ➲ *Gays and lesbians, until fairly recently, were the **least** visible of all groups.*

In the last few years, there has been a growing interest in gays and lesbians. Their politically correct designation is the LGBT community, standing for lesbians, gays, bisexuals and transgender people, though the "B" and the "T" are often ignored in real-world marketing.

Programs like *Will and Grace* and *Queer as Folk* have helped make mainstream America comfortable with having gays in their homes, at least on television. The result is gay and lesbian multicultural marketing, and increasingly companies are looking at gays as another multicultural segment that deserves attention. Still, there are many pitfalls in targeting or not targeting LGBT consumers. Gays and radical religious right organizations have been in a constant and acrimonious tug of war: gays, on one hand, saying they deserve honest representation, and groups like the Mississippi-based American Family Association (AFA), threatening to punish companies for vocal support of such "degenerates." Groups like AFA are on the wrong side of history, however, and later I will explain how dancing with bigots is an increasingly losing battle for corporate America.

## Hitting the bull's eye

Multicultural marketing is a fluid thing. Those of us trying to hit the multicultural bull's eye are constantly confronted with a moving target. There are emerging multicultural markets that are getting more attention today—Eastern Europeans, Middle Easterners, and Africans, for example, and there will be more in the future. Today's multicultural groups may assimilate into the mainstream or change it so profoundly that they will no longer be considered part of multicultural marketing's sphere of interest. Just where that bull's eye is today, and where it will be in the future, are the two fundamental questions that the following chapters will endeavor to answer.

➲ *Scores of marketers don't understand what makes the new Americans **tick**.*

The problem is that there are scores of marketers who don't understand what makes the new Americans tick. Some are daunted by the prospect of marketing to an unfamiliar consumer group; others make stupid mistakes.

In my experience, some of the world's best marketers, the large global corporations, are whizzes at marketing around the planet. They source materials around the world, have plants and labor forces in multiple countries, sell their products via sophisticated distribution networks, and seamlessly adapt their marketing campaigns to the idiosyncrasies of local markets while remaining faithful to a core marketing strategy. Yet when it comes to marketing to gays, or African Americans, Hispanics, or Asian Americans, they go glassy-eyed. It is my sincere hope that after reading these pages, you will have a deeper, richer understanding of today's newest consumers, and what it means for your business. I'll look at what motivates multicultural consumers to faithfully buy certain products or brands and boycott others. I'll also give some insight into what makes the multicultural marketing industry tick and how big multicultural dollars mean that those in charge of spending don't always act in their own best interest or that of their clients. Ultimately, my goal is that you will be sufficiently armed with the rules of the new American to not fear it, but to support and nurture it. If you can make an honest buck in the process, even better.

# two

# Hispanic Americans

There have been Hispanics living in the present-day United States since the Spanish started roaming around Florida looking for the Fountain of Youth. But it was the 1980 Census that led some white Americans to wonder whether the country was "browning." The Census made headlines when it proclaimed that there were 14.6 million Hispanics living in the U.S., an increase of over 50 percent from 1970. By 1990, the number, largely driven by immigration, had increased to 22.4 million. Headlines were made again, big time, when the 2000 Census showed that there were 35.3 million, meaning that Hispanics had surpassed African Americans as the largest minority in the country. In 2008, that number was about 48 million. It is expected to grow to 133 million by 2050, at which time Hispanics will make up 30 percent of the population.

As a country, we are becoming more Hispanic. More specifically, we are becoming more Mexican. Nearly three-quarters of the Hispanic growth from 1970 to 2000 came from Mexicans alone, whose population in the United States increased fivefold, from 4.6 million to 23.4 million. Mexicans now make up about two-thirds of the U.S. Hispanic population. Despite doubling in numbers since 1970, Puerto Ricans and Cubans have lost share, now comprising only about 9 percent and 4 percent of Hispanics respectively. And despite substantial immigration from other Latin American countries, particularly El Salvador, the Dominican Republic, Colombia, and Peru, the "Other" slice of the Hispanic pie has shrunk, too, the result of the remarkable influx of Mexicans.

And it's not just immigration that's fueling the growth of the Hispanic population. According to the National Center for Health Statistics, from 2000 to 2007 the Hispanic population grew by 10.2 million—58.6 percent of this growth came from natural increase (births over deaths). The total U.S. population grew 20.2 million so Hispanics drove half of the total organic growth in the United States. And Hispanics, particularly Mexicans, are showing up in unconventional places, especially the Southeast. This trend has been going on for some time. Between 1990 and 2000, seven of the eight states experiencing the largest percentage growth in their Hispanic populations were in the Southeast: North Carolina (394 percent growth), Arkansas (337 percent), Georgia (300 percent), Tennessee (278 percent), South Carolina (211 percent), Alabama (208 percent), and Kentucky (173 percent); Nevada ranked fifth with growth of 217 percent. From 2000 to 2004, Hispanic populations grew by more than 40 percent in six metropolitan areas: Atlanta; Cape Coral, Florida; Charlotte; Indianapolis; Nashville; and Raleigh.

A 2008 USA Today article pointed out that the Hispanic baby boom is transforming rural America in big ways. The influx of Hispanics into parts of the country previously unaccustomed to immigration has intensified during this decade. From 2000 to 2005, 221

> ➲ The influx of Hispanics into parts of the country previously **unaccustomed** to immigration has intensified during this decade.

counties would not have grown except for Hispanics, according to research published by Kenneth M. Johnson at Loyola and Daniel T. Lichter at Cornell University. For declining counties, many in the Great Plains, the growth of young Hispanics may be the only way out of a population downward spiral.

The Latino influx has been so much, so fast, that we are bombarded with assertions that the United States is becoming a "Latino nation." One can hear these phrases from Hispanic marketers and in the Hispanic media from commentators like Jorge Ramos, anchorman for the leading Spanish-language television network Univision. In his book *The Latino Wave*, (Rayo, 2005), Ramos writes that Latinos are different than other Americans; that they are "rapidly integrating themselves into this society . . . but they will not completely and fully assimilate culturally." It's the party line among Hispanic marketers who regard statements that Hispanics might assimilate as heresy.

On this point, Hispanic marketers and media types have found strange bedfellows among disgruntled non-Hispanics like Patrick Buchanan, author of *The Death of the West* (St. Martin's Press, 2002). Buchanan complains, "Mexicans not only come from another culture, but millions are of another race. History and experience teach us that different races are far more difficult to assimilate. The 60 million Americans who claim German ancestry are fully assimilated, while millions from Africa and Asia are still not full participants in American society." Harvard professor Samuel P. Huntington agrees. In his article "The Hispanic Challenge" he writes that Hispanics, particularly Mexicans, are dividing America into "two peoples, two cultures, and two languages." He warned of Hispanics "rejecting the Anglo-Protestant values that built the American dream" and that the United States "ignores this challenge at its peril."

His warnings are wrong. Hispanics *will* assimilate, though they will do it on their own terms. They will not assimilate to a monolithic America that is Anglo-Saxon and white; rather, they will assimilate to a new and improved multicultural America, a multicolored version that revels in its own diversity. Like the immigrants of old, assimilation will take time. Today three-quarters of Hispanics are either immigrants or children of immigrants. Assimilation has never occurred as quickly as some would have us believe.

> ➲ *Hispanics* will ***assimilate***, *though they will do it on their own terms.*

Given the magnitude of immigration from Latin America, Hispanic immigration will look different than immigration from other times and other places. And the children of today's immigrants are proudly proclaiming their *Hispanidad*, their Hispanic-ness.

It wasn't always this way. In one of our research studies, I met a second-generation Mexican-American woman, Paula, who was stunningly beautiful with her cropped black hair and chiseled cheek-bones. She was a former Miss East Los Angeles and in the course of our interview, she read the acceptance speech she had given. "I accept this award as a Latina, a proud Latina, with deep respect for my community," she began. She went on to describe her process of self-acceptance. When she was younger, she was embarrassed to be Latin. Her mother would pick her up at school in a 1969 Chevy with Mexican music blaring from the radio. She would tell her mother to meet her around the corner. Today, Paula is proud of her mother who she says made great sacrifices for her family. Paula's own greatest pleasure, she says, is helping immigrant Hispanics adjust to life in Los Angeles. The Miss East Los Angeles pageant was her turning point, the moment when she could stand up publicly and acknowledge her roots.

Paula is typical of second- and third-generation Hispanics who grew up prior to the 1980s and 1990s. Many were told by their parents not to speak Spanish. Teachers often advised parents to speak only English in front of the children so they would not grow up speaking with Spanish accents. I've met many who were sent to the principal's office at school or punished at home for speaking Spanish. Raquel Welch, for instance, born and raised Raquel Tejada, talks openly about having to deny her Latin heritage. Her Bolivian father forbade Spanish at home and any discussion about the family's Latin heritage. As she told *Hispanic Magazine* in 2003, "I understood when I looked in the mirror that I was not Mary Jane Pringle. I was somebody different." She now says that her single goal in life is to speak Spanish more fluently.

This yearning by second-, third-, and even fourth-generation Americans for their roots is termed "retro-acculturation," a phrase popularized by the author of *Marketing to American Latinos*, (Paramount

Market Publishing, 2000) M. Isabel Valdés. Retro-acculturation is not unique to Hispanics. It encompasses many assimilated ethnics, such as Jews I have known, raised on English, who have decided to learn Yiddish, the language of their grandparents. Another example of retro-acculturation is the Lebanese-German-Hungarian American young man described in a 2004 *New York Times* article who makes a point of telling people about his Arab ancestry: "No one would know I was Arab American if I didn't bring it up. But it's a whole identity thing. I have different ethnicities in me, but this is the one that feels tangible. It's important to me, and it's something I want people to know and understand about me."

It may very well be that retro-acculturation will be irrelevant to Hispanics born in the United States in the last twenty years. It may be that for them and their children, there will be no lost Hispanic culture to retro-acculturate to. Unlike Raquel Tejada or Paula, young Hispanics are taught to embrace their culture and their Latin identity. In our experience, most are spoken to in Spanish by their parents who realize that learning English will happen inevitably once their kids start going to school. A New American Dimensions study, "Made in America," conducted among U.S.-born Hispanics found that most have mostly Hispanic friends—88 percent of second-generation and 66 percent of third-generation young Hispanics say that at least half of their friends are Hispanic. The same study asked respondents to name their top ten television programs in either language; among these, third-generation respondents included three Spanish-language television shows. This was despite the fact that these same respondents indicated very little Spanish language ability. Today's third-generation Hispanics may be losing their Spanish but they are certainly not becoming *gringos*.

It's easy to embrace a Hispanic identity because it's cool to be Hispanic today, a theme hammered home at every Hispanic marketing conference I have ever attended. The assertion nonetheless has a lot of validity. Top-forty types have embraced singers like Ricky

Martin, Cristina Aguilera, Enrique Iglesias, and Paulina Rubio, while artists like Daddy Yankee, Tego Calderon, and Don Omar appeal to Latinos with a more urban sensibility. Then there is George Lopez, the third Hispanic, following Desi Arnaz and Freddie Prinze to star in a mainstream television show. And, there is America Ferrera, 2007's Hispanic Woman of the Year, the Emmy-winning star of *Ugly Betty*, the U.S. version of the Colombian *telenovela*, *Yo Soy Betty La Fea*.

One of the latest surveys my company conducted demonstrates that the common notion that Hispanics do not want to integrate into U.S. society is false. The telephone survey of 1,000 Hispanic respondents aged 18 to 64, showed that, despite common perceptions to the contrary, three-quarters of Hispanic immigrants agreed that immigrants should learn English if they plan to stay in this country.

> ➲ *The common notion that Hispanics do not want to integrate into U.S. society is **false**.*

The survey also pointed out that there was big interest in the 2008 presidential election. Among Hispanic citizens, 83 percent expressed an intention of voting. Of the non-citizens, seven in ten stated that the recent debate about immigration has made them more interested in pursuing citizenship.

The bottom line is, Hispanic immigrants are learning English, raising their children as Hispanic Americans, and engaging in the political process.

## *Tu Ciudad* Magazine and the Boundaries of Assimilation

In June 2008, three years after its debut, *Tu Ciudad,* the glossy Los Angeles magazine aimed at affluent, assimilated Latinos shut down. *Tu Ciudad* magazine was hailed as a bold experiment in targeting an enormous but elusive demographic: children and grandchildren of immigrants who still feel connected to their cultural roots. As in any media failure, especially in the volatile publishing industry, questions arise about what led to the demise. Many are now asking whether a specialty magazine like this could be viable at all, and, more specifically, whether this audience wants a publication that caters to their "Latin side."

Even the man who developed the magazine's marketing and editorial plan has his doubts. "Frankly, this experience has left me with the feeling that the jury is still out," *Tu Ciudad* editorial director Angelo Figueroa told the *L.A. Times*. "I'm not convinced that highly assimilated, U.S.-born, English-dominant Hispanics necessarily want to be separated and marketed to as a group. They don't want a Latino *L.A. Times*; they just want to be included in the *L.A. Times*."

*Kansas City Star* editorial writer Mary Sanchez had some ideas about why the magazine failed. Her opinion: no, assimilated, well-educated, affluent Latinos do not want to be marketed to as a group:

Despite the fear in some quarters that new Latino immigrants are not assimilating, the fact is that most of us in the second generation and beyond—especially those of us in the middle class—are so highly assimilated that we're becoming difficult to capture as a niche market. I believe that cultural values and traits are passed on, but in subtle ways. A family might lose its Spanish language as the generations pass but still retain an attitude about respect and a way of speaking that is far less staccato and direct than standard American English. Most of my Latino friends can retell incidents where they realized they were acting from their family's culture rather than thinking from their American upbringing. One of the benefits of being "bicultural" is that you notice things others might not. You question assumptions and habits of both cultures. You choose who you're going to be. And guess what most of us are choosing. Clearly, we have a love of the U.S., but with a deep respect for the immigrant relatives who got us here.

## The new immigrants

Undocumented immigrants are a political hot potato. Given the demographic changes in the United States, the "browning of America," no political party can afford to bash, or look like they're bashing, Hispanics, illegal or not. Studies have shown that the party that woos Hispanics most effectively can control electoral politics as far as the eye can see. Strange, then, that Univision, the major Spanish-language TV network, had to cancel a Republican presidential debate because only one candidate out of nine was willing to come. The rest of the candidates walked a fine line between appeasing their socially conservative base with calls for a Fortress America, while making at least token gestures to reach out to Latinos. The irony was not lost on comedian Carlos Mencia, who wondered about the proposed fence that politicians claim will keep all the illegal aliens out. "I just have one question," he asks. "Who's going to build the fence?"

Marketers, too, find the issue of illegal immigrants, or to use the politically correct term, unauthorized migrants, to be a conundrum. In early 2007, Bank of America, then the country's second-largest bank, "quietly" began offering credit cards to "customers without Social Security numbers—typically illegal immigrants," *The Wall Street Journal* reported. The pilot program, aimed at Hispanics in Los Angeles and Orange counties in California, was an effort to tap a fast-growing market, the bank said. The reaction was unusually harsh, with critics saying things like, "Bank of America is an oxymoron" and insisting that the program effectively endorsed illegal immigration and could even foster identity theft, money laundering, and terrorism. It's not unusual for banks to offer checking accounts, and even mortgages, to undocumented immigrants, most of whom are Hispanic. Hundreds of financial institutions now accept a *matrícula consular* (consular registration), an official identification card issued by the Mexican government, or other foreign forms of identification. In fact, in 2004, Congress voted down a motion to prevent banks from accepting these IDs. But these immigrants generally haven't been able to get major credit cards like the one being offered by Bank of America, making it hard for them to develop a credit history and expand their purchasing power. B of A's program was, apparently, one step over the line for many critics.

After a coalition called for a boycott of the bank, Bank of America Chief Executive Kenneth Lewis defended the program in an op-ed in *The Wall Street Journal*. "Bank of America's roots date to San Francisco in 1904. That year, Amedeo Giannini, a son of Italian immigrants, founded the Bank of Italy to serve 'the little guys,' including immigrants that other banks wouldn't touch." While he pledged to continue the card program, which he said complies with the USA Patriot Act and other laws, he expressed regret at being caught in the "heated" national immigration debate, and that he was "feeling the passion."

Another company to find itself smack in the middle of the immigration debate was Western Union. When the shares of its parent company First Data Corporation fell in 2006, its Chairman and CEO Ric Duques attributed it to immigrants who were worried about wiring money because of anti-immigrant hostilities whipped up in the recent debate. "The last thing these people want is to find themselves the target of controversy or suspicion," he said. "Many immigrants feel backlash as a result of all the controversy, whether they are documented or not, and may now even be more fearful about law enforcement and a possibility of being deported."

Advocates of immigration reform didn't see Western Union as a victim. In September 2007, a network of over 150 immigrant organizations across the country launched a boycott of the company, accusing it of charging immigrants exorbitant fees and non-standard exchange rates when they sent money home. Within a week, the money transfer giant, which boasts 17 percent of the global remittance business, announced a five-year philanthropic initiative to help migrant families.

MTV, not a company to shun controversy, decided to take the immigration issue head-on by sponsoring an Immigration Forum on MTV Tr3s (pronounced *tres*, the Spanish word for three) which targets young Latinos. The forum brought together audiences in the studio and at home who submitted questions online, as well as pop culture and political figures like writer Gustavo Arellano who writes an irreverent syndicated column called *Ask a Mexican*, actress Betty Ortiz of the show *Ugly Betty*, rapper Malverde, and U.S. Representative Xavier Becerra of California. MTV Tr3s cites research that in a poll of young Latinos, 60 percent said immigration was the most important issue for young Hispanics and 76 percent said they would make their decision to support a candidate based on their immigration stance.

## Immigration by the Numbers

In 2006, the Pew Hispanic Center published a study called "Estimates of the Size and Characteristics of the Undocumented Population." Some findings:

- In 2005 there were approximately 11 million undocumented residents in the United States, meaning that about 30 percent of the foreign-born population was undocumented. Of the total undocumented, Mexicans numbered more than 6 million, accounting for 57 percent.

- About 80 to 85 percent of the migration from Mexico in recent years has been undocumented.

- The most rapid growth in the undocumented population has been in states that traditionally had small immigrant populations. To give some perspective, in 1990, 88 percent of the undocumented population lived in six states: California, New York, Texas, Illinois, Florida, and New Jersey. By 2004, only 61 percent of the undocumented lived in these states.

## Culture clash

In 2006, as the illegal immigration issue heated up in Congress and in the population, a series of protests throughout the country not only showed the immense support that illegal immigrants have, but also the contradictory attitudes that many immigrants have about the United States. The media made a big ruckus about the flag, specifically, the fact that there were so many Mexican and Central American flags flying at these rallies. At Montebello High School in California, a Mexican flag was raised on a flagpole above a United States flag flying in the distressed (or upside-down) position. In addition, California's Oceanside Unified School District banned flags and signs from its campuses after Mexican flag-wavers clashed with U.S. flag-wavers. Because of the controversy, organizers of the protests encouraged protesters to leave their Mexican flags at home. Cardinal Roger Mahoney asked Los Angeles protesters to not fly any flag other than the United States flag because that does not "help us get the legislation we need." Since the initial marches in spring of 2006, protests have featured fewer red, white, and green flags and more of the red, white, and blue variety.

Waving Old Glory might help calm *gringo* sensibilities, but it can't completely disguise the fact that most immigrants from Latin America have mixed feelings about the United States. They want their children to grow up in a land of affluence where they can aspire to heights impossible to achieve in Latin America, but they also worry that too much of American culture will rub off on their children.

Latin Americans have always had a love-hate relationship with the Anglo-Saxon country to the north. In the collective psyche of the region, perceptions of the United States have alternated between admiration and scorn. American influence, for better or for worse, has forever been a constant in Latin America. With the exception of Puerto Rico, which became a commonwealth of the United States in 1952, no country has been more closely coupled to the North American giant than Mexico. With the Treaty of Guadalupe Hidalgo that ended the Mexican-American War (known to Mexicans as the North American Invasion) in 1848, Mexico lost half of its land, including the states that are now California, Nevada, Arizona, Utah, New Mexico, Colorado, and Texas. It is no wonder that Mexicans have an expression that when "the United States sneezes, Mexico catches a cold." My favorite, a statement attributed to the Mexican writer Miguel Leon Portilla, "Poor Mexico. So far from God, so close to the United States."

But Mexico is just one among many countries that have felt the wrath of American gunboat diplomacy. At the end of the 19th century and the beginning of the 20th century, the United States carried on numerous military interventions in Latin America known as The Banana Wars. Between the end of the Spanish-American War and the beginning of the Depression, the United States sent troops to Latin American countries thirty-two times, all in the name of the Roosevelt Corollary to the Monroe Doctrine, in which Teddy Roosevelt proclaimed that the United States, as a "civilized nation," had the right to intervene throughout Latin America. Needless to say, the idea of an imperialistic, dangerous and warmongering United States has hardly gone away.

There are also cultural factors that contribute to the ambivalence of our neighbors to the south. In 1922, the Uruguayan writer José Enrique Rodó wrote an influential book Ariel, in which he criticized the awe with which so many Latin Americans of his time viewed the United States. He articulated a vision of the United States as being utilitarianism personified, materially wealthy but spiritually and morally devoid. He wrote of life in North America as being "the ceaseless seeking for well-being that has no object outside of itself."

Despite being vilified in the psyche of Latin America, *gringos* are also held in certain esteem. There is an expression in Mexico, *malinchismo*, which means a preference for things foreign, particularly things American. La *Malinche*, whose Spanish name was Doña Marina, was the native woman who served as mistress and translator to Cortés. Mexicans have an ambivalent and complex relationship with Doña Marina. On the one hand, by selling out her people, she is seen as the ultimate traitor. On the other hand, since she and Cortés are said to have had a son, she is the progenitor of the *mestizo* race, the mother of all Mexicans.

The majority of post-1964 immigrants come from Latin America, specifically Mexico, and most of them come here to work and raise a family in a safe and stable environment. When Latin Americans emigrate, their motivations are mostly economic; the United States is a desirable destination because of the opportunities it offers to improve one's lot. But they see *gringos* as being very different than themselves. To quote an expression that Hispanics use all the time, "*Gringos* live to work. Latinos work to live." Hard work is a fundamental Hispanic value. It is not an end itself.

> ⮑ To **quote** an expression that Hispanics use all the time, "Gringos live to work. Latinos work to live."

Take the case of Francisco, a Colombian immigrant in Miami, who has been living in the United States for about 17 years. He married in Colombia and his wife Gloria arrived five years later, pregnant with their first child. Francisco has done well for himself; a few years ago he opened his own mechanic shop. When asked to describe a typical Anglo household he has trouble; he doesn't really know any. However, he imagines a home where everyone is doing his or her own thing. "There's not the togetherness you find in a Hispanic family," he tells me. "We do everything for our children. *Gringos* are more concerned with themselves. They're more about material things then we are." I ask him why he thinks that is. "It's living in this country that makes them that way. In Colombia, a family always eats meals together. We talk. Neighbors know each other. In the United States, it's all about work. Hispanics here have to work two jobs to make ends meet. We work hard for our families, but at the same time, the family life suffers."

A question we often ask Hispanics during focus groups is, "What part of your culture are you most proud of?" The music is a common response, as much a reference to traditional Latin American music like salsa, merengue, bachata, and norteña, as to a love of dancing. Food comes up a lot, be it *carne asada* for Mexicans, *arroz con pollo* for Cubans, *mofongos* for Puerto Ricans, *mangú* for Dominicans, or *arepas* for Colombians and Venezuelans. But usually, the number one answer is "our values."

When asked what their values are, most responses relate to the centrality of family in Hispanic life and Hispanic identity. Some will talk about the idea of *respeto* (respect). Hispanics are taught from an early age to respect other people, especially their elders, whether

> ➲ Hispanics are taught from an early age to **respect** other people, especially their elders, whether parents, grandparents, or teachers.

parents, grandparents, or teachers. Others will talk about discipline and how their fathers taught them with an iron hand, but always with love. Still others will talk about *educación*, which often has little to do with anything scholastic and everything to do with having a proper upbringing. *Educación* is about being polite, well behaved, and sensitive to the needs of others. When Hispanic values are discussed, *los gringos* are often brought up as a point of contrast, as a group of people who at best, have different values; at worst, inferior values.

For Hispanics, family is central, a fact that can't be ignored in the realm of marketing. It is typical for an immigrant Hispanic mother to spend her entire day preparing fresh meals for her family. She'll go shopping in the morning once her kids have been packed off to school and her husband to work, and she'll buy everything she needs for that day. She makes several stops: she'll go to a *carnicería* (a butcher shop) for fresh meat, a *panadería* (a bakery) for fresh bread, and a local market for fresh produce. And though this behavior disappears, usually by the second generation, the underlying value, the idea that family is supreme gets passed on from one generation to the next.

Because of the importance of family and the persistence of traditional gender roles, advertising images that center on the family tend to be the most durable. Throughout Latin America, the mother is regarded as sacred, ever compassionate and nurturing. A woman learns from an early age that her role is to sacrifice everything for her family, a concept that has been called *marianismo*, the female counterpart of the much maligned word *machismo*. And though *machismo* has taken on a negative connotation today, it occupies a hallowed space in the ethos of Latinos: the long-suffering and hard working father, who cries on the inside in the face of a hostile world, and only lets his sadness show in song, such as in the *corridos* of Mexico.

> ⤳ *Our research shows that the focus of recent arrivals remains on Latin America and a **nostalgia** for the past.*

Our research shows that the focus of recent arrivals remains on Latin America and a nostalgia for the past. They are more interested in its sports, its popular culture, and its politics than they are in life in the United States. A majority plans to return home one day, a fact that is evidenced by the billions of dollars sent to Latin American countries every year in remittances. But things often don't work out as planned. Their kids are born in the United States, and are raised on hip-hop, trips to the shopping mall, and reruns of *The Cosby Show*. They grow up eating Lucky Charms cereal, Chuck E. Cheese pizza, and Baskin-Robbins ice cream. Their friends live here. Many feel like foreigners in the countries of their parents.

For their part, the parents feel more and more comfortable in their adopted country and Latin America seems increasingly remote. When they do go back, they find that things have changed, and that they are not quite as they left them. At some point they realize that they have also changed. They've gotten used to the comfort, conveniences, safety, and stability of life in the United States. Besides, they would never dream of leaving their kids and grandkids behind.

## Viva la Familia

Two market research firms, Packaged Facts and Silver Stork Research, teamed up to produce a report titled *The U.S. Hispanic Mom Market*. The report combines original quantitative and qualitative research, as well as secondary sources. Here's a condensed version of some of the insights:

1. Hispanic moms have the highest birth rates and the largest families. They are the youngest moms, and are the fastest growing mom segment.

2. The Hispanic mom takes pride in her role as mother. When given the choice between family and friends, or family and alone time, she'll pick family.

3. Retaining her heritage and passing it on is an important motivator. Though acculturation is evident in language and eating, ethnic culture and identity run strong.

4. Hispanic moms respond to positive images of motherhood and gravitate to information as to how they can do a better job.

5. The goal is a happy family, not wealth or individual success. She wants her kids to be given as much opportunity as any other American child.

6. She faces challenges such as discrimination, lack of acceptance of Spanish, and stereotyping. She also has to struggle with adapting to American culture without letting go of her own.

7. Her cultural influences come from two worlds—Hispanic and American. Successful marketers understand the marriage of these influencers and how best to incorporate them into their brands.

One factor not mentioned above is that for the Hispanic mom, keeping her family healthy is one of her primary motivations. However, what she considers to be healthy may not be the same thing that a typical Anglo American, or for that matter the scientific community, considers to be healthy. For instance, according to the *American Journal of Public Health*, Hispanic mothers tend to think that a chubby child is a happy and healthy child, which may be a contributing factor to high childhood obesity rates. According to their research, 14 percent of Hispanic infants take a bottle to bed, which experts say encourages overeating, compared with six percent of white children and four percent of African-American children.

> ⮑ *In the immigrant Hispanic view, anything natural is good while **artificial** is always bad.*

In our experience, in the immigrant Hispanic view, anything natural is good while artificial is always bad. It's what I call the "fried lard" phenomenon. A freshly prepared meal with freshly purchased ingredients made with mother's love, and fried with lard and loaded with salt is good. A frozen Healthy Choice dinner is bad; it's processed and therefore has got to be loaded with chemicals. I've heard many recent immigrants say that low fat milk is bad, especially for kids, since removing the fat must mean removing the vitamins. As a general rule, Hispanics, particularly immigrants, are more concerned about preservatives and other additives than about fat. From a marketing perspective, that means that educating Hispanics about nutrition might be an efficacious approach to get them to try healthy products that might not match their idea of healthy. It's also an opportunity for producers of junk food to get some brownie points for doing something good, by promoting healthy eating and a healthy lifestyle, given the heat that many of them are taking from government and other agencies in charge of promoting healthy lifestyles.

In their book *Hispanic Marketing: A Cultural Perspective*, (Elsevier 2005), Felipe and Betty Ann Korzenny identify some of the archetypes within Hispanic culture and how they impact the way that

Hispanics respond to marketing. For instance, Hispanics tend to possess a deeply ingrained parental guilt and a firm belief that it is the duty of parents to endure sacrifices for their children. So an ad campaign that emphasizes rewarding oneself first or enjoying time away from the kids can backfire. Beliefs in *curanderos* or healers and a faith in folk remedies present challenges to those in the health care or pharmaceutical industry. Negative associations with money and the idea that people without money are "poor but proud" can make financial services a tough sell if you emphasize the profits to be made. Hispanic immigrants tend to pay cash for everything; "credit is a vice" is a common expression, a belief that Bank of America and other financial institutions are hoping to turn around. In terms of saving for the future, for Hispanics, their children are their retirement plan. They expect to be taken care of the way children have taken care of parents in their family for generations.

Hispanic culture is based on hierarchy and a respect for rank, and the family is no exception. Older people are treated with reverence, especially one's parents. Nursing homes are for *los gringos*. Compared with the United States, status tends to be conferred based on one's position rather than accomplishments. Women are doted on by men, even in the office, in a way that modern Americans would find to be bordering on sexual harassment.

➲ *Hispanic **culture** is based on hierarchy and a respect for rank, and the family is no exception.*

One of the most comprehensive studies of Latinos is the Pew Hispanic Center's "2002 National Study of Hispanics." The study found that Hispanic immigrants had significantly stronger "family oriented values and conservative attitudes toward gender roles than those born in the United States." With acculturation, these values start to change, and become more like mainstream American values. In the study, Hispanic immigrants were much more likely than their U.S. born counterparts to strongly agree that "it is better for children to live in their parents' home until they get married" (77 percent vs. 33 percent), that "elderly parents should live with their adult children" (52 percent vs. 33 percent), that "relatives are more important than friends (81 percent vs. 64 percent), and that "in general the husband should have the final say in family matters" (22 percent vs. 13 percent).

Not that the U.S.-born Hispanics stop thinking like Hispanics. The study concludes that Hispanics born in the United States, even those "whose families have been in the United States for multiple generations," are still more likely than non-Hispanics to emphasize the importance of family. As Hispanics acculturate, they will retain certain aspects of their culture and eliminate others. As the Pew study shows, values change but not completely. Other things, like shopping behavior, change drastically. When it comes to food, the Hispanic diet evolves. Typically, when Hispanics first immigrate, most meals are traditional. With acculturation, they begin to incorporate more elements of American food into their daily repertoires. Still, the overall importance of traditional food never completely goes away.

## Shopping

A 2005 study co-sponsored by ADVO, FMI, and New American Dimensions focused on the shopping habits of English- and Spanish-speaking Hispanics in the top ten markets across the U.S. Here are some of the highlights.

1. Hispanics spend significantly more money on food than non-Hispanics—almost $130 a week, versus $91 a week—and they shop for groceries more often. They also spend a much higher percentage of their total food dollars at non-supermarkets such as butcher shops, bakeries, bodegas, convenience stores, drug stores, specialty shops and warehouses—over 30 percent versus 18 percent for all U.S. shoppers.

2. As Hispanics acculturate, they buy more of their food at main-

stream supermarkets. In half of the markets studied, the supermarket of choice for less acculturated Hispanics was a store with a Hispanic format. By contrast, more acculturated Hispanics preferred more mainline supermarkets in nine out of the ten markets studied. Still, they continue to shop at traditional venues.

3. Less acculturated Hispanics are looking for a Spanish shopping experience. Nearly 90 percent of less acculturated Hispanics said that having Spanish-speaking employees was a very important factor in deciding where to shop, double the number of acculturated Hispanics. Looking at the data a little differently, nearly half of acculturated Hispanics rated the presence of Spanish-speaking employees as being very important; they might not need them, but it is a strong indication that they, as Hispanics, are recognized.

---

## Lies, damned lies, and the Hispanic advertising industry

The theme for the Association of Hispanic Advertising Agencies' (AHAA) biannual conference in the fall of 2007 was "Is Hispanic Advertising Dead?" It was, of course, a rhetorical question, since if the answer were in the affirmative, no one would have attended the conference in the first place. The dramatic theme of the conference reflects the turmoil in the organization and a growing need to question what the role of Hispanic advertising agencies should be as Hispanic consumers become increasingly acculturated.

If you check out the academic and public policy research, evidence of assimilation, or at least linguistic assimilation, is conclusive. Study after study shows that by the third generation, a majority of Hispanics become English-speaking monolinguals. Here are some examples:

- A study published in 2005 by the University of Albany's Mumford Center concluded that even though Hispanics are retaining their Spanish longer than the earlier European immigrant groups and the Asian immigrants of today, English monolingualism is the predominate pattern by the third generation. Based on an analysis of U.S. Census data, the study found that 72 percent of third-generation Hispanic children spoke only English at home.

- In the largest longitudinal study of its kind, sociologists Alejandro Portes and Rubén Rumbaut demonstrated what writer Gregory Rodriguez has called "the overwhelming allure of English." Over 2,000 second-generation teens in San Diego and Miami were interviewed twice: in 1992 as freshmen and in 1996 as seniors. As freshmen, about half the Mexicans and three-quarters of the other Hispanics preferred to speak English. Four years later, three-quarters of the Mexicans preferred English, while the number for the other Hispanics had risen well into the 90th percentile.

- The Pew Hispanic Center's 2002 survey found that 78 percent of third-generation Hispanic adults were English Dominant, the remaining 22 percent being bilingual. Among the second generation, 47 percent were bilingual, 46 percent were English dominant and only 7 percent were Spanish dominant.

Despite the evidence, many establishment Hispanic marketers try to spin their own research to show the primacy of Spanish for generations of U.S. born Hispanics. In the words of Benjamin Disraeli: "There are three kinds of lies: lies, damned lies, and statistics." A lot of the research I've seen coming from Hispanic marketers lies somewhere along that spectrum.

Take the notorious "Spanish vs. English Advertising Effectiveness" study of 1994, conducted by Peter Roslow. This oft-touted body of research was for years the darling of traditional Hispanic marketers. It claimed to prove the persuasiveness of Spanish-language advertising and continues to be cited as evidence that marketing to Hispanics should be done in Spanish. Interestingly, according to the publication *Hispanic Market Weekly*, the studies were funded by Univision, a company that stands to lose millions of dollars in advertising revenue if advertisers decide that they can reach acculturated Hispanics on English-language media.

Roslow's methodology seems to have been designed to mislead. He asked respondents to rate ads that were in English and Spanish, yet he included respondents who spoke no English, excluding those who spoke no Spanish. So his sample was already biased toward people with a Spanish preference. Furthermore, most of the Spanish and English ads used in the experiment were different; the only thing they had in common was that they were for the same brand. It's no wonder that respondents preferred the Spanish ads—they were designed for Hispanic consumers. The English ads were not.

In 2000, Roslow repeated his study, this time with teens. He again concluded that English advertising is less persuasive than Spanish, which he attributes to the fact that many teens are foreign born. He's partly right; a quarter of these teens are foreign born. But I've never seen any research besides his that concludes that Hispanic teens prefer Spanish.

It is not just in linguistics that stereotyping is rampant—it's cultural too. The stereotyping of Latinos in the Spanish-language media was brought to the forefront in a PBS documentary by Phillip Rodriguez, first aired in September 2007 and titled *Brown is the New Green: George Lopez and the American Dream*. In it, Lopez and Rodriguez explored how corporate America and Hispanic marketers packaged up a stereotypical image of Latinos in order to reap corporate profits. In the words of Rodriguez, "The Latino image is stage-managed by marketers and media companies" while Latinos are "caught in a netherworld." He added, "Mainstream media have largely ignored them, while Span-

> ➲ *It is not just in linguistics that **stereotyping** is rampant—it's cultural, too.*

ish-language networks and Hispanic ad companies have served up an exoticized image that has no basis in contemporary American reality." The film argued that rather than helping Hispanics move into the mainstream, the agenda of Hispanic marketers has been to promote the image of a separate Hispanic America with "folkloric commercials to cheesy Latin American soap operas to butt-shakin' bicultural music videos."

> *The real challenge facing Hispanic ad agencies today is the younger **generation**, for whom the old way of doing business may not continue to work.*

The real challenge facing Hispanic ad agencies today—and Spanish-language media—is the younger generation, for whom the old way of doing business may not continue to work. A 2006 study commissioned by Spanish-language Telemundo's youth-oriented and bilingual network, Mun2 (pronounced mun-DOSE), found that 79 percent of 14-to-34-year-old Hispanics couldn't identify a brand that accurately portrays young Latinos. They just can't relate to the stereotypes of themselves that they see on Spanish-language television. According to Sharon Lee, founder of Look-Look, the company that conducted the study, "Over and over, we heard young Latinos complain that they didn't want to be defined by looks—darker hair, eyes or skin—and that they were tired of being asked to prove they were Hispanic by speaking Spanish."

Why are advertisers missing this important market? Our qualitative research has shown that U.S.-born Hispanics do watch Spanish-language TV because it offers them the opportunity to see Hispanic culture portrayed on the air, with all its passion and steaminess. It's not that they don't speak English. It's just that when they watch English-language television, they don't see themselves. The problem for many marketers that want to advertise in English, especially on TV, is that there has been no large-scale outlet yet to reach English-speaking Hispanics. The bilingual and English-language Hispanic networks are still relatively small, and until now haven't delivered the audience numbers advertisers would get with a campaign on a mainstream network. Univision can deliver the numbers but only in Spanish—the network does not accept commercials in English.

At the forefront of Hispanic marketing today is a new wave of media operating with the understanding that acculturation and a preference for English do not necessarily mean a diminishment of Latino identity. One of the originals is *Latina* magazine, founded by Christy Haubegger in 1996 after she successfully pitched the idea of a magazine for Hispanic women to Ed Lewis, Chairman and CEO of Essence Communications (the publisher of *Essence Magazine*). *Latina's* format uses Spanglish and is full of ads like the one that reads "Looking great doesn't have to cost a *fortuna*."

English and Spanglish networks aimed at Latinos are taking off on television as well. SíTV, whose tagline is "Speak English, Live Latin," was founded in 1997 by writer, producer, and standup comedian Jeff Valdez, with the stated mission of delivering "authentic and original programming in English while portraying Latinos in non-stereotypical roles." Los Angeles–based mun2, owned by NBC Universal and the sibling of Spanish-language network Telemundo, features bilingual programming aimed at an 18-to-34-year-old, second- and third-generation audiences. Other networks targeting younger, U.S. born Latinos include Los Angeles-based LATV with its bilingual, Spanglish-speaking music format and AIM Tell-A-Vision, a New York-based syndicator of English programs like *American Latino* TV and *LatiNation*.

Catering to the young Hispanic American market has already paid off for the cable network Nickelodeon. *Dora the Explorer* is a popular animated children's series aimed at the pre-school set. It features Dora Marquez,

➲ *Catering to the young Hispanic American market has already paid off for **Nickelodeon**.*

a seven-year-old bilingual Latina. Though the program is aimed at a mainstream audience, it has special significance for young Latino children who are able to see themselves through the eyes of the young Dora. Speaking in English, she teaches viewers Spanish words during her half-hour adventures.

MTV Tr3s has made amazing inroads among an older (but still youthful) demographic. When it was launched in September, 2006, MTV President Christina Norman said that it "will change the way young Latinos are served in this country." Because their target demographic is English-dominant, yet comfortable with both languages, the founders of MTV Tr3s decided to program in English and Spanish. If an artist on a show wants to speak Spanish, he speaks Spanish. At its launch, Gonzalo Perez, formerly the senior director of consumer insights for MTV Tr3s said that the target audience lives a bicultural reality, and easily steps back and forth between Anglo and Hispanic cultures. "We don't talk about language as an issue," Perez explained. "It's more organic. The network is more about cultural identity, which isn't necessarily about language."

The battle over the future of the Spanish language in Hispanic marketing has been a hot and bitter one. MTV took a stand with MTV Tr3s and it appears to be paying off for them. In my opinion, what they did right was realize that it was a battle that was driven by concerns more political and commercial than linguistic and cultural.

## Hispanic Marketing, Version 2.0

Carl Kravetz, who founded the Hispanic advertising agency Cruz/Kravetz IDEAS, has been struggling with how to push Hispanic marketers to meet the needs of consumers while avoiding the inevitable advertising turf wars of English versus Spanish. In 2006, when he began his term as president of the Association of Hispanic Advertising Agencies (AHAA), Kravetz unveiled the "Latino Identity Project," which consisted of 400 academic studies of Hispanic identity. The purpose was to pursue a discussion about why Latinos behave the way they do. "What we found was that spirituality, family, interpersonal relations, and to a lesser extent, national origin, play important roles in the decision making of the Hispanic consumer," Kravetz explained. In other words, Latino identity went a lot deeper than language. But Univision wasn't buying it, despite a lengthy period of discussions with the broadcasting giant in order to move forward the idea of Latin culture, not language, as a driving force. "Our goal is to make them understand that ad agencies are in a different business than broadcasters, and that we are not a threat to them."

Kravetz points out that Hispanic advertising and marketing is in a period of transition. "We are in Hispanic Marketing 2.0. There are no established rules yet and we are in the midst of experimentation. It's important to remember that the change won't happen overnight. It took 30 years for the idea of Spanish-language marketing to fully take hold. But you can't sell a stereotype anymore. There is no one way to reach 45 to 50 million Hispanic consumers, so we better start finding ways of dividing it up."

Manuel Gonzalez, who manages the Hispanic practice at abecé/ Hill Holiday Hispanic, a large, general-market advertising agency, has been at the forefront of advocating that advertising agencies recognize that Spanish is not always the way to reach Hispanic consumers. "In the last five years there has been a blurring of the lines between general market and ethnic media. That echoes the ability of Hispanics themselves to migrate easily between English and Spanish worlds. Companies must be aware of cultural nuances, but they shouldn't develop strategies for those nuances in a silo." Gonzalez agrees with Kravetz that successful ad agencies are finally grasping the complexity and diversity of lifestyles of the Hispanic segment. But most, he insists, are playing catch up. Once they catch up, agencies face another uphill battle convincing their clients that Hispanic market does not mean "Spanish-language market."

Today's generation of young Latinos embrace American culture and its idioms like never before, and, partly because of their sheer numbers, youth are re-defining what it means to be Latino today. Many in the anti-immigration movement incorrectly characterize all Hispanics as rejecters of English who resist the impulse to

> *The majority of second-
> and third-generation
> Latinos, rather than
> resisting U.S. media
> and language,*
> **unequivocally**
> *embrace it.*

become American. The majority of second- and third-generation Latinos, rather than resisting U.S. media and language, unequivocally embrace it. But they also do so by exhibiting their own unique cultural imprint, experiences, and identities. These attitudes and behaviors confound the myth that a majority of Latinos' media consumption habits are defined by a single-language preference. Although they may participate in the popular culture of two different languages, there is a clear preference for English—and Spanglish.

Political analyst and journalist Michael Barone concluded that it took white ethnic immigrants about 100 years to fully assimilate into the American mainstream. So if we date the age of the new Hispanic immigration to have started around 1975, and if the past is any measure of the future, we can expect Hispanic marketing to be around until at least 2075. By that time, our grandkids will be horrified by the inundation of America by another ethnic group, as scholars study the assimilation of early 21st century Hispanics into the mainstream. And for certain, the multicultural marketing pundits will declare that the new immigrants are different, that they are special, and that they are nothing like the earlier immigrants, including Hispanics, who came to America in search of their dreams. And they will be partly right.

# three

■ ■ ■ ■ ■ ■ ■ ■ ■ ■ ■ ■ ■ ■ ■ ■ ■ ■ ■ ■ ■ ■ ■ ■ ■ ■ ■ ■ ■ ■ ■ ■ ■ ■ ■ ■ ■ ■ ■ ■ ■

# African Americans

In January, 2008, Senator Barack Obama had a ten- to twelve-point lead over Senator Hillary Clinton in the New Hampshire presidential primary polls, yet he lost that primary by three points. For weeks the pundits debated whether the polling error was due to the so-called "Bradley Effect," named for former Los Angeles mayor Tom Bradley, an African-American politician whose lead in polls dried up at the ballot box, and the "Wilder Effect," whose namesake, another African-American man who saw his ten point advantage vanish as Virginians cast their ballots for governor in 1989.

Had Americans lied to pollsters about their willingness to vote for an African-American candidate? Did deep-seated, perhaps barely conscious racism take hold of them behind closed doors and convince them to vote for a white candidate over a black one? Or were there other explanations? Had Clinton, as some proclaimed, simply done a better job of getting out the women's vote in the wee hours of the campaign?

Race was always an underlying factor in the 2008 election, ever since Obama emerged as a black candidate with a real shot at the office. Throughout the primary, Democratic contenders downplayed his race. However, when an incendiary video of Obama's former pastor, the Rev. Jeremiah Wright, emerged, Obama took race head on, in a speech in Philadelphia in March, 2008. It was partly a CYA speech (Reverend Wright did not speak for me when he said "God damn America"), and partly an opportunity to open up the discussion about a subject that was about as discussed as the emperor's new clothes. Obama could have left it at that. Instead he used the media frenzy to open a discussion about race. The speech received multi-million hits on YouTube, making it one of the most watched videos of all time on that forum.

The speech put out the media firestorm, for a while, anyway, until Wright himself emerged in person and gave a press conference that embarrassed Obama. After that, Obama denounced Wright completely. But the discussion about race was not over. Did Rev. Wright, who excoriated white America for its oppression, speak for all African Americans, or all black churches? Or were his angry sermons a throwback to an earlier time, when African Americans didn't take today's rights for granted (a world in which Barack Obama, who grew up in Hawaii and largely away from the Civil Rights struggle, didn't live)?

The presidential election of 2008 truly was a watershed election in terms of race and gender: By February, the Democratic field of contenders was narrowed down to a black man (Obama) and a woman (Clinton). Obama prevailed in a hard-fought primary to become the first presidential nominee of color in U.S. history, and, finally, the first black president (to be accurate, its first mulatto president). The ripple effect of this race will be felt for many years as it continues to change not only whites' perception of blacks, but more importantly, blacks' perception of themselves.

Although Obama is technically half-black, the mainstream media and most voters consider him to be African American. Throughout the race there were subtle, and not-so-subtle questions about what kinds of white voters would vote for a black (or half-black) candidate. From the moment he was declared the winner in the first Democratic caucus—Iowa, one of the most Caucasian states in the union—pundits of all kinds were scratching their heads. How could a black man be winning over white people, and working class white people (who, as the suggestion goes, are supposed to be racist)? But win them over he did.

Still, there was a persistent notion that racism would sink Obama's chances in the general election. There was plenty of anecdotal evidence for this view. In September 2008 National Public Radio ran a series of conversations with voters in York, Pennsylvania, about race and its role in the 2008 presidential election. Steve Inskeep and Michele Norris met with a group of 13 voters—a mix of whites, blacks, and Latinos—several times to get their attitudes about race and how it affected their voting decision. York was also home to a race riot in 1969.

What came through from interviewees were some pretty well ingrained attitudes about race. Several said they believed America was not ready for a black president. One woman, a retired factory worker, said she couldn't trust Obama because she was sure he was a Muslim and nobody could convince her he wasn't. The interviews exposed a racial divide, reported NPR: "But after the voters spent more time debating that divide—again, all the voters of color behind Obama, and almost all the white voters behind John McCain—most came to a reluctant conclusion. Does race matter on a subconscious level? There was a series of exasperated utterances of "yes."

Then there was a September 2008 AP-Yahoo poll that suggested Obama's race would cost him 2.5 percentage points—more than the final difference between the candidates in 2004. More than a third of all white Democrats and independents—voters without whom Obama couldn't win the White House—agreed with at least one negative adjective about blacks, according to the survey, and they were significantly less likely to vote for Obama than those who didn't have such views. And statistical models derived from the poll suggested that the election would be a blowout for Obama, instead of a likely squeaker, if there were no white racial prejudice. "There are a lot fewer bigots than there were 50 years ago, but that doesn't mean there's only a few bigots," said Stanford political scientist Paul Sniderman who helped analyze the survey.

In the end, the election wasn't a squeaker or a landslide, but a decisive 365 electoral vote victory for Obama, who picked off states Democrats hadn't carried in more than 30 years, such as North Carolina and Virginia. But Virginia and North Carolina may be special cases as far as the South is concerned, and outside of relatively affluent and educated areas—mostly along the Atlantic coast—racism in the South did cost Obama votes.

The *New York Times* map of county-by-county voting pattern shifts showed that many counties in West Virginia, Arkansas, Oklahoma, Alabama, Louisiana, and the Appalachian sections of Kentucky and Tennessee voted more heavily Republican in 2008 than in 2004. Obama won in only 44 counties in the Appalachian belt of 410 counties that runs from New York to Mississippi. Many of those counties, according to the *Times*, are rural and isolated, and have "been less exposed to the diversity, educational achievement and economic progress experienced by more prosperous areas." A day after the historic election, the *New York Times* stated, flat out, that Obama's race appears to have been the critical deciding factor in pushing a large number of white Southerners away from the Democrats:

> "Here in Alabama, where Mr. McCain won 60.4 percent of the vote in his best Southern showing, he had the support of nearly 9 in 10 whites, according to exit polls, a figure comparable to other Southern states. Alabama analysts pointed to the persistence of traditional white Southern attitudes on race as the deciding factor in Mr. McCain's strong margin. Mr. Obama won in Jefferson County, which includes the city of Birmingham, and in the Black Belt, but he made few inroads elsewhere.
>
> "Race continues to play a major role in the state," said Glenn Feldman, a historian at the University of Alabama,

Birmingham. "Alabama, unfortunately, continues to remain shackled to the bonds of yesterday." David Bositis, senior political analyst at the Joint Center for Political and Economic Studies, pointed out that the 18 percent share of whites that voted for Senator John Kerry in 2004 was almost cut in half for Mr. Obama. "There's no other explanation than race," he said.

In the final analysis, Obama won the popular vote by six points, 52 percent to 46 percent, exactly where many of the final polls showed the race going. According to the exit poll data, Obama won 43 percent of the white vote, a slight improvement on John Kerry's 41 percent in 2004. Obama won 95 percent of the black vote, which made up 13 percent of the electorate, compared to Kerry's 88 percent of black voters, who made up 11 percent of the total vote in 2004. Obama won Hispanics by 66 percent to 32 percent, compared with Kerry's 53 percent to 44 percent showing.

## Two Americas

The history of America's first black President has yet to be written. However, that Obama was elected by a majority of Americans is monumental. So many of my generation grew up with the certainty that we would never live to see a black president, the way the pre-Kennedy generation never dreamed a Catholic president would be possible.

The election raises fundamental questions about the mindset of Americans, both black and white. Has the mindset and rhetoric of the Civil Rights movement, and its modern day advocates, the Jesse Jacksons and Al Sharptons, become irrelevant? Have the stereotypes of white America been confined to the coffins of past generations? What does it mean to be black in America today? And most relevant to this book, in the America of Barack Obama, how can companies most effectively make a connection with African Americans? Has the need to be acknowledged become less pressing, or has it become more of an imperative than ever?

## What's in a Name?

In 2001 the *Gallup Newswire* found that nearly half of African Americans say they had no preferences between the terms "black" or "African American." There is a slight difference, however. When asked what term they preferred being called on a personal level, the term "black" won out over "African American" by a slight majority. However, when asked what they preferred the race to be called, the majority of blacks preferred the term "African American." A 2008 study by Radio One and Yankelovich reported that black Americans are equally divided on how they are referenced: 44 percent prefer African-American and 42 percent prefer black.

---

When once asked to define jazz, Louis Armstrong replied: "Man, if you don't know, don't mess with it." The same could be said about race. For earlier generations, race, like religion or politics, was not seen as fair game for polite dinner conversation. At least not among whites. Things have always been different for African Americans, who at least in the company of each other, have always tended to talk freely about race and racism. Blacks have had their group identity forged in the fires of slavery and Jim Crow, a couple of words whites are not sure it's even okay to mention. Race has been an integral part of the daily lives of most African Americans and its derivative, racism, is experienced in myriad forms: unemployment, incarceration, crime, getting turned down for loans, and missed taxicabs. For blacks, race has always been a subject that demands to be addressed.

A 2000 study conducted by the *New York Times* highlighted in the book, *How Race is Lived in America*, found that blacks were four times more likely than whites to say they thought blacks were treated less fairly, and three times less likely to agree that too much has been made of the problems facing black people. Differences were so profound they led the authors to conclude that on issues of race and inequality, blacks and whites "seemed to be living on different planets." Similarly, in Yankelovich's 2005 MONITOR Multicultural Marketing Study, 56 percent of blacks compared with 17 percent of whites agreed with the statement that, "In the past I have felt a security guard/store clerk was watching me more closely than other shoppers." Eighty-eight percent of African Americans said that discrimination is still a part of most African-Americans' day-to-day lives. And it doesn't just occur in the United States, as many of us learned in 2005 when Oprah Winfrey was not allowed to enter a Hermès shop in Paris.

But that was all before the 2008 elections. A Rasmussen poll taken two days after Barack Obama was elected President, showed a dramatic improvement in the perception of America. The percentage of black voters in that telephone poll who viewed American society as fair and decent jumped 18 points to 42 percent. Just

➲ *A Rasmussen poll taken two days after Barack Obama was elected President, showed a dramatic improvement in the **perception** of America.*

a month earlier, only 24 percent of black voters viewed American society as fair and decent. Another post-election Rasmussen survey found that 70 percent of African-American voters think relations between blacks and whites are getting better, up from 37 percent in September. By comparison, 73 percent of whites said, post-election, that race relations are better now, while 68 percent thought so in September.

In 1968, the Kerner Commission warned of America becoming two nations, one black and one white, separate and unequal. Clearly, after Obama, the rift is narrowing. However, it is hard to dispute that on key quality-of-life indices, the findings of the Kerner Commission still hold true. For African Americans, it is difficult to sing "Kumbaya" about the state of things in America when the median household income for blacks is $30,000 per year compared to $50,000 for whites. It is impossible to relegate racial discrimination to the confines of history when study after study affirms that African Americans are more likely to be victims of racial profiling by police, denied housing or incarcerated more often than whites for the same crimes. It is too much of a stretch to accept that whites are colorblind, when ignoring racial disparities only serves to maintain a structurally unequal society.

Blacks are significantly worse off than whites according to the National Urban League's annual report "The State of Black America." In 2008, according to the study's Equality Index, the status of African Americans in America is 73 percent of their white counterparts, a composite score based on rankings on six attributes.

**Economics: Score: 57 percent.** Fewer than 50 percent of black families own their own homes, versus 76 percent of whites. Blacks are three times more likely to get high priced loans, 55 percent versus 17 percent.

**Health: Score: 78 percent.** On average blacks are twice as likely to die from disease, accident, and homicide as whites. Life expectancy is 72 years for blacks, 78 years for whites.

**Education: Score: 78 percent.** Teachers with fewer than 3 years' experience teach in minority schools at twice the rate as in white schools.

**Social Justice: Score: 66 percent.** Blacks, who are incarcerated at seven times the rate of whites, are more likely to get convicted and incarcerated longer for the same crimes as whites.

**Civic Engagement: Score: 104 percent.** Largely reflective of the higher percentage of blacks in the military.

In health matters, for African-American men especially, the mortality gap is clear. The average life span for black men today is 6.2 years less than for white men. Homicide is the leading cause of death for black men aged 15 to 34, followed by unintentional injuries. (For white men in those ages, unintentional injuries are the leading cause of death, followed by suicide.) Once they become sick, blacks are more likely to suffer worse consequences and die sooner of the disease. The death rate from heart disease is about 30 percent higher among blacks than whites, according to the Centers for Disease Control and Prevention. The prevalence of diabetes is about 70 percent higher, and diabetes significantly increases the risk of heart disease. Beyond these bleak statistics lies a new theory, that racism itself is detrimental to health. According to a *Los Angeles Times* article:

> "We have always thought of race-based discrimination as producing a kind of attitude," says Vickie Mays, psychologist and director of the UCLA Center on Research, Education, Training and Strategic Communication on Minority Health Disparities. "Now we think we have sufficient information to say that it's more than just affecting your attitude. A person experiences it, has a response, and the response brings about a physiological reaction." The reaction contributes to a chain of biological events known as the stress response, which can put people at higher risk of cardiovascular disease, diabetes and infectious disease, says Namdi Barnes, a researcher with the UCLA Center. For many African Americans, these responses may occur so frequently that they eventually result in a breakdown of the physiological system.

Race and poverty are not the same. But there is a correlation. Seeing the predominately black population outside the Superdome in New Orleans, screaming for help and dying, literally, in front of television cameras,

➲ *Race and poverty are not the same. But there is a* **correlation**.

was shocking for white America; it stripped away the lie that we are really one America, and forced them and the media to face, at least for a few days, the uncomfortable effects of economic disparities, which correlate highly with race. For many blacks in the Ninth Ward, the reaction was fear, anger, and, later, a too-familiar feeling of resignation. In a promotional TV appearance for the NBC telethon to raise money for Katrina victims, black singer Kanye West went off his prepared teleprompter speech and shouted, "George Bush doesn't care about black people!" NBC was quick to issue an apology for his off-the-cuff remarks. But Kayne West's comments were more than one man's opinion, and certainly numerous African Americans felt that neither does the rest of white America.

Blacks and whites, as a rule, still don't live in the same neighborhoods. Dissimilarity indices, a measure of integration, reveal a residentially segregated nation, despite improvements from a decade past. As an example, in cities like New York, Chicago, Milwaukee and Detroit, 80 percent of African Americans would need to relocate in order for the cities' black and white populations to be evenly distributed. A majority of blacks and whites go to separate schools, worship at different churches, watch and play different sports, and consume different media. Though intermarriage rates are soaring between whites, Hispanics, and Asian Americans, they remain remarkably low with blacks. We even think differently, as we learned during the O. J. Simpson trial (the first one) that split Americans along racial lines with a huge majority of whites convinced of his guilt, and African Americans certain he was a victim. Even when presented with the same set of facts and circumstances, African Americans and whites can reach very different conclusions.

In their book, By the Color of Our Skin: The Illusion of Integration and the Reality of Race, (Dutton, 1999), authors Leonard Steinhorn and Barbara Diggs-Brown wrote, "The reality is that blacks and whites today are not much closer to living together, learning together, relaxing together, praying together, and playing together than they were a generation ago. The law might bring people together, but in matters of choice, blacks and whites are simply going their own ways."

And let's not ignore the fact that when it comes to using the English language, we speak it differently. In 2004, DiversityInc magazine published an article on linguistic profiling. According to the article, linguistic profiling is a way of "determining characteristics such as socioeconomic status from the way a person uses language." It's something we all do.

Professor Dennis Preston of Michigan State University has studied how language is used to discriminate, particularly by violating fair housing laws. Preston said in housing discrimination, linguistic profiling occurs when an African-American, Latino or Middle-Eastern sounding prospective renter calls the landlord or representative of the property, and is told the property is no longer available just because of the way certain words have been pronounced. "In linguistic profiling, we know that it happens . . . we know that people are treated differently based on people's perception of them over the telephone," says Nancy Haynes, executive director of the Fair Housing Center of Greater Grand Rapids, Michigan. "If someone believes you're African American, whether or not you're African American, you are going to be treated differently." African Americans are more likely to be discriminated against than Latinos with an accent, the research found. "The discrimination rate against Spanish-accented speakers is a little less than the discrimination against African Americans. Apparently, African Americans are seen by some landlords as less desirable renters than Latin Americans," said Preston.

Even names can be the source of discrimination. Economics professor Marianne Bertrand of the University of Chicago found in a recent study that employers apparently do discriminate based on whether names on résumés sound "white" or "black"—even when other credentials are equal. They found that résumés with white-sounding names generated twice as many callbacks as those with conspicuously "black" names like Jamal. For many African Americans, the possibility that names could hold their children back does affect their decisions.

➲ *Résumés with white-sounding names generated twice as many callbacks as those with **conspicuously** "black" names*

## Racism and Tipping

A 2008 study published in the *Yale Law Journal* found extreme racial discrimination in taxicab tipping. The study included data on more than 1,000 taxicab rides in New Haven, Connecticut, and found that white drivers were tipped 61 percent more than black drivers. Black drivers also were 80 percent more likely to be stiffed than white drivers. When making a fast decision about a tip, passengers of all races tend to round up for white drivers and down for black drivers.

To make sure quality of service wasn't influencing tipping, the authors conducted some "secret auditing" of cab drivers. Their testers rated quality of service higher for black drivers (4.5 out of 5 total points) than white drivers (3.3 out of 5 total points).

---

Despite obvious disparities between the races, in my experience with whites, and I have a lot, a majority see themselves as color-blind and resent that blacks insist on making race such an issue. Pointing to civil rights legislation, the rarity of overt expressions of racism in society, and the fact they may not harbor any personal malice towards blacks, whites are content to believe in the idea of American egalitarianism and equal opportunity. Embracing the individualism embedded in the American ethos, they point to successful, integrated blacks and wonder why others haven't done the same.

For African Americans, on the other hand, race and racial disparities are issues that demand to be addressed, and history is something to be embraced, not ignored. African Americans take pride in their history. It is no coincidence that the month that the media devotes so much time to African Americans is Black History Month. And to understand how to effectively market to African Americans in the present and future, an examination of the past is required.

## History matters

We have inherited the legacy of black and white from our forebear-
ers, and though biologically irrelevant, it has managed to survive
well beyond the Civil Rights era. The "One Drop" rule, the absurd
doctrine that one drop of black blood made you black, a doctrine
developed to enslave or segregate the offspring of black and white
unions, continues to influence how multiracial people see themselves and are seen by others.

The boundaries were drawn on the basis not of biology—geno-
type and phenotype—but of descent. For purposes of the laws of
nine southern and border states in the early part of the 20th century,
a "Negro" was defined as someone with a single Negro great-grand-
parent; in three other southern states, a Negro great-great-grand-
parent would suffice. That is, a person with 15 white ancestors four
generations back and a single Negro ancestor at the same remove
was reckoned a Negro in the eyes of the law.

Race is a social construct. It has been constructed
in different ways in different times and places. In 1870,
the U.S. Bureau of the Census divided up the American

> ⮑ *Race is a **social**
> construct.*

population into five racial groups: white, colored (blacks), colored
(Mulattoes), Chinese, and Indian. In 1950, the census categories
reflected a different social understanding: white, black, and other.
By 1980, the census categories reflected the ethnic blossoming of
the prior two decades: white, black, Hispanic, Japanese, Chinese,
Filipino, Korean, Vietnamese, American Indian, Asian Indian, Hawaiian, Guamanian, Samoan, Eskimo, Aleut, and Other.

How future generations of America will relate to race is uncer-
tain. Hispanics are now the nation's largest minority, a group for
whom the dichotomy of black and white just doesn't fit, especially
when considering the racial mixing or *mestizaje* that has occurred in
Latin America over the centuries. In the 2000 Census, four in ten
Hispanics indicated a racial categorization of "SOR," Some Other

Race. This group will inevitably challenge our current racial boundaries.

## Who is Black?

Are Africans living in the United States African Americans? In the 1990s in the United States, the number of blacks with recent roots in sub-Saharan Africa nearly tripled, and the number of blacks with origins in the Caribbean grew by more than 60 percent. Things got heated after Barack Obama's speech at the Democratic National Convention in 2004. Alan Keyes, who ran against Obama for his seat in the U.S. Senate, said on *This Week with George Stephanolpolous,* "Barack Obama claims an African-American heritage. He and I have the same race—that is, physical characteristics. We are not from the same heritage. My ancestors toiled in slavery in this country. My consciousness, who I am as a person, has been shaped by my struggle, deeply emotional and deeply painful, with the reality of that heritage."

According to the *New York Times,* the article in which the above quotation appears, many African Americans feel that black immigrants are laying claim to the fruits of the civil rights movement, without bearing the burden of a history rooted in slavery. Several studies suggest that black immigrants and their children are already achieving at higher levels than native-born blacks. A study based on 2000 census data conducted by John R. Logan and Glenn Deane at SUNY–Albany found that African immigrants typically had more education and higher median incomes than did native-born blacks.

Sociologists say foreign-born blacks from majority-black countries are less psychologically handicapped by the stigma of race and, they often encounter less discrimination.

## Black and white TV

James Baldwin wrote, "The country's image of the Negro, which hasn't very much to do with the Negro, has never failed to reflect with a kind of frightening accuracy the state of the mind of the country." Nowhere has the country's schizophrenic relationship with race been more telling than in the movies and on television. And though the image of blacks has improved over the years, their depiction was best described in the title of a book by Donald Bogle: *Toms, Coons, Mulattoes, Mammies and Bucks,* (Continuum International Publishing Group, 2003).

The depiction to have the most longevity in the nation's consciousness was the minstrel show. It was created in the 1830s by white actor Thomas Dartmouth Rice, who imitated the song and dance of a slave boy that he had reputedly seen perform on a street corner. The format, which would remain the most popular form of American entertainment until supplanted by vaudeville eighty years later, consisted of a troupe of white men in black face, and lots of singing, banjo and tambourine playing, rapid-fire jokes, gags, and comedy skits. Ironically, minstrel shows excluded black actors from performances.

With the dawn of motion pictures, African Americans would continue to be portrayed by white actors. Many of the earliest portrayals of blacks were as sinister, evil, and vice-ridden, in films such as *The Wooing and Wedding of a Coon* (1905), *The Masher* (1907) and *The Nigger* (1915). D.W. Griffith's depiction of blacks in *Birth of a Nation* in 1916 is the most notorious example.

By the 1930s, it would be the harmless, lazy, but loyal, happy-go-lucky image of the "coon" that would become the most prevalent as portrayed by actors like Stepin Fetchit, and the "mammie," best personified by Hattie McDaniel in her Oscar-winning performance in *Gone with the Wind.* Following World War II and into the fifties, there was a shift in how African Americans were portrayed, initiated by black soldiers returning home from the front to the segregated country they called home, and fueled by the Civil Rights movement, which served to raise the consciousness of the mainstream which until now had been content to be blissfully unaware of or indifferent to the disparity between how African Americans were portrayed and reality.

When television took off in the late 1940s and early 1950s, it reached back to the earlier stereotypical images of the pre-war days for its images of African Americans. In 1950, three television shows debuted which featured African Americans in the role of domestic servants—Beulah, The Jack Benny Show, and The Stu Erwin Show. In 1951, the first program with an all-black cast, Amos 'n Andy debuted, a shift from the white actors that had appeared in the radio program. Amos 'n Andy was cancelled two years later, after protests from the NAACP for portraying African Americans as "inferior, lazy, dumb, and dishonest." Despite the stereotypes, many African Americans watched these shows, and the appearance of an African American on television was enough to trigger phone calls alerting friends and relatives to tune in. Stereotypical or not, blacks had been excluded from everywhere but the fringe of American popular culture, and many marveled at seeing images of themselves on the air.

In the 1960s, African Americans appeared more on television and were seen as idealized characters. Bill Cosby's erudite portrayal of Scottie in I Spy (1965–68) marked the first appearance of an African American in a non-stereotypical leading role. Soon there were others: Linc Hayes in The Mod Squad (1968–73) and Pete Dixon in Room 222 (1969–74). In 1968, Diahann Carroll became the first African-American woman to star in her own comedy series, portraying a widow, mother and nurse in the series Julia (1968–71). By the end of the decade, All in the Family's Edith Bunker, when asked how she felt about black people, replied: "Well you sure gotta hand it to 'em. I mean, two years ago they was nothing but servants and janitors. Now they're teachers and doctors and lawyers. They've sure come a long way on TV."

The 1970s would mark the beginning of blacks being portrayed as regular working class people. Significantly, these characters had their own lives, apart from whites. *Sanford and Son* (1972–77), *Good Times* (1974–79), *That's My Mama* (1974–75), *The Jeffersons* (1975–85), and *What's Happening!!* (1976–79) all featured characters "full of jivin', jammin', streetwise style stuff that is the worst kind of stereotyping," as one black critic wrote. Stereotyped, perhaps, but the shows projected authenticity, a quality that had always been missing from the world of blacks on television. Realism would peak with two television specials, *The Autobiography of Miss Jane Pitman* (1974) and *Roots* (1977) that would shock America with vivid, human portrayals of slavery and black oppression.

In the 1980s, *The Cosby Show* (1984–92), based on a sophisticated upper-middle-class African-American family, would change the dialog forever about the portrayal of "blackness" on television. The program's appeal was in part due to its positive representation of African Americans. It wasn't above reproach, however. Many blacks criticized it for creating a new stereotype—the well-to-do African American.

Research commissioned by Bill and Camille Cosby and presented in the book *Enlightened Racism: The Cosby Show, Audiences, and the Myth of the American Dream* (Westview Press, 1992) found that the program's success was due to allowing both blacks and whites entry into a deceptive world where African Americans are successful and prosperous, a misleading picture of what life is really like. According to the authors, "The problem with this response is that it accepts the assumption that, on television, a positive image is a prosperous image." Any representation that was less than exemplary became unacceptable.

When it came to racial authenticity in the eighties, maybe America wasn't quite ready. *Frank's Place* (1987–88), a comedy-drama produced by Tim Reid, tackled serious subject matter, but was cancelled in its first season. Wrote Henry Louis Gates, "*Frank's Place* was the closest thing to the reality I experienced growing up and the reality that I experience now as a person of color in American society that I have encountered on television. I don't think that the average white American is prepared to encounter the full complexity of that reality. They want to encounter fictions of that reality which are palatable to them."

➲ *With the multitude of broadcast and cable networks on the air, blacks and whites are tuning in to **different** programs.*

In the pre-cable days, for better or for worse, African Americans and whites watched the same shows. There simply were no alternatives available. Because whites represented the larger audience, programming was directed at their sensibilities. Today, with the multitude of broadcast and cable networks on the air, blacks and whites are tuning in to different programs. The overall trend, at least on cable, is toward greater segmentation. Most of BET's acquired shows like *The Parkers*, *Girlfriends*, and *Soul Food* are not big winners with white audiences, and the newer and smaller networks, TV One and the Gospel Music Channel have even less cross-over appeal.

## Advertising

One of the earliest and most systematic studies to look at the portrayal of African Americans in the media was conducted by UCLA Professor Harold H. Kassarjian in a paper called "The Negro and American Advertising, 1945–1965." Kassarjian studied about 150,000 pages of magazines published during three years—1946, 1956, and 1965—and found big changes in how blacks were portrayed in the ads.

In 1946, about eight in ten of the black models he found were depicted in servile jobs: "maid, waiter, slave, field hand, personal servant, the Aunt Jemima, or the Uncle Tom." Only one ad portrayed an African American in a professional occupation. In 1956, only half of the ads portrayed blacks in servile positions, while over a third depicted them as sports heroes or entertainers. By 1965, the number of ads that depicted black athletes or entertainers had climbed to 60 percent, while the number of actors portrayed in servile jobs dropped to 13 percent. Significantly, the percentage found in professional and managerial type jobs rose from nearly nothing to 9 percent.

Kassarjian's study revealed a U-shaped distribution in the number of ads featuring blacks over the twenty-year period—the number of blacks dropped significantly from 1946 to 1956 and went up again in 1965. His explanation was that in 1946, few were threatened by the depiction of blacks in servile roles, so advertisers gravitated to these images. By 1956, the Civil Rights movement heated up, and the Uncle Tom images of old had become unacceptable. But depicting blacks as anything but servants or entertainers was still not attainable. So advertisers took the easy way out; they stopped using blacks in ads. In 1965, it became unacceptable not to use blacks, so advertisers did, though now apparently in a more positive manner.

## Marketing through the filter of black experience

Perhaps more than any other group, African Americans are acutely sensitive to how they are portrayed in the media, and given history, it's not surprising. According to Pepper Miller and Herb Kemp in their seminal book *What's Black About It?* African Americans run their experience through a filter, a way of perceiving the world as a result of past experience with slavery, post slavery and discrimination:

"The Filter is the nucleus of the black experience and black culture. . . . It has predisposed many African Americans to become overly sensitive about feeling stereotyped and not feeling valued, respected, included, and welcomed. It also explains why many African Americans want to be seen as a heterogeneous rather than homogeneous group, to desire real inclusion, to see more and see differently when it comes to marketing communications, to rely upon word-of-mouth, to use general market media, but to embrace black media. . . . As a result, many African Americans care about how they are represented, and how white Americans perceive them."

> ⮞ *Blacks, especially black men, have suffered **disproportionate** stereotyping for a longer period of time.*

So how do blacks want to be perceived? First, and most important, *they do not want to be stereotyped*. This goes for all cultural groups, but blacks, especially black men, have suffered disproportionate stereotyping for a longer period of time. Of course, we've come a long way from such images. But that still doesn't mean blacks are depicted in the ways they want to be seen. There are images of African Americans created for white people by white people and there are images of African Americans created for African Americans. And there's a big difference. Our research shows that African Americans like to see themselves portrayed in all their diversity.

Related to this is the intense desire to be shown as "normal." Not normal in the sense of mediocre, and certainly not normal in the sense of white. Normalcy refers to a portrayal of African Americans as regular people, with jobs and families, and the same aspirations as the rest of Americans. It is the antithesis of all those years of being portrayed as abnormal. It means an accurate portrayal of African-American life as it is lived today by African Americans, without the need to sanitize or "white wash" it. It is important to point out that rappers and sports heroes, while admired by many, are not normal. Miller and Kemp write:

"We have observed that the impact of the Filter may cause many African Americans to feel they are excluded from particular opportunities and their desire for inclusion is heightened. When those same black respondents were asked which advertising messages grabbed their attention, nearly all agreed that ads depicting an all-black cast spoke best to them. They further qualified their answers by saying that situations that speak directly to them should be non-stereotypical, positively reflect who they are, and connect them to the African-American culture."

In 2007, my company conducted a series of interviews with African-American men in a venue that has always been an important one in the community—the barbershop. We wanted to get their thoughts and perspectives on media and marketing with an honesty that we rarely obtain in controlled focus group environments, especially among African-American men, who are often the most skeptical toward traditional research methods. Among the key themes and thoughts expressed by our respondents:

- **Acknowledge us. Represent us. Respect us.** One man commented, "Black people are so hungry to be respected and to be considered in the decisions of what's said and marketed to us . . . we've become passionate about the stuff that relates to us." Another participant told us that he always looks for black representation in commercials, but never sees it and is offended by that.

- **Show us as we are. Portray the rich spectrum of African Americans and our experiences. Avoid the worn clichés and stereotypes.** One participant plainly told marketers to "respect African Americans by showing all representations of us. We have diversity. Don't just show a slice of who we are. Show all of who we are."

- **Be authentic. Get to know us. Show you understand us.** "We know junk when we see it," said one man. "We know when you just put something out there and say, 'Well, we did do a commercial using you guys.'"

This research, and other research we have done for clients, demonstrates that targeted efforts are still important in the African-American market. In the words of one respondent:

> "At first, we were satisfied just to see our faces on TV, even if they were in black face or whatever. Then we got excited about Uncle Toms. Then the Jeffersons. Black people were so excited to finally see Cosby, to see a black husband and wife who were a doctor and a lawyer. Because that's what we have in our community."

## Racism, advertising and the myth of mainstream marketing

> ➲ *African-American buying power is projected to reach $1 trillion by 2010.*

African-American buying power is projected to reach $1 trillion by 2010. Still, too many marketers don't seem to get, or want to get, this segment. Or, if they used to get it, they don't anymore, as evidenced by the dwindling dollars that make their way toward African-American marketing.

When the racial climate heated up in the late sixties, the pressure to include African Americans in advertising was coming from all directions: civil rights activists, the government, the press, and consumers themselves. In a 1969 *New York Times* article titled "For Advertising, Signs of Change," the author wrote that with governmental pressure, companies were smartening up to "the need not only to hire the disadvantaged but also to feature Negro and Puerto Rican talent in their advertising." The March 1970 issue of *Ebony* magazine contained an ad with the headline "Why Johnny Can't

Read Your Ads." The article stated, "Johnny, you see, has trouble identifying with . . . all-American types. They may be all-American in your neighborhood, but not in Johnny's. So Johnny doesn't get past the pictures to the words. He knows they're not meant for him." The clamor to represent people of color in advertising was getting louder. For the first time, the fear of outraged black consumers began to outweigh the risk of a white backlash.

Today's African-American advertising agencies face increased competition from general-market agencies that have successfully convinced advertisers that they can deliver the same services. Additionally, the fast growing Hispanic market is attracting the lion's share of "multicultural" marketing budgets, further threatening the viability of black agencies. In 2004, *Black Enterprise* magazine noted, "As focus on the ethnic market increased, African-American-owned ad agencies continued to compete with general-market rivals for a controlling stake in the urban market. Last year, in an increasing trend, some black-owned agencies formed strategic partnerships with general-market shops to target brass ring accounts."

Marketers still need to better understand what moves African American consumers. Without fully appreciating how they consume media, and, more importantly, the Filter through which they see their

> ➲ *Marketers still need to better **understand** what moves African American consumers.*

experience, a marketer's efforts will, at best, fall flat. Said Eugene Morris, head of E. Morris Communications, a Chicago-based company that specializes in targeting African Americans: "Marketers assume that their message reaches African Americans. But reaching them is not selling them. African-American agencies develop culturally relevant messages." He goes on to point out the widely divergent media habits between blacks and the general market. "I can tell you that, for years, *Seinfeld* was the number one TV show. I've never seen it."

## How do African Americans behave as consumers?

Here are some highlights from Packaged Fact's 2008 report called "The African-American Market in the U.S."

- African American consumers allocate a greater portion of their budgets to eating at home. They are more likely to spend money on cereals and baking products, meats, poultry, fish, eggs, processed fruits and vegetables and non-alcoholic beverages. They also spend a higher percentage of their money on laundry and cleaning supplies, telephone services, apparel (particularly dress clothes and athletic shoes), automobile expenses, television, radio and sound equipment, and many personal care products.

- African Americans are trendsetters and influencers. They are more likely to say that they are the first among their friends to try new styles (17 percent versus 9 percent) and that people come to them for advice before buying (26 percent versus 20 percent). They are less likely to indicate that they ask advice before buying new things (36 percent versus 46 percent).

- African-American shoppers devote more time to shopping, visit a larger variety of stores, are more likely to enjoy shopping and spend more time browsing, and are less likely to postpone purchases until items go on sale. They are brick-and-mortar shoppers and are much less likely to have made a purchase on the Internet in the last year (26 percent versus 44 percent).

- BET is the most popular cable outlet among African American viewers—about half of African Americans reported watching it in the last seven days. Many of the once-a-week network television programs that are popular with non-African Americans are also popular with African Americans. However, many are not. In Spring 2007, many shows appeared in the top-25 list of shows for African Americans that did not appear for the general market including *Everybody Hates Chris, Girlfriends, My Wife and Kids,*

and *America's Most Wanted*. When looked at by gender, *20/20,
Dateline NBC Friday, Prison Break, WWE Friday Night Smackdown*
and *It's Showtime at the Apollo* appear in the top-25 list for Afri-
can-American men but don't appear for others; *All of Us, So You
Think You Can Dance, Wheel of Fortune* and *America's Next Top
Model* appear only for African-American women.

- Fewer African Americans say they don't like advertising (18 percent versus 39 percent) or feel that it is a waste of their time (15
  percent versus 28 percent). They are also more likely to depend
  on ads to make purchasing decisions and to remember brand
  names of products used in TV shows and movies.

As ad agencies compete for "ethnic dollars," it's the African-
American segment that's getting overlooked. "After all, African
Americans speak English," goes the argument. "We'll reach them
with our general market campaign." As a result, Pepper Miller
writes, "marketing executives adopt erroneous notions about how
to market to African Americans that underestimate the value of
the African-American consumer and ultimately lead to ineffective
marketing messages." As marketers see less and less of a need to
reach out to African Americans, they are in danger of reinforcing
and compounding a long-held belief system in the black community: *they* just don't give a damn about *us*.

## Consequences of stereotyping

Racial stereotypes have had a direct negative impact
on the buying habits of black consumers, according
to a NiaPulse survey of 606 black men and women.
Over half of those surveyed said they have boycotted
a product to let a company know that a show it sponsored was
offensive. Sponsors of programming or content using controversial
racial stereotypes and language are taking a real risk with black

> ➲ *Racial stereotypes
> have had a direct
> **negative** impact on
> the buying habits of
> black consumers.*

consumers, especially those consumers who are middle class or affluent. The higher the income, the more likely they are to view racially offensive images or words in the media as reflecting upon the sponsors.

Boycotting is the most popular method used by blacks to let a company know that a show it sponsors is offensive to them. Rather than voice their opinions, they are more likely to simply stop buying or watching. Higher-income respondents were more likely to report boycotting. Of those respondents with annual incomes of $25,000 and above, 59 percent said they have boycotted a product, compared with 38 percent of respondents with incomes under $25,000 a year. Blacks will also boycott a company if they have heard of a racial discrimination complaint against it. Fifty-five percent said they had stopped buying a product because of a racial discrimination allegation, and among the companies cited were Denny's, Cracker Barrel, and Tommy Hilfiger (which was subject to an unfounded Internet rumor about discriminatory remarks by its founder).

## Life after Obama

In the November 8, 2008 edition of the *Washington Post*, commentator Jonetta Rose Barris said that, with the election of Barack Obama, African Americans have entered the "no-excuse zone," that they have arrived as fully equal citizens but also need to recognize that there are challenges that go along with the election. Barris suggested that it marks the beginning of a post-racial America, where young black people have come of age un-burdened by and not tied to the identity politics of the civil rights movement of the 1960s, 70s, and 80s.

> "Obama is already constructing a new black political and cultural narrative—gathering together the best of the past,

including the coalition politics that characterized the early civil rights movement and an image of strong black males that doesn't involve bling-bling or hip-hop misogyny. He has decried the low-hanging pants fashion so popular with young black men, blasted rapper Ludacris for offensive song lyrics and called on fathers to take responsibility for their families. Are African Americans ready to accept all this and respond positively? Are they ready for a truly post-racial America?

"The answer isn't clear. Just a few days after Obama's stunning win, black America is already divided over what his election means, arguing about what it should expect from a 'black President'—and about whether his first obligation is to black America or to all America. It's an argument that reflects the continuing cleft within the community, between those who hew to the race-based politics advanced chiefly by the black power movement of the 1970s and 1980s and the so-called Millennial or race-neutral generation, which appreciates but isn't imprisoned by African American history."

*Washington Post* columnist Clarence Page agreed that Obama's election marks a sea change in blacks' perception of themselves, but he rejected the term "post-racial." Page told NPR that he prefers the term multi-racial, and said that Obama's election raises America's baseline of presumptions regarding race. "We used to say, 'if we can put a man on the moon, we can do _____ (fill in the blank). Now we will say, if we can put a black man in the White House, we can do _____ (fill in the blank)."

Michael Omi, a professor of ethnic studies at UC Berkeley told the *Chronicle*: "The prospect of having an African-American presidential candidate has led some people to think we're now in a post-racial society. What's disturbing are the ways in which that ignores the persistence of racial inequalities—in health care, home-mortgage loan rates—it shouldn't make us think we've gotten beyond that."

The expanding conversation about race that has been prompted by Obama's candidacy and his complex heritage could advance America's understanding about race. The discussion about Obama's racial lineage and appearance—light skinned, and not "too dark"—reveals how racism remains a powerful factor in the political make-up of the nation. Racial inequality may be receding but it still exerts tremendous force in our political system and in the lives of Americans. Still, although Obama looks unlike any of the previous 43 presidents, he looks like what America, demographically speaking is becoming.

In the introduction to his eminent book *Race Matters*, Cornel West writes, "our truncated public discussions of race suppress the best of who and what we are as a people because they fail to confront the complexity of the issue in a candid and critical manner." If we ignore the intricacies of race, if we shy away from the difficulties or inconveniences that it imposes, we risk faulty judgment and simplistic understanding, something that as marketers (and human beings) we cannot afford to do.

The results of election 2008 will be felt for generations to come. To what extent will Obama's election and administration heal the black/nonblack divide in the U.S., if at all? How, exactly, will Obama's presidency change blacks' perceptions of themselves, and to what extent will that be reflected in the prisms of our society (advertising, TV programming and marketing in general)? We do not yet know. But one thing is clear: people are talking about race in terms more honest than ever before. And that alone is a huge win for all races.

# four

## Asian Americans

There was a recurring skit on Fox Television's *Mad* TV, called "Average Asian." The hero is Hideki, played by Korean-American comedian Bobby Lee. He's a twenty-something Asian-American guy who speaks English, doesn't have Ninja friends, doesn't know sumo wrestling, and doesn't have herbal remedies to cure bad backs. But his "friends" aren't buying the fact that he's just a regular American. Each skit shows him as the center of attention, for all the wrong reasons, often at a party, and the stereotypes fly fast and furiously. Party-goers force him to do origami and karate moves; they assume the bottle of wine he brought contains a magic dragon. Though he suffers more bizarre stereotyping than most Asian Americans do in real life, there is more than a grain of truth to the skit. Not only do Americans often demonstrate a baffling misunderstanding of Asians, it appears to be socially acceptable in some circles to openly stereotype them (e.g., "but they really *are* bad drivers").

Apparel company, Blacklava, takes some stereotypes of Asian Americans head on with a line of t-shirts, buttons, and stickers with slogans that evoke common stereotypes of Asian Americans. Their "I hate math" t-shirt is an assertion that not all Asians are stereotypical math geeks. Another shirt, "I speak English" refers to the stereotype of the perpetual foreigner, and that many Americans can't seem to get it straight that Asian Americans look as American as anyone else. Their "I am not a terrorist" message is particularly relevant for South Asians in the post-9/11 world. And a shirt bearing the phrase "I will not love you long time" refers to the lines uttered by a Vietnamese prostitute in Stanley Kubrik's movie *Full Metal Jacket*—"Me so horny. Me love you long time." According to Blacklava's website, the shirt "confronts the notion of the submissive lotus flower sex slave dragon lady."

In American popular culture, the image of the Asian has run the gamut, from exotic orientalism to turn of the century fears of the Yellow Peril; from the sexually emasculated Chinese laundryman to the lascivious and predatory Chinatown shopkeeper; from the Viet Cong to the Japanese corporate samurai. Frank H. Wu writes in his book, *Yellow: Race in America Beyond Black and White* (Basic Books, 2002), that growing up Asian in America carried with it a bundle of stereotypes, some friendly, some benign, and some outright harmful. In the eyes of white America, because of his race, he could find himself converted into any one of dozens of images attributed to Asians:

> "I could turn around and find myself transformed into Genghis Khan, Tojo, Charlie Chan, Fu Manchu, Hop Sing, Mr. Sulu, Kato, Bruce Lee, Arnold on *Happy Days*, Sam on *Quincy*, M.E. I was the Number One Son, intoning "Ah so," bending at the waist and shuffling backwards out of the room, with opium smoking, incense burning, and ancestor worshipping. . . . My mother and my girl cousins were Madame Butterfly from the mail order bride catalog, dying in their service to the masculinity of the West, and the dragon lady in a kimono, taking vengeance for her sisters. They became the television newscaster, look-alikes, with their flawlessly permed hair."

What makes today's Asian stereotypes unique is that they lack the perniciousness of other stereotypes, at least at face value. In the American psyche, Asians are thought of as highly intelligent, technically skilled, hard working, disciplined, serious, and thrifty, all solid

American values. Asian students are expected to exceed their allotment of spaces at top universities, fill the upper economic brackets, and quietly fall into the shadows of society's consciousness.

Asian Americans, at least ones who do not come from countries with a high refugee exodus, tend to support that stereotype. In 2007, over one in four Asian-American college graduates graduated from a Top-40 university (as defined by US *News and World Report*). The FBI says that Asian Americans have the lowest rates of being arrested. Nationally, Asian Americans tend to get higher grades and have lower rates of drug use and premarital sex. Over 25 percent of Asian Americans over age 25 hold a bachelor's degree compared with only 16 percent of the general American population. Communities with a high number of refugees, however—Cambodians, Vietnamese, Laotians, and Hmong—have much lower levels of education, and a much higher unemployment rate.

In general, the impression that Asian Americans as a group are very success-oriented, led to the coining of the phrase "model minority" to describe them. Critics of this terminology point to the struggling refugee populations to show that the label is overly broad and damaging to Asian communities that need assistance. Others assert that the persistent and unrealistic expectation that "all Asians are smart" puts too much pressure on many Asian Americans.

> The impression that Asian Americans as a group are very **success-oriented,** led to the coining of the phrase "model minority" to describe them.

Still, the stereotype of Asian super achiever persists. The attitude of media taste makers and marketers has been that there's nothing wrong with employing these stereotypes. This logic is especially attractive to advertisers, for whom stereotypes serve a purpose. They help convey a complex message in a 30- or 60-second package, a "shorthand which helps to convey ideas and images quickly and easily," to use the words of Alice Courtney and Thomas Whipple.

Stereotyping Asians might be great for marketing to a mainstream audience, particularly if it gets a laugh, but it is not always funny to the group being stereotyped. For Asian Americans,

stereotypes are a stark reminder that in the psyche of popular consciousness, they are different; they are foreign. For those who feel
themselves to be part of the red, white, and blue, stereotypes are
a reminder that those who trace their ancestry to Asia are of a
different hue. In the book, *The Asian American Movement* (Temple
University Press, 1993), William Wei writes, "Whether negative or
positive, stereotypes are essentially false images that obscure the
complexity and diversity that is an inherent feature of Asian Americans as well as other people. Whether it be the Chinese launderer,
the Korean grocery store owner, or the South Asian Maharaja, this
kind of imagery reinforces the stereotype in the American mind that
Asians, American or not, are 'other.'"

➲ *Asian Americans
consistently want to be
shown in the media
and in ads as they
really are.*

Our research shows that Asian Americans consistently want to be shown in the media and in ads
as they really are. I recently worked with a beverage
company to identify which messages would connect
the most with American-born Chinese (also known
as ABCs). We showed participants a variety of concept boards with
different types of ads, some with no Asians, some with all Asians,
and some with a mix. When the ads did not include Asians they
brought it up, without any ire, as if to say, "That is what we are
used to." They responded positively to ads that showed Asians represented as part of a multicultural cast. Many responded negatively
to ads that had a purely Asian cast.

The dislike of the purely Asian ads was complex. Many expressed
that they felt like they were being "marketed to," in the sense of being
targeted by marketers because of their ethnicity. Others expressed
a cultural dislike of standing out from the group—in this case, the
mainstream. As we probed deeper, a more profound theme seemed
to emerge. Many of our Chinese-American respondents, particularly
those with mostly non-Asian American friends, expressed that being
singled out from the group happened to them a lot, because of

the way they looked. Their aspiration, to be included as part of the group, was often denied to them because of race.

## The perpetual foreigner

"Where are you from?"

"No, I mean, where are you *really* from?"

These are questions that many Asian Americans must confront constantly. Poughkeepsie is never the right answer. It's a guileless question, often a conversation starter, and a reflection of our American obsession with race. Some use it as a way of inquiring about an Asian American person's ethnicity or what country their ancestors came from. For others, it reflects the simple attitude that Asians can't possibly be from here. When that's the case, it's often followed by the compliment "You speak such beautiful English," even if the person was born and raised in the heartland.

But "where are you really from?" brings up feelings of alienation. As Frank H. Wu wrote in the *Civil Rights Journal*, "everyone with an Asian face who lives in America is afflicted by the perpetual foreigner syndrome. We are figuratively and even literally returned to Asia and ejected from America."

Asian Americans don't *look* American, at least not the way most Americans visualize. I look American, though my great grandparents certainly didn't, donned in the vestments of the Eastern European ghettos from whence they came. But Asian Americans, no matter how assimilated they might be, just don't look the part. When Chinese-American figure skater Michelle Kwan finished second to Tara Lipinski in the 1998 Olympics, MSNBC's headlines read, "American beats Kwan." In the eyes of that news network, only Lipinski looked American enough to be called American.

Most of the time, racism is no more virulent than "where are you really from?" Other times, it's ugly. In 1994, New York Senator Alfonse D'Amato was a guest on the politically incorrect *Imus in the Morning Show*. When asked how the O.J. Simpson trial was going, D'Amato expressed his impatience with the pace of the trial by mocking Judge Lance Ito with a ridiculous rendition of a Japanese accent. Judge Ito is a third-generation Japanese American who speaks perfect unaccented American English.

In January 2005, a horrible and vulgar "parody" called "The Tsunami Song" aired on New York's influential hip-hop radio station Hot 97. The tune, set to the music of "We Are the World," was played repeatedly over a one-week period during the *Miss Jones in the Morning Show*. It included the following lovely lyrics:

> All at once you could hear the screaming chinks
> And no one was safe from the wave
> There were Africans drowning
> Little Chinamen swept away
> You could hear God laughing "swim you bitches swim"
> So now you're screwed, it's the tsunami
> You better run or kiss your ass away, go find your mommy
> I just saw her float by, a tree went through her head
> And now the children will be sold to child slavery.

According to reports, the station's newsreader, an Asian American named Miss Info, objected to the song, only to be bashed by deejay "Miss Jones" who said "I know you feel you're superior because you're Asian, but you're not." The program's co-host added, "I'm going to start shooting Asians." Students, community leaders, and groups such as Asian Media Watch and the Japanese American Citizen's League denounced the song and demanded that the station make amends. The station responded by firing the co-host and producer, donating $1 million to tsunami relief and suspending the show's crew for two weeks. Advocacy groups succeeded in persuading some sponsors including McDonald's, Toyota, and Sprint to pull their ads.

Rosie O'Donnell, who has a much larger following than Hot 97, received national attention (and ire) when she used the expression "ching chong" to describe Chinese people talking about Danny DeVito's drunken appearance on *The View*, a show she was co-hosting. "The fact is that it's news all over the world. That you know, you can imagine in China it's like: 'Ching chong . . . ching chong. Danny DeVito, ching chong, chong, chong, chong. Drunk. *The View*. Ching chong," O'Donnell said on a December 5, 2006 episode of *The View*. John C. Liu, a New York City councilman, fired off a letter to *The View* co-host Barbara Walters condemning the "ching-chong" gag. "It really hits a raw nerve for many people in the community—many like myself, who grew up with these kinds of taunts. We all know that it never ends at the taunts," he said. O'Donnell issued a weak apology of the "I'm sorry if you were offended" variety.

A few years ago Abercrombie & Fitch came out with a line of t-shirts that were truly insulting to Asians. One featured a slogan "Wong Brothers Laundry Service—Two Wongs Can Make it White" with two smiling Chinese men with conical hats harking back to the early twentieth century. Another read "Wok-N-Bowl—Let the Good Times Roll—Chinese Food and Bowling" with similar stereotypical images. A third t-shirt gaffed "Abercrombie & Fitch Buddha Bash—Get Your Buddha on the Floor." According to an article in the *San Francisco Chronicle*, the retailer actually thought that Asian Americans would like the t-shirts. But they didn't. The protest started with Stanford University's Asian American Students' Association. Said its vice chairman Michael Chang, "The stereotypes they depict are more than a century old. You're seeing laundry service. You're seeing basically an entire religion and philosophy being trivialized." The outcry grew, fueled by word of mouth and e-mails, culminating in a boycott. Ultimately, the retailer discontinued the line and apologized.

The event that shocked and mobilized Asian Americans more than any other was the 1982 murder of Vincent Chin, a Chinese

American, who was killed in the Detroit, Michigan, suburb of High-land Park by two white autoworkers, Ronald Ebens and Michael Nitz. Chin was having a bachelor party at a strip club when the two autoworkers called him a "Jap," and one yelled, "It's because of you (expletive deleted) that we're out of work." A fight broke out and Chin left the bar, but Ebens and Nitz hunted him down in the streets and bludgeoned him with a baseball bat. Chin lapsed into a coma and died four days later. Ebens and Nitz were found guilty, yet served no jail time, were given a mere three years probation, fined $3,000 and ordered to pay $780 in court costs. At the time, racial hatred towards Asians was especially strong in Detroit because the domestic auto industry was being threatened by Japanese imports. The fact that Chin was a Chinese American didn't matter. Chin's "mistake" was having Asian features and living in a region that held charity events that let people pay to smash Japanese cars to fight back at Asia.

The Chin murder was a flashpoint for Asian-American indigna-tion, a symbol of discrimination suffered by all Asian Americans, and for many, the realization that when it comes to anti-Asian racism, all were in the same boat. Outrage over Chin's murder stimulated the pan-Asian American community nationwide to use the media, raise money, garner support from elected officials, and educate the public about a side of racism that few Americans acknowledged.

It has been suggested that the Chin murder, more than any other event, except perhaps the internment of Japanese Americans during the Second World War, led to the emergence of a pan-Asian identity based largely on race. Sociologist Mia Tuan, in her book, *Forever Foreigners or Honorary Whites?* (Rutgers University Press, 1998), writes, "All Asian-Americans are *potential victims* of racially motivated inci-dents that can unite persons of Asian ancestry and thereby activate or enhance ethnic salience even if they have not personally suffered from a hate crime, racism, or prejudice in their own lives."

In her research, based on 100 in-depth interviews, Tuan identifies four characteristics of how the Asian-American experience differs from the white ethnic experience:

1. Asian ethnics exercise a great deal of flexibility regarding the cultural elements they wish to keep or discard from their *personal lives*. What they have retained by way of cultural traditions is largely symbolic and a novelty.

2. How they choose to identify, however, is not a private affair and they experience pressure to identify in ethnic or racial terms.

3. Despite their generational longevity in this country, an assumption of foreignness stubbornly clings to them.

4. Asian ethnics are not considered "real" Americans. They have not been incorporated into the collective memory of who qualifies as a "real" American.

Tuan's interview transcripts are revealing as to how Asian Americans feel about themselves. While some feel pride and a normalcy about being Asian, for others, it is more of a struggle. She identifies the racial composition of the area where respondents were raised as being a defining variable—those raised in areas with many other Asians seem to have a much easier time of it. She quotes one respondent, a Korean American whom she calls Tony, who talks about being a teenager in a mostly white area:

"At times I looked in the mirror and I go, gee, I looked Asian but I eat their food, dance their dance, I read English, am I really that different? But because they assign so much to differences, they go (more) by outward differences than what counts. We learn to hate people who are different and that's not (because of) anything that I did. . . . They never (knew) me. So how do I feel? . . . I grew up hating myself. I was a no good lousy Jap. But I never hated Japanese. I never did."

Tony was Korean, not Japanese, but to the whites he knew, there was no difference. Or if there was, they didn't care. Compare his comments to Frank, a fifth-generation Chinese American who grew up in Chinatown in San Francisco:

"If you lived in San Francisco, Chinatown, you are completely absorbed in the culture as well as language. So in that sense it was normal. I don't know if you were really conscious of it. I guess my parents' family and ourselves, we were pretty proud of the fact that we were Chinese and Americans at the same time. . . . Perfectly fluent English. . . . But at the same time we all preferred to live in the Chinese culture and pursue it, and the Chinese customs and food of course, and our friends were predominately Chinese."

Clearly, different Asian Americans relate differently to the experience of growing up Asian in the United States. However, all have been exposed to the stereotypes on one occasion or another, if not in real life, than certainly on the media. As we've seen with other markets, the cost of offending Asian Americans is dear, and the benefit that can be obtained by respectfully including them in a company's marketing efforts can greatly pay off. As in the case of Hispanics, marketing to the U.S.-born generation can be tricky and the desire to market to these consumers brings up questions that are not easily answered. Are they so assimilated, as some think, that there is no point in doing any kind of targeted marketing outreach? Or is there something sufficiently unique about them that makes targeting them desirable or necessary? How do you reach them without being stereotypical, or specifically in the case of Asian Americans, how do you reach them without making them feel "singled out." In order to answer these questions, it's useful to gain an understanding of who these U.S.-born Asians are and what makes them tick.

➲ *The benefit that can be obtained by* **respectfully** *including Asian Americans in a company's marketing efforts can greatly pay off.*

## The Ballad of East and West

In our research, values emerge at the forefront of what makes the Asian American experience unique. In "The Ballad of East and West," Rudyard Kipling wrote the now famous lines "East is East, and West is West, and never the twain shall meet." Globalization and the growing influence of Asian culture (and demographics) on the United States are proving his adage anachronistic. But Kipling did have a point. There are distinct differences between Asian and Western culture; where they do meet is in the lives of Asian Americans.

> ➲ *There are distinct differences between Asian and Western **culture**; where they do meet is in the lives of Asian Americans.*

According to psychologist May Pao-may Tung, these cultural differences are also a source of conflict for Asian Americans. In her book, *Chinese Americans and Their Immigrant Parents* (Haworth Clinical Practice Press, 2000), she relates some of the common themes she encounters while conducting psychotherapy with young Chinese Americans. She writes that these themes include "a sense of parental disapproval or emotional withholding ('It's never good enough'), inadequate or mistaken guidance (from parents), role reversals, and puzzling beliefs and behaviors. In relation to society at large, they often feel unsure of themselves, not knowing who they are. The sense of being 'invisible' or overlooked is pervasive. I began to see that much of the intergenerational and societal conflicts basically stem from the intercultural misunderstandings and antagonism."

In our research, when we go for a deeper line of questioning with Asian-American participants, there are common problems that many have faced and continue to face based on cultural differences. One is the lack of assertiveness, either in school or on the job. American children are taught to develop their own opinions, to speak up, to assert themselves. Asian children are generally taught not to speak their minds. Chinese children, for example, according to Tung are taught to *ting hua*, literally, "listen to the speech/talk/words of elders, implying obedience." A corollary is the Western belief in individualism and the collectivist spirit of many Asians; Japanese children, for instance, are taught that the nail sticking up will be hammered down.

One Asian value, one that frequently causes misunderstandings with Westerners is the desire to maintain harmony at all costs. That Japanese will say "yes" when they mean "no" is well known. In Japanese, the "yes" is often an indication that the person follows what is being said, and not necessarily that he or she is agreeing with it. To disagree would cause a loss of face, it would create disharmony. Harmony must be upheld at all times.

In Japan, at least when I lived there, if you lost your wallet, chances were almost certain that it would be returned to you or the police with everything intact. Nearly every time it rained and I was without an umbrella, someone insisted on giving me theirs. In highly collectivist cultures like Japan, people take care of each other.

> *Because Asians as a whole are **affluent**, they are a popular segment for financial institutions to target*

Because Asians as a whole are affluent—although as I point out later, affluence blesses some nationalities far more than others—they are a popular segment for financial institutions to target, and as a result, my company has done a lot of work in this area. A common theme is the importance of thrift to Asians, which also translates into a consumer who is hungry for a bargain. This doesn't mean, however, that Asian consumers are willing to sacrifice on quality. On the contrary, Asians will often pay a premium, but if and only if they feel that they are getting value for their money.

I recently conducted an interview with a Chinese-American woman who was an officer with a San Francisco branch of a large American finance company. I was trying to understand what was important to her Chinese customers. "Do you know what a Jew is?" she asked me. I told her that I did, that in fact I was one. "Oh," she said knowingly. "Then you can understand that like Jews, Chinese will never let you get away with charging a price that is too high." I had a vivid image of my grandmother arguing with the kosher butcher and I knew exactly what she was talking about.

These cultural beliefs are a filter through which marketing messages are filtered and interpreted. In order to be successful, it's important to keep them in mind when developing marketing messages, or better yet, hire experts who are in tune with the particular group that you are targeting. Themes like individualism and assertiveness, which might play out well with a Western consumer, will have different resonance with an Asian American, particularly an immigrant. Conversely, images with a collectivist or patient feel may work well. As always, the most important thing to do is to test your concepts with real consumers.

## Upscale Asians

The ethnic enclaves characterized as Chinatowns are largely tourism-generating artifacts of the past. True, many Chinese Americans still live in these communities, but to a large extent, recent immigrants and particularly second- and third-generation Chinese and more affluent Chinese Americans now reside in suburban communities commonly known as "ethnoburbs" or mixed "Asiatowns."

And, of course, if they have the money, Asian Americans can live anywhere they choose. And, increasingly, affluent urban Asians are doing so. According to an article in the *New York Times,* American young professionals are at the forefront of demographic shifts in Long Island City and downtown Brooklyn. Asian Americans, the story reports, account for 15 to 50 percent of the initial sales in some of the new condominiums under construction in those neighborhoods, even though Asians account for only 10 percent of the city's population. Now some developers are trying to accelerate this trend by marketing heavily in the local Chinese and Korean media.

Does this demographic shift suggest that satellite Chinatowns and Koreatowns will pop up around these neighborhoods? Just the opposite, according to the article: Asians, at least in New York, are going mainstream at an ever-increasing rate. From the *Times:* "The relatively high concentrations of Asians moving to these neighborhoods may just be a sign that like their counterparts who grew up in the early-20th-century Italian and Jewish enclaves on the Lower East Side, these young Asian-Americans have more buying power than their parents' generation and they are using it to meld into mainstream New York."

## The Pan-Asian segment: the ties that bind

Despite the fact that Asian Americans represent so many different ethnic identities, U.S.-born Asians and acculturated Asian Americans of different ancestries find that they have many things in common with each other—similar experiences with immigrant parents who struggled to adapt to a new and very different country, parents who stressed similar cultural values like education, discipline, respect for family, and more mundane pursuits like after-school language lessons, and piano training. Many U.S.-born Asians, like Hispanics, undergo a return to their ethnic roots. To quote an article in *Time* magazine, today's young Asian Americans often follow "the path of a boomerang: early isolation, rapid immersion and assimilation, and then a re-appreciation of ethnic roots."

### What Does it Mean to be Asian?

Jeff Yang, who writes a column for the *San Francisco Chronicle* on Asian popular culture, asked his readers what it meant to them to be Asian American. Here are some of the responses that he received:

• I save napkins and plastic utensils from restaurants.

- I cook Chinese food, like wonton soup, tomato beef and sticky rice.

- I push my kids to get good grades.

- I've eaten with chopsticks because that was the "Asian thing to do," even though Filipinos don't eat with chopsticks.

- I fight for the dinner bill at the restaurant with my other Asian friends.

- I've taken ten Caucasian colleagues to lunch in a dim sum restaurant and ordered in Cantonese.

- In America, when I'm with Caucasians or other races, I feel like I'm Asian. But when I'm trying to work with Asians who don't speak Vietnamese or English, I don't feel Asian.

- My parents would describe themselves as Indian Americans when talking to non-Indians. Among Indians, they'd describe themselves as Gujarati. I always described myself as Indian American right up until I started working in national politics, when I started using the term Asian American. Now I do think of myself as Asian American—though I'm not sure that Indian people are always accepted in that terminology.

Wang concludes "If there's one thing my unscientific survey made clear, it's that Asian means many things to many people."

---

Perhaps the greatest indicator of an emerging pan-Asian American identity has been borne out of the research by sociologists Shinagawa and Pang, which shows that *intraracial* marriage rates between Asian Americans of different ethnicities now outnumber *interracial* marriages with whites for all subgroups except Japanese-American women. So as more and more Asian Americans, say Chinese, start families with Asian Americans of another ethnic group, say Korean, a pan-Asian sensibility can only be expected to grow, at least among the U.S.-born generation.

That a pan-Asian identity is emerging is a clear indication that Asian Americans feel that there is much that binds them together. But it is only with acculturation that this pan-ethnic identity develops. According to the U.S. Census, Asians are people from the East Asian nations or territories of China, Taiwan, Hong Kong (which was under British control from 1840 until 1997 when it reverted to the Chinese), Japan, and Korea; the South Asian nations of India, Pakistan, Bangladesh, Sri Lanka, Nepal, Bhutan and Maldives; and the Southeast Asian nations of the Philippines, Vietnam, Laos, Cambodia, Thailand, Indonesia, Malaysia, Myanmar, Singapore and Brunei.

Here are some facts about the Asian American market:

- There were 15 million Asian Americans in 2007. In 1970, there were fewer than a million. Between 2000 and 2005, this population grew by 19.8 percent (the Hispanic population grew by 20.9 percent). Nearly half of all Asians live in either California or New York.

- Chinese make up the largest subgroup of Asians (the Census tracks ten); they make up about 23 percent of the Asian population (excluding Taiwanese), followed by Asian Indians and Filipinos who make up 19 percent and 18 percent, respectively. The two fastest growing subgroups are Pakistanis and Asian Indians, which grew by 36 percent and 34 percent respectively between 2000 and 2005.

- As a group, Asian Americans are educated and affluent. Nearly half have a bachelor's degree or more and they are the most likely group to work in managerial or professional jobs (46 percent compared with 38 percent of non-Hispanic whites). The median income of Asian American households is 26 percent higher than the average. Still, there are disparities

➲ *As a **group**, Asian Americans are educated and affluent.*

between different ethnic groups. For instance, the median annual household income for Asian Indians and Filipinos is $69,000 and $66,000, respectively. For Cambodians, it's $36, 000 and for Hmong it's $32,000.

- Asian Americans are primarily an immigrant population, with slightly over two-thirds being foreign born. As is the case with income, there are differences by ethnicity. About three-quarters of Koreans and Asian Indians are foreign born, compared with about two-thirds of Chinese and Filipinos. Nearly six in ten Japanese Americans were born in the United States. Also, there are big differences by age. While 80 percent of Asian adults are immigrants, about 80 percent of Asians under the age of 19 were born in the United States.

The Asian-American market, if such a thing does exist, is extremely diverse. Even within certain groups there are huge disparities. The Chinese market consists of Mandarin speakers from Taiwan and Mainland China; it also consists of Cantonese speakers from Hong Kong and the southern provinces. Taiwanese tend to be high wage earners, higher than people from Mainland China. Cantonese speakers include poor people from the southern provinces of Mainland China and, prior to the People's Republic of China's occupation of Hong Kong in 1997, many wealthy people who came in great numbers to the United States and Canada.

In 2006, Packaged Facts released a report on the Asian American market titled "Asian Americans in the U.S." It's a comprehensive analysis of data from multiple sources including the Census Bureau and other government agencies, Simmons' 2005 National Consumer Surveys (NCS) for kids, teens, and adults, plus information collected from firms active in the Asian American market. Some highlights:

- Asian Americans enjoy shopping, significantly more so than the national average. Compared with the average American consumer, Asian Americans are more frequent shoppers and more likely to pay attention to advertising.

- As consumers, Asian Americans are more driven by price and more likely to seek out bargains where they shop. Compared with U.S. adults as a whole, they are more drawn to stores they don't usually frequent because of sales and coupons, travel an hour or more to factory outlet stores, and postpone buying things until they are on sale.

> ➲ *As consumers, Asian Americans are more driven by **price** and more likely to seek out bargains.*

- They over-index in credit cards, allocate more of their budgets to designer clothing, are health conscious about food and have a preference for prescription medicine carrying a brand name.

- Asian Americans are big consumers of electronics, and are far more likely than the average consumer to say they keep up with developments in technology.

- Asian Americans are far more likely to say that the Internet has changed the way they shop and get information about products. They buy more on the Internet and are more than twice as likely to have spent $1,000 or more on the Internet in the year before the survey.

Given that so many Asian Americans today are foreign born, it's not surprising that many prefer to be marketed to in their own languages. A 2005 poll conducted for New California Media found that 80 percent of Korean, Chinese, and Vietnamese adults read an ethnic newspaper on a regular basis. The study, which is ongoing, also concluded that Chinese and Koreans are watching in-language television more frequently. About a quarter indicated watching television in either Chinese or Korean more often than in English—impressive given that large numbers of Koreans and Chinese do speak English.

## Japanese pop culture: techno-geek chic

In 1980, when I was a sophomore at the University of New Hampshire, my friends thought I was insane for opting to study Japanese. It simply wasn't done, at least not in Durham, New Hampshire. To begin with, the department was so small, it was part of the Russian studies department (don't ask me why). The class was taught by a graduate student who just happened to be Japanese, and besides me, there were three others in the class.

Given the economic explosion that was taking place, it was certainly a practical choice. But that was the furthest thing from my mind. I was fascinated by Japanese culture—the samurai, the martial arts, and Zen Buddhism. When I decided to move to Japan after graduation, everyone was convinced that I was crazy, especially the Japanese living in Kobe, Japan. There were few *gaijin*—foreigners—living there at the time and we were oddities. I vividly remember how strange I felt when I saw my reflection alongside another *gaijin* in the mirror on the side of the train platform. "The Japanese are right," I would think to myself. "We do all look the same."

Today, things are different. According to *Japan Today*, nearly three million people were learning the Japanese language in 133 countries in 2006, up 26 percent from 2003. And perhaps for the first time in its history, Japan is a giant exporter of popular culture, not just cars, appliances, and other gadgets.

> ➲ For the first time in its history, Japan is a giant **exporter** of popular culture, not just cars, appliances, and other gadgets.

Take the explosion of manga, Japanese print cartoons, and anime, Japanese style animation. Their obsessive followers, known as *otaku*, a word borrowed from the Japanese and best translated as "geek" or "nerd," number in the tens of thousands, but they have achieved an amazing mainstream following—the Japan External Trade Organization (JETRO) believes that manga and anime will grow into a $100 billion global market. Unlike my days of staring into train platform mirrors, Japanese geek-chic is hot these days, a fact that is not lost on America's "model minority."

Asian culture, Japanese and otherwise, is cool, and young Asian Americans are forging a unique popular culture in the United States, adopting everything from Indian Bollywood videos and Gujarati hip-hop music, to Chinese-character tattoos and revved up high performance cars, not to forget cuisines as varied as Thai, Vietnamese, and Cambodian. In the United States, Asian and American popular cultures are merging and Asian Americans are the ambassadors of this hybrid culture. It's something that they are proud of, not surprising, given their former status as well-behaved technoids.

## Asian Echo-Boomers

According to results of a survey conducted with over 538 Asian American teens and "echo-boomers" — between the ages of 14 and 28 years—by New American Dimensions and interTrend Communications, an Asian-American advertising agency, Asian-American young people are likely to see themselves as trendsetters in three distinct cultural categories: technology and gadgetry, anime and manga, and video-gaming.

Among the major findings:

- Close to 80 percent of respondents identify "technology/gadgets" and "anime/manga" as the top two areas where Asian Americans are influencing trends, while 72 percent of respondents cite "video gaming" as the third major area. Asian-American youth also cite "food and culinary arts" and the visual arts as highly influential.

- A diverse array of musical genres forms the listening habits of Asian youth, but with distinct differences according to their acculturation levels and generation. While first-generation respondents preferred "Pop/Top 40" music, second-generation

Asian Americans exhibited a strong preference for hip-hop and Alternative music.

- Asian-American youth are more likely to identify and seek out trends through word-of-mouth messaging than through any other media channel or network. This is particularly true for second-generation Asian Americans who indicate they are twice as likely as their first-generation counterparts to learn about trends via word of mouth. Among the first-generation cohort, television holds the greatest influence in helping them learn about new trends.

- Among single Asians that were U.S. born, two-thirds date interracially, and only 45 percent indicated that they intended to marry another Asian.

---

"Hip, techno-savvy, game-building and game-using Asian Americans represent the future for marketers who want to make stronger inroads in the Asian American market. The way to reach (this segment) is not through traditional media, but through exciting concerts and events, peer to peer grass root marketing campaigns, celebrity endorsements and online techniques," according to Giancarlo Pacheco, president and co-founder at Plan C Agency, which creates strategies for reaching Asian youth. One way for savvy marketers to tap into the emerging Asian American pop culture scene is by sponsoring events that are frequented by young Asian American trendsetters. Plan C specializes in helping its clients connect with Asian Americans by sponsoring hip "Asian nights" at clubs doing guerilla marketing, product placement, and using celebrity endorsements.

> ➲ *One way for savvy marketers to tap into the emerging Asian American pop culture scene is by **sponsoring** events that are frequented by young Asian American trendsetters.*

One of the sources of Plan C's success is that U.S.-born Asians have been, for the most part, ignored by marketers, perhaps with reason. MTV tried several networks: MTV Chi, targeting U.S.-born Chinese Americans, MTV K, targeting Korean Americans and MTV Desi targeting Indian Americans. MTV cancelled these channels after less than two years, claiming the ratings didn't justify the cost. Then again, these channels were only available on premium service conduits such as DirecTV. They were never available on non-premium channels where the big audiences are. Comcast's AZN Television, which billed itself as "the network for Asian America" had its plug pulled in 2008. The only two channels of note today that target Asian Americans are ImaginAsian Entertainment and TFC, The Filipino Channel.

## To see and be seen: portrayals of Asians in the media

The experience of being either ignored or stereotyped in advertisers' collective vision of America has made Asian Americans sensitive to how they are portrayed. Still, marketers and media types haven't quite gotten the message that it's simply not okay to stereotype Asian Americans. Like the other segments we've seen, Asian Americans want to be included in commercials, and shown as they really are. Our research does indicate subtle differences in how Asian Americans tend to want to see themselves. While African Americans, Hispanics, and gays seem to relish a commercial featuring themselves as stars, many Asian Americans are okay if they're merely seen, as long as that representation is tactful and truthful.

That does not mean that Asian Americans are ambivalent about seeing themselves represented in the media. On the contrary, they take such portrayals very seriously. In the first four decades of TV programming in the United States, there were few Asians at all. Beyond George Takei on *Star Trek*, Pat Morita on *Happy Days*, Kam Fong and Harry Endo on *Hawaii Five-0*, and Robert Ito on *Quincy, M.E.*, it's hard to come up with other Asian American actors in long-running series.

It wasn't until 1994 that a prime-time series focused on an Asian-American family. Lasting one season, the sitcom *All American Girl* was critically panned. But it has received an afterlife by Margaret Cho, a notoriously irreverent and scathing Korean-American comedienne, who trashes the show and the Hollywood system in her stand-up routines. When it was cancelled, the Hollywood sitcom machine seemed to learn the lesson that America didn't care to see Asian families depicted: there have been no sitcoms or dramas depicting Asian families since then. TV producers and network executives could have learned another, more reasonable lesson, as Cho points out. That is, to simply make better and funnier sitcoms.

While there were no recurring Asian characters on the 1990's sitcom *Seinfeld*, the show did make at least one trenchant observation about Asians (and races in general). In one episode, Jerry gets a wrong number; the person on the other end says she's Donna Chang. After hanging up, he considers calling her back, because, as he tells Elaine, he loves Chinese women. "Isn't that just a little racist?" Elaine chides. He replies with a question that anyone who has ever considered Asians the model minority might ask: "If I like their race, how can that be racist?"

There has been a steady increase in Asian faces cast in regular roles in prime time television shows, including *Lost* and *Grey's Anatomy*, leading some to wonder whether diversity is becoming more mainstream. Yet the presence of Asian faces doesn't necessarily mean

➲ *There has been a steady increase in Asian **faces** cast in regular roles in **prime time** television shows.*

that Asian-American experiences are being portrayed on television. The Asian characters on television now are primarily doctors, or (name the profession) who just *happen* to be Asian American. Says Sandra Oh about her character, Christina: "It's nice to see a woman who can't commit and who is emotionally stunted, because there's a lot of us who are." By us, she means women or even people in general, not Asian Americans. *Lost*, another ensemble cast where characters from different types of environments and backgrounds

are forced to work together, also features prominent Asian characters. Yet, again, their Asian identity is not something that's explored.
It's their Asian face that's used to promote diversity. The show *Heroes*,
on the other hand, has developed storylines where the character's
Asian-ness is a crucial factor in the plot. A huge hit in its first season, *Heroes* featured Masi Oka and Sendhil Ramamurthy. In *Heroes*,
the characters' Asian-ness does create some story lines: Oka's character Hiro has a friend in Japan: Ando, played by James Kyson Lee.
Meanwhile, Hiro has a subplot involving his father, so they bring
in George Takei.

> ⊃ *Asian Americans*
> *consider Asians on*
> *television to be a*
> ***measure*** *of integrating*
> *themselves into the*
> *fabric of American*
> *culture.*

Asian Americans consider Asians on television
to be a measure of integrating themselves into the
fabric of American culture. That belief imbues every
Asian face on television with crucial importance. As
director Jeff Adachi puts it, "While it's true that 40
percent of the doctors coming out of medical school
are of Asian descent, [they] don't really exist in the minds of many
people unless [they're] on ER. Political power is often defined by
the reach one has to shape one's image or the perceptions of other
people. If Asian Americans are excluded from popular culture and
media, then we are excluded from society and access to it."

It is the "dumb teen stoner comedy" film genre that appears to
be pushing the envelope of post-ethnic America with the Harold
and Kumar series. *Harold and Kumar Go to White Castle*, a movie
about a pot-fueled, nightlong, surreal odyssey, was a smash hit, on
DVD if not at the theater. The sequel, *Harold and Kumar Escape from
Guantanamo Bay*, used the easy target of overzealous and stupid
Homeland Security agents for its humor. It wasn't their ethnicity that
was exceptional. It was the way their ethnicity was treated—unex-
ceptionally.

In the first film, they were simply two guys who got stoned
and had adventures and happened to be Asian American (and not
much is made of their ethnicity). In *Harold and Kumar Escape From*

*Guantanamo Bay*, Kumar's ethnicity is important, insofar as it helps him land in detention (the over zealous Feds assume that, because he's somewhat vaguely Middle Eastern, of course he must be a terrorist). Yet ethnicity in that film is used to make fun of America's Middle East phobia, rather than say anything about the character himself.

In a *Los Angeles Times* article, Marc Olson said Harold and Kumar push the limits of multiculturalism:

> "At the time, many wrote off the low-budget movie as just another stoner comedy. But to others, the characters of Harold and Kumar—weed-smoking and wisecracking but very much of color—right away read as something different. Somehow, in featuring the misadventures of two regular guys who just happened to not be white, the pair pushed the limits of multiculturalism in contemporary cinema, bringing film closer to speed with changes that seemed to have already taken hold in the world of casting for television."

Building a goofball comedy around two Asian guys—they were not just "the Korean Guy" sidekick/cameo character but leading men who were fully Americanized and just happened to be Asian—was something different. Hollywood is notoriously risk-averse and doesn't like to mess with success, so it's safe to expect more multicultural young dudes in comedies (and, of course, as always, more young stoner dudes).

## Which group to focus on?

Marketers need to be clear on which Asian ethnicity they plan to target as well as what level of acculturation makes the most sense. Many companies have been successful narrowing their scope, for instance by focusing on Chinese or Koreans. Others have targeted more than one Asian segment. Many have focused on newly arrived

Asian-American immigrants, while still others have focused on more acculturated immigrants or even U.S.-born Asian Americans. However, in spite of the diversity of cultures lived and languages spoken in the Asian segment, the real future of Asian marketing is through English. This is borne out by recent reports such as one by Packaged Facts, which points out that 78 percent of foreign-born Asians speak English, compared with only 52 percent of foreign-born Latinos. In addition, New American Dimensions' research has shown that only about half of second-generation Asians speak an Asian language, compared with three-quarters of their Hispanic counterparts who speak Spanish.

➲ *78 percent of foreign-born Asians speak* **English***, compared with only 52 percent of foreign-born Latinos.*

## Asian Indians in the U.S.: Quickly Acculturating

Asian Indians in the U.S. are becoming increasingly attractive to marketers, due to their rising population and purchasing power and other appealing demographics.

In 2008, New American Dimensions and interTrend Communications explored first-generation Indian Americans. Our research showed that, though relatively new to the U.S., first-generation Indian Americans show many signs of advanced acculturation. Specifically:

- They are generally proud of their heritage, but consider themselves to be both Indian and American, despite having lived in the U.S. for an average of only about one-third of their lives.

- Most express interest in enjoying Indian food, music, and entertainment and in preserving their native language (the latter, a means of staying connected with family and friends back in India). However, they tend to ascribe less importance to retaining other aspects of their culture, such as traditional clothing, vegetarianism, arranged marriages, and religious holidays and rituals.

- Despite their fairly recent arrival, first-generation Indian Americans appear to be quite comfortable with life in the United States. The majority indicated that they're comfortable with non-Indians and feel completely at home. Most said they're valued in the workplace, treated well in American culture, and portrayed positively by U.S. media.

- A high number said they felt welcome in stores and are willing to shop retailers that aren't close to home or that don't speak their native language. They tend to make purchase decisions independently without relying on recommendations from family or friends, and are receptive to American brands, including those that aren't well known.

- They're likely to use media in English, and with American content, not surprising given their proficiency in English and the greater availability of those media, relative to Indian-language vehicles.

- Family is a top priority of first-generation Indian Americans, and appears to be a factor that motivates them to set and fulfill financial goals. The importance they ascribe to family is reflected in a strong desire to provide a college education for their kids. In our experience, this is a desire that may also be tied to the notion that education brings honor, which runs deep in Indian culture. They also have a belief that it's their responsibility to care for their elderly parents.

## The end of the model minority?

A quiet, high-achieving math or science major at MIT. Or Stanford. Or Caltech. That's an enduring stereotype of Asian-American students. But according to a 2008 report, "Facts, Not Fiction: Setting the Record Straight," that image is not completely accurate, given the diversity of Asian-American students.

The report, by New York University, the College Board and a commission of mostly Asian-American educators and community leaders, dispelled the perception that Asian Americans and Pacific Islanders cluster in science, technology, engineering, and math. "Certainly there's a lot of Asians doing well, at the top of the curve, and that's a point of pride, but there are just as many struggling at the bottom of the curve, and we wanted to draw attention to that," Robert T. Teranishi, the N.Y.U. education professor who wrote the report, told the *New York Times*.

➲ *Like those of other Americans, Asian students' academic **achievement** correlates with the income level and education of their parents.*

The report, based on federal education, immigration and census data, as well as statistics from the College Board, noted that like those of other Americans, Asian students' academic achievement correlates with the income level and education of their parents. And, contrary to the notion that Asians major in math, science, or technology at highly selective universities, the report found that more Asian Americans received bachelor's degrees in social sciences and humanities, and the majority were enrolled in community colleges rather than four-year public or private universities.

In an interview with *Inside Higher Education* magazine, author Rosalind Chou discussed similarities and differences in the treatment of Asian, black, and Hispanic students:

"The similarities start with the shared history of racial oppression and labor exploitation. Early Asian immigrants were brought to this country for their cheap labor, just as African slaves and Mexican *braceros* were. They were also lynched just as the African American and Latino American. Today, these students still live in a society that is racially stratified. Unfortunately, many students do not know about this shared history and then do not apply this knowledge to our current racial hierarchy.

"The major differences in the treatment of these students are how they are stereotyped. Asian Americans are associated with academic excellence and overachievement, whereas black and Latino students are negatively stereotyped in academia. Either way, these stereotypes are externally imposed and can have a great affect on individual students internally, but also may impact other students, their teachers, professors, and administrators. Stereotyping, whether positive or negative, can be damaging."

In a sense, the tragic shootings at the Virginia Tech campus in March 2007 put a bit of distance between Asians and the model minority stereotype. Here was a Korean student who was anything but a model minority (although he was smart and skilled enough to be admitted to an academically rigorous university). A month after the killings, the University of Maryland sponsored a panel entitled "The End of the Model Minority Myth." The panel featured mostly Asian university professors, community activists, and students who reflected on their reactions to the tragedy and the media's role in the racism that minorities face after an individual from a certain ethnic group commits a crime.

Students at the panel agreed that, even though the shooter looked like them, they didn't have to apologize for his actions. One panel participant, Yixin Li, a University of Maryland freshman, said he prayed the shooter, Seung Hui Cho, would be Korean or Vietnamese and not a fellow Chinese. "I was praying, which I knew was wrong of me, that he was not Chinese. I was praying that he would be Korean or Vietnamese," said Li, an economics major. But he added, any wholesale comparisons between himself, Cho or any other Asian is wrong.

"I am not a model minority," Li said. "I am me, I am myself."

# five

................................

## LGBT Americans

Lesbian, Gay, Bisexual, and Transgendered

For decades, Judy Garland was the ultimate icon for the gay community, so much so that in gay parlance, someone gay was referred to as being a "friend of Dorothy," referring to Garland's role in *The Wizard of Oz*. It was a code word, a necessary thing for gays, who had to live an underground existence, meeting in shady clubs in the nastier parts of town, risking alternating police raids and gangs of gay bashers out for a little fun.

The Tudor Café in Manchester, New Hampshire, was one such place, or so it was rumored to be. It was hidden away on Pine Street, two blocks away from the public library where the indigents would gather on winter days to get out of the cold. The Tudor Café was a scary place to any kid growing up in that mill-town where decaying shoe factories overlooked the Merrimack River in the 1970s. To me, the Tudor was the domain of lonely, lecherous old men lurking in the shadows, the butt of jokes.

I first went in the Tudor when I was fourteen, on a bet. My closet had lead walls around it in those days. For twenty dollars, a friend and I rang the bell hidden away in the back alley. We got buzzed in and we warily walked through the door. Rather than being a den of desperation and depravity, it was abuzz with blasting disco music, men dancing with men and women with women. It seemed to be a parallel universe of people having fun. A blond bartender with an earring and bulging biceps told us to leave. The next day, we each collected our twenty dollars. No one could know it at the time, but things would be soon changing. The Stonewall Riots in New York's Greenwich Village had occurred just six years earlier, and the explosion of the movement for gay rights was well under way. Yet it would take a while to take root in the mainstream.

In 1985, while working at American Honda, I had a meeting scheduled with a market research supplier I'll call Jim, whom I had known for two years. I was hoping to hire him to conduct a customer satisfaction study. "You'd better sit down," I was told by a colleague. It turned out that Jim, a man over six feet two, in his mid-forties, was now named Michelle. When I met Michelle, she walked on unsteady heels and wore an unflattering wig and equally unflattering designer clothing. We conducted the study, though I had to lecture a couple of people in my department on proper office etiquette and catcalls did not fit the bill. When it came time to present the results of our study to management, my boss's boss refused to attend the meeting. Things had changed, but not completely.

Today gay men who wear women's clothes and/or identify as essentially female are not called drag queens, at least not in polite company. They are transgender people, the "T" in LGBT, which stands for lesbians, gays, bisexuals, and transgender people. (Straight men who like to wear women's clothes are called cross dressers or transvestites). There are some who add a "Q" to LGBT, which stands for the queer movement, a group unto itself, proudly taking its name from a word that was, for many decades, used as a pejorative. Some even add an extra Q for those who are "questioning."

Today there are no catcalls, at least not in the conference rooms of corporate America. Gay life that consisted of a Saturday night in a hidden away bar is now a broad and diverse movement of all kinds of gay "lifestyles," including, increasingly, parenthood. What was once a hidden group is now powerful, proud, and savvy, as well as recognized (and highly coveted) by businesses.

➲ *Gay life that consisted of a Saturday night in a hidden away bar is now a broad and diverse movement of all kinds of gay **"lifestyles."***

According to a 2008 Packaged Facts study, there are 15 to 16 million LGBT adults living in the United States with a purchasing power of $712 billion. That's about six to seven percent of the entire adult population, a few percentage points shy of the proverbial one-in-ten ration popularized by Kinsey more than half a century ago.

Kinsey was talking about sexual behavior, however, whereas the Packaged Facts study (and this book) refers to LGBT individuals as people who identify themselves as belonging to a community. There's a difference. In fact, I would propose that LGBT marketing has nothing to do with homosexual behavior, despite what many on the political far right might have us believe. It's about belonging to a group with a shared sense of history and a vision of unity, despite the tremendous diversity that exists within the LGBT community. It is this sense of gay identity that means opportunity for marketers. If they can touch it, if they can hook into it, they stand to make a lot of money, as many large corporations are coming to realize. If they miss the mark, and as we'll see, many have, they stand to lose big time.

## It's not easy being gay

Comedian Judy Carter jokes: "It's a lot easier being black than gay. At least if you're black you don't have to tell your parents." I don't agree with the first part, but I can tell you from experience, telling the parents is no fun. And despite the diversity within the gay market, coming out of the closet is one experience that all openly gay people share.

> ➲ *Like African Americans, the collective **history** of gays has not been without its stings.*

Like African Americans, the collective history of gays has not been without its stings. Unlike African Americans, most gays don't have gay parents to teach them about injustices, both past and present. And like African Americans, a majority of gays have experienced discrimination—two-thirds according to a 2007 study by New American Dimensions. Like African Americans, the depiction of gays and lesbians in popular culture has been, until fairly recently painfully stereotypical.

In *The Celluloid Closet*, a film about the way gays and lesbians have been portrayed in the movies, Shirley MacLaine recounts making *The Children's Hour*, a 1961 film in which she played a tortured, closeted lesbian in love with fellow schoolteacher Audrey Hepburn. In the end, her character hangs herself. "We didn't do the picture right," says MacLaine in the interview. "These days, she would fight for her budding preference. We were unaware. We didn't understand what we were doing."

*The Celluloid Closet* also examines how coded any gay references had to be. In one interview, Gore Vidal discusses contriving to add some homoerotic spice to the 1959 film *Ben-Hur*. Vidal recalls how one scene in particular, involving actors Charlton Heston and Stephen Boyd, was a little bit lifeless. So, to spice things up, and what the heck, have a little fun at the same time, Vidal, the screenwriter suggested to director William Wyler to add a subtext that one or both of the characters was homosexual, or at the very least, attracted to each other. All that the audience members would know—except, possibly, for some savvy gay men—would be that there was *something* deeper about the characters' relationship. Vidal got Wyler to buy into the idea—partially. "Talk to Boyd," Wyler said, "but don't say anything to Heston. Chuck will fall apart." It worked. To this day, film enthusiasts and gays marvel at how a few word choices and acting tweaks from Vidal managed to transform *Ben-Hur* from a Christian epic into a gay romance, with Charlton Heston none the wiser.

As the interviews from *The Celluloid Closet* demonstrate, gays weren't completely absent from the movies, despite censorship laws. Sometimes they were stereotyped as swishy and flamboyant queens or lesbian vampires. At other times, gay writers like Vidal cleverly injected gay culture or sexuality, with cloaked references that only other gays or culturally astute straights could pick up on. The gay presence was like the wizard in *The Wizard of Oz*, disguised and hidden behind a curtain.

The interview with MacLaine shows the more painful side of the equation; in the movies, gays and lesbians that acted on their homosexual impulses often met with tragic endings, the implication being that they were evil and needed to be punished. When MacLaine says that they did the movie wrong, she is referring to the fact that in the early sixties, it just never occurred to anyone that being gay was a legitimate choice.

## Yep, I'm gay

"Yep, I'm Gay," read the cover of *Time* magazine on April 14, 1997. After months of hinting and an unprecedented publicity campaign, Ellen DeGeneres came out—on her show and in real life. *Ellen* became the first network television show with a gay person in the leading role. Not that gays were unheard of on American television. Mike Wallace hosted CBS *Reports: The Homosexuals* in 1967, the first network news special about homosexuality. *All in the Family* was the first sitcom to tackle the subject when Archie Bunker discovered his drinking buddy was gay in a 1971 episode. TV dramas from the 1970s, such as *Medical Center, Police Woman*, and *Marcus Welby, M.D.*, featured an occasional episode that dealt with gay themes. As time went on, there were even some recurring gay characters. Billy Crystal played one on *Soap* in the late seventies. Steven Carrington wrestled with his homosexuality on *Dynasty* in the eighties. In the nineties, there were regular gay characters on *Northern Exposure, Melrose Place*, and *Roseanne.*

But Ellen's coming out was significant. Story lines on the show began to center on gay themes. Ellen dated women. And there were gay in-jokes, especially about relationship-crazed lesbians ("What does a lesbian bring on a second date? A U-Haul."). In the words of former Vice President Al Gore, "When the character Ellen came out, millions of Americans were forced to look at sexual orientation in a more open light."

In April 1998, a year after the coming out episode, ABC announced that *Ellen* would be cancelled. Perhaps it was too much too fast—"too gay" as many said. Ellen told *Entertainment Tonight*, "I'm gay, the character's gay, that's the problem everyone has with the show. It's just too controversial." Controversial it was, but Ellen paved the way for programs with lesbians and gays in the spotlight. First there was *Will and Grace*'s debut on NBC in 1998; followed by Showtime's *Queer as Folk* in 2000, Bravo's *Queer Eye for the Straight Guy* in 2003, and Showtime's *The L Word* in 2004. In 2005, Viacom launched the first 24-hour gay network, Logo. The latter would be a milestone, in that for the first time, there was a major television network that could feature ads specifically targeting gays.

Gay characters on these shows were instrumental in shaping a new generation to believe that homosexuality is no big deal. A 2007 Pew survey showed that support for gay marriage among the Millennial generation (generally aged 18 to 29) was nearly twenty points higher than for all adults. In an August, 2005 Greenberg Quinlan Rosner (GQR) survey of 18-to-25-year-olds, 82 percent reported that they personally knew or worked with someone who was gay, lesbian, bisexual, or transgender.

Pro-gay sentiment, to the extent it exists in America, is, strictly speaking, generational. An entire generation is coming of age in an era where being gay or lesbian is no big deal. Consequently these younger consumers, the Millennials, don't have to undo the anti-gay prejudice that other generations learned. They simply never learned that gay was bad.

> ➲ *An entire **generation** is coming of age in an era where being gay or lesbian is no big deal.*

Of course, this is a sweeping generalization. But polling bears out the idea that young adults across the board see homosexuality as rather benign. In May 2008, California became the second state to offer full marriage equality for gays and lesbians, through the state supreme court. Predictably, right wing and religious groups pushed through a ballot measure to outlaw it in November 2008. But the anti-marriage forces have been surprised to find some fierce and growing opposition, especially from young voters. In August 2008, an editorial in the *Los Angeles Times* opined:

> "With same-sex marriage, as with gay rights generally, the younger generation is leading the way. Last month's Field poll found that opposition to Proposition 8 was greatest among voters under 30 years of age. That was consistent with a finding by the Pew Forum on Religion and Public Life that roughly half of adults under 30 supported same-sex marriage. The trend is clear: Support for gay rights and same-sex marriage is being driven by generational change."

But differences among age groups cannot completely explain the greater tolerance for gays and lesbians. Thanks to the gay-rights movement, Americans of all ages are more likely to have openly homosexual relatives, neighbors and co-workers. Those personal contacts make it harder for decent people to accept discrimination against gays and lesbians—including at the ballot box.

> ➲ *A 2008 Zogby International survey showed that more than six in ten Americans were open to a gay* **President**.

The growing acceptance of gays and lesbians showed up in various polls, including a 2008 Zogby International survey, which showed that more than six in ten Americans were open to a gay President. It underscored a 2007 Gallup poll, which also showed a majority of Americans willing to support a gay or lesbian president. Interestingly, the only kind of candidate a majority of Americans could NOT support, (of Catholic, Jewish, African American, female, Hispanic, Muslim, married three times, over 72 years of age, or gay) was an atheist. For gays and lesbians, the shift in attitudes in a relatively short amount of time represents huge progress. The trend is clear: we are moving toward a society where sexual orientation is openly discussed and tolerated.

It could be, in less than a generation, that the U.S. will enter a post-gay era. If and when that youthful nonchalant attitude of sexuality becomes the prevailing societal view, it could spell the end of so-called gay culture as we've come to know it.

## Is Gay the New Black?

Advertising to gays and lesbians in the gay and lesbian press is booming, but it is emerging in mainstream media as well. A couple of television ads that have made the rounds:

- A man in colonial dress awaits the arrival of his beloved outside of Independence Hall with a bouquet of flowers in hand. He ignores the glance of an attractive girl that passes him as an announcer says "Philadelphia and its countryside have a long history of making everyone feel welcome and free." Another man walks up to him, to whom he gives the bouquet. The tagline proclaims, "Come to Philadelphia. Get your history straight, and your nightlife gay."

- Two Snapple bottles, dressed up like a bride and groom, are marching down the aisle to the "Wedding March." Suddenly, in a take off on *The Graduate*, the ceremony is interrupted by another Snapple character, a noisy man in the balcony, setting off a flurry of gasps and groans among the attendees. The organist faints. In the next scene, the two men leave the church together to the "Wedding March," the guests, limo, and abandoned bride behind them.

Some companies have been very successful in reaching out to gays and lesbians, either overtly or covertly. Ikea has been successful in not just showing gays as stereotypical single, party people, but it also pioneered in showing the nesting behavior of many gay men. In 1994 Ikea and its ad agency, Deutsch, launched an ad with a gay male couple, showing them shopping together and discussing how they met, with one finishing the other's sentence; in other words, a typical couple that just happened to be gay. The ad aired only once before being pulled—for safety reasons. One of its American stores received bomb threats due to the commercial. It is still remembered by the gay community, even by people who only heard about the ad but never saw it.

Twelve years later, Ikea launched a new spot including another gay pair, this time with a child. Following a rainbow of families, the black and Asian male couple joined by their golden retriever and daughter, snuggle in domestic bliss. An ending voiceover asks: "Why shouldn't sofas come in flavors, just like families?" The commercial, also created by Deutsch, aired on national cable networks. However, no ads appeared in gay media. In fact, for all its goodwill with the gay community, the company has never advertised in the gay media. A spokesperson for Ikea told Commercial Closet–founder Mike Wilke that there was "not even a debate" to include the male couple again. "It was sort of a no-brainer. Gays are part of the world we live in." She adds that, when casting the men, "we went with the people we felt were right," and that they were of different ethnicities was incidental.

> ⊃ *Ikea shows gays as being part of an ad's* **ensemble**.

Ikea, which has used gay and lesbian characters in many commercials, shows gays as being part of an ad's ensemble. For instance, including a same-sex couple with a heterosexual couple is a way of showing that your company recognizes that gays are "normal," that they are part of the diversity that makes up America. This inclusion is still rare in advertising. That's what makes it a real opportunity to demonstrate a company's awareness of gays as being part of the landscape.

In 2007, Levi Strauss & Co. and its agency BBH New York

created a provocative commercial using the same protagonist in two different versions of a commercial. In the first version, the hero, with a tug of his jeans over his hips, is thrust through the floor of his office to an exciting new world, complete with a beautiful fantasy woman waiting in a phone booth. The second version is the same, shot for shot, until it comes to the phone booth. The fantasy woman is instead a fantasy man.

The ad, created by BBH New York, was placed on the 24-hour gay network Logo, and was scheduled to appear later on other cable channels such as Bravo and HGTV. According to openly-gay VP of marketing Robert Cameron, the company wanted to talk to communities that are leading fashion, like African Americans and gay men. As Cameron explained to Michael Wilke, "The message is, 'we see you, we support you, just like any other human being.'"

Other companies are investing in "branded" entertainment. In 2005, Subaru, a charter sponsor of Logo, created two-minute mini-movie interstitials for Logo about Subaru owners, like a female couple who are triathletes and expedition racers. In 2006, Pernod Ricard USA's Stolichnaya vodka produced a 53-minute documentary called "Be Real—Stories from Queer America," about six gays and lesbians who made a difference in their communities. The film ran at 19 gay film festivals and won an award from the Association of National Advertisers. Moving to other media, "Be Real" aired on Logo, and in spring 2007 was turned into a series of half-hour programs on the network.

Many of these efforts have been wildly successful; some, less so. In other cases, company policies and boneheaded corporate moves have sent out mixed messages that have made gays and lesbians wonder about the company's true motivations and ask the question, "Do they just want my money, or do they really care about me?" Many companies are finding out the hard way that gays and lesbians, more than any group, need to be convinced of the latter, before they will give up

➲ *Simply put, gays and lesbians **support** brands that support them.*

their hard earned dollars. Simply put, gays and lesbians support brands that support them. They are early adopters, trendsetters, and very brand loyal. And brand loyalty, building relationships for life, is the brass ring in marketing.

## LGBTs by the Numbers

In 2007 Packaged Facts came out with a broad and comprehensive study of the gay and lesbian population in the United States. The study concluded:

- An estimated 8.7 million gay men account for a majority of the gay and lesbian population. Surveys indicate that more than 80 percent of self-identified gay men are less than 50 years of age.

- Gay men are much more likely than lesbians to live in central cities in large metropolitan areas, and gay-male couples tend to cluster in neighborhoods with a high concentration of couples like themselves.

- Gay men earn less than heterosexual men but more than lesbians. They are more likely to be employed in managerial and professional jobs but in lower-paying occupations within those categories.

- Lesbians are more likely than gay men to have children but an increasing number of gay-male couples are adopting children.

- Compared with gay women, gay men affiliate more strongly with the gay community. They are more likely to read gay print media, visit gay websites, and participate in gay community events.

- Compared with other consumer segments, gay men are more likely to shop for luxury goods and be early adopters of new consumer electronics products.

## Getting your company's house in order

Although marketers covet the dollars of LGBT consumers, and have been making great strides in reaching out to them—through advertising, community events, PR, and online—some are beginning to learn that such efforts fall far short of expectations. The reason is that outreach is not enough. Perhaps more than any other group, the LGBT community closely watches what companies do behind the scenes. Gays insist that businesses walk the walk, not just talk the talk, and they will collectively shun a company if its corporate policies don't match up with its outward gay friendliness. A company that does not measure up will not be making significant inroads in the gay community.

> ➲ *Gays **insist** that businesses walk the walk, not just talk the talk*

For eight years running, HRC has published an annual report, called the Corporate Equality Index, which shows how companies fare on a number of issues of importance to gays and lesbians. The 2009 report showed a record number of the largest U.S. companies are increasingly competing to expand benefits and protections for their gay, lesbian, bisexual, and transgender employees and consumers. An unprecedented 260 major U.S. companies earned the top rating of 100 percent. That number is up from 195 in the 2008 report, and has grown tenfold in six years.

HRC has found that, instead of fearing backlash from antigay groups for their pro-gay policies, companies are fiercely competitive within their industries for the top rating, triggering quick actions to improve company policies and benefits. According to HRC president Joe Solmonese, "CEOs are very much aware of their score and its impact on their business. They know that a top score means a healthier work environment, greater productivity and the ability to recruit top talent. They also know that a bad score will hurt their bottom line." Beyond recruiting and retaining talent, a good score is, increasingly, something that a company's LGBT consumers look for as well.

My friend Chris Lehtonen whose agency asterixGROUP helps companies make their brands "gay-friendly," suggests that advertising to LGBTs, while arguably the most visible sign of outreach to a community, should be the cherry on top of marketing efforts to gays and lesbians.

> "Ads are not enough to reach gays and lesbians. First, you need to get your house in order. Build a relationship with the LGBT segment, and put your money where your mouth is. Look at your internal policies. Are you giving to AIDS causes and to gay causes? What events can you sponsor? Are you in dialogue in companies on how to treat LGBT people? If you are a motel chain, do you have a company policy for front desk clerks to ask, 'Would you like one bed or two?' when faced with a same sex couple."

In 2004, Home Depot found out the necessity of putting gays first (or at least ahead of animals). When it was reported that the company offered insurance for employees' pets, while refusing to cover gay employees' domestic partners, the Atlanta-based Fortune 500 company came under fire from HRC and other gay rights groups. In less than a day after HRC gave Home Depot a failing grade on its Corporate Index, the home improvement chain did a *mea culpa*, and announced that it would provide domestic partnership benefits for its gay employees. The company needed to do a little spin as well, to ensure that it was merely an oversight, after the issue hit the gay and mainstream press. Home Depot's vice president of diversity and inclusion, told the *Atlanta Journal Constitution* that when she saw the policy, it "looked funny to me, too."

## United we stand

Outreach to the LGBT community is about more than being politically correct. It's about money. One of the first groups to grasp this and jump on the LGBT bandwagon was the travel industry. American Airlines was one of the first to reach out, though it was the result of getting off to a bad start.

In their book *Business Inside Out: Capturing Millions of Brand Loyal Gay Consumers* (Kaplan, 2006), Robert Witeck and Wesley Combs recount how American Airlines came to their agency, Witeck-Combs, to improve its image in 1993. The flashpoint was an incident where an American Airlines crew in Chicago, fearing for the passengers' safety, removed a man living with AIDS from a flight. Word got out, and it turned into a public relations disaster. The agency worked with American to rebuild trust and communicate the company's values. The airline's first test came in 1994, with the 25th anniversary of the Stonewall Riots and the Gay Games. Thousands of LGBT travelers would be in New York to celebrate both events in June. To prepare, the airline updated its training for employees in dealing with passengers living with HIV or AIDS. Witeck-Combs and the airline educated employees on the importance of such events. The instructional video touched gay and lesbian airline employees, but also solidified American's culture as welcoming and nondiscriminatory. According to Witeck and Combs, "incorporating LGBT issues into the diversity strategy of the company reaped huge dividends for American Airlines. Over the past 12 years, American can attribute millions in revenue from its targeted outreach to gay and lesbian consumers. Doing the right thing is truly good for business."

By the mid-nineties the commitment was already starting to turn around American's reputation. Seeing this success, United Airlines sought to copy American, and began packaging vacations for gay travelers, advertising in gay media, and prominently supporting gay-events.

But United stumbled, badly. Again, it wasn't the outreach. It's what was going on behind the scenes that caught the attention and garnered the wrath of the gay community. In June 1997, the

San Francisco Board of Supervisors passed a law that required companies doing business with the city to provide the same benefits to workers with domestic partners as they give to married employees. United, the largest airline carrier in San Francisco, with 20,000 employees, fought it. It joined the Air Transport Association, a group representing the nations' major airlines, in a lawsuit seeking to ban San Francisco from forcing the airlines to comply with the ordinance. The airlines contended that they only have to follow federal government mandates.

Even more galling to gay leaders was that Pat Robertson's American Center for Law and Justice, an organization with a history of vigorously attacking pro-gay policies, sided with United in the fight. In fairness, all major airlines had joined in the lawsuit against the San Francisco ordinance, but because United's lease was the first to expire at the city's airport, only it attracted attention.

In the spring of 1999, HRC launched a boycott against United. The group Equal Benefits Advocates (EBA) supported it, running television commercials in San Francisco and Los Angeles. In the words of the commercial's producer, the ads were created to "stamp United Airlines and Pat Robertson as leaders in anti-gay discrimination in the minds of gay people across the country." While the boycott was on, United's efforts to reach out to gays and lesbians were ignored and derided. The company sponsored community events but it was loudly booed. In August of that year, United Airlines gave in and offered its gay and lesbian employees the full array of domestic-partners-benefits, even as the company remained locked in litigation. Six days later, American Airlines—which had begun to suffer scrutiny because it didn't offer full benefits—vowed to follow United's lead. One day after that, US Airways announced that it would be the third.

United redoubled its efforts to get back into the good graces of gays and lesbians, many of whom were still skeptical about the airline's motives. Through sponsorships, increased gay advertising, tie-ins, and community events, the airline made a strong effort to show that the friendly skies were gay-friendly as well. Bowing to gay organizations, United even declared it would no longer accept ads in its in-flight magazine for radio personality Dr. Laura Schlessinger, who had made disparaging remarks about gays.

Simply put, gays and lesbians support companies that support them.

## Dirty Dancing with the Religious Right

Supporting the gay community is not without its risks. That's one reason why support is so appreciated by LGBT consumers. The staunchly antigay American Family Association (AFA), a right wing organization, regularly does battle against what it calls the "radical homosexual agenda" and is notorious for urging boy-cotts of companies that support the gay community like Procter & Gamble, Kraft, Walgreen, Johnson & Johnson, Orbitz, Avis, Motorola, Allstate, and Ford Motor Company.

> Supporting the gay community is not without its risks. That's one reason why support is so **appreciated** by LGBT consumers.

The AFA can be vicious. In 2000, P&G Canada took out an ad in a Toronto gay publication, *Xtra*, for Downy wrinkle releaser. The ad showed two men in bed, with their wrinkled clothing strewn about. The caption read "You were more concerned with taking them off than folding them up." Aside from the Toronto gay market, the ad went largely unnoticed. Until four years later when P&G came out in support of a measure to repeal a 1993 amendment to the Cincinnati city charter which forbade providing protection to gays. The AFA decided to go to war, and set up a website, PGBoycott. com, to highlight the ad and spotlight what it considered to be the company's dirty laundry. After describing the ad, the website said, "There should be no doubt P&G is aggressively promoting the homosexual agenda. A company doesn't create and run an ad that leaves the impression that homosexual sex is thrilling and exciting unless they support the homosexual agenda." The website asked its constituency to boycott three P&G products: Crest toothpaste, Tide detergent, and Pampers diapers.

It is hard to measure how effective consumer boycotts have been. However, *The Wall Street Journal* noted that AFA's boycott of P&G after that company backed gay rights legislation in Cincinnati did have an effect:

> "P&G officials won't talk publicly about the boycott," the *Journal*'s Alan Murray wrote. "But privately, they acknowledge the groups turned out to be larger, better funded, better organized and more sophisticated than the company had imagined. And there is little doubt the boycott hit its mark. Tim Wildmon, president of the American Family Association, says 360,000 families signed petitions to boycott P&G products. Subsequently, P&G's advertising disappeared from gay magazines and Web sites and gay-oriented television shows."

While some companies are willing to ask, "How high?" when organizations like the AFA say "jump," they soon find out that the backlash from gays and lesbians (who often make up a sizable chunk of their consumers) can cause infinitely more grief. In May 2005, Ford Motor Company joined the large and distinguished group of companies threatened with an AFA boycott due to its pro-gay company policies. In December of that year, the AFA lifted the boycott completely, just after Ford decided not to renew advertising campaigns for its Jaguar and Land Rover brands in gay publications.

When gay leaders got word of a prepared statement suggesting that Ford's decision was linked to AFA pressure, they were furious. Further suspicion was cast on the alleged Ford-AFA deal after an auto industry publication reported that the ad decision was part of a larger deal with AFA that included Ford's agreement to no longer sponsor gay and lesbian events and a promise that its Volvo brand would advertise in the gay media only without messages tailored to gays and lesbians. True or not, it appeared that a small, publicity-seeking antigay group had yanked around pro-gay Ford, which had received a 100 percent rating from HRC. A Ford spokesman asserted that the company's decision was "for business reasons, not a social statement."

The gay community would not accept the spin. A coalition of 19 LGBT advocacy organizations sent a joint letter to Ford, expressing dismay and anger that the company would cave in to anti-gay pressure. Ford met with LGBT leaders and again reaffirmed its commitment to gay rights, and disavowed any ties to Wildmon.

Microsoft, a long time friend to the gay community—it boasts the oldest LGBT employee group in America—made a significantly dumb move when a series of flip flops made it look like a homophobic preacher might have more influence on company policy than its gay and gay-friendly employees, gay-friendly consumers, and increasingly gay-friendly public opinion. In early 2006, it was revealed that the software giant had taken a neutral stance on gay rights legislation in its home state of Washington. Bill 1515, which would have banned discrimination against gays and lesbians in housing, employment, and insurance, had died by a single vote in the state Senate a month before. It was largely believed that Microsoft quietly pulling its support led to the defeat. Gay leaders, bloggers and other activists were even more incensed when they learned that Microsoft brass had met with the Rev. Ken Hutcherson, pastor of a Redmond, Washington, church, who reportedly threatened a national boycott if the software giant continued supporting the bill (as it had for years). The Los Angeles Gay and Lesbian Center took the bold step of demanding that Microsoft return a corporate vision award for its forward-looking approach to LGBT issues.

After two weeks of receiving holy hell from gay community leaders as well as (gay and straight) Microsoft employees and the gay press, Microsoft's Chief Executive Officer Steve Ballmer announced the company's renewed backing of the legislation in an e-mail to all U.S. employees: "After looking at the question from all sides, I've concluded that diversity in the workplace is such an important issue for our business that it should be included in our legislative agenda," Ballmer wrote. Ballmer went on to admit that the company had made a mistake, though he did not mention the pastor, nor did he indicate who was behind the decision to go neutral on a bill the company had strongly supported for years.

Perhaps Kraft Foods learned from the blunders of Microsoft and Ford when AFA targeted it for sponsoring the 2006 Gay Games in Chicago. An e-mail from AFA encouraged its 500,000 members to make a personal call to Kraft and "tell them to pull their financial support from the 2006 Gay Games." Unlike its previous strong-arm tactics, the group did not call for an official boycott of Kraft or other corporate sponsors. The games went on, and Wildmon moved on to the next pro-gay company, no doubt claiming victory for his efforts at Kraft, despite no visible success.

Wes Combs has stark advice for companies who care about reaching LGBTs: "The bottom line: Don't negotiate with conservative organizations. It's a no win situation. You can't meet your business needs and their demands."

## African American and gay

My company recently conducted multiple focus groups on the African American LGBT market, half with gay men and half with lesbians. Each segment was divided by age; the first group included 18-to-24-year-olds, and the second, 25-to-45-year-olds.

As was expected, there were big similarities as well as differences between the groups. For instance, men and women in both groups felt that they were at once gay and African American, but more than anything else, they were gay African Americans. Respondents in all the groups talked of the difficulty of coming out of the closet in the African-American community, at church, with their friends, and with most difficulty, to their parents. Many did not date interracially. Those that did, spoke of the problems inherent in an interracial relationship, even a gay one. And many of the respondents were churchgoers, attending both predominately gay and mainstream African-American congregations.

Despite commonalities, each group had its particularities. More typical of lesbians than gay men in general, many of the women had children and were in partnered relationships. Like lesbians in general, the women were equally as likely to identify strongly with being women; for men, identification was more about race and sexual orientation. The men were able to point with pride to the recently cancelled Logo program *Noah's Arc*, which focused on gay African-American men living in Los Angeles. African-American lesbians felt pretty certain that no company would dare to focus on them; it would be too much of a stretch, too scandalous.

Another big difference between the men and the women was that the women identified strongly with clearly delineated groups, specifically "Studs," who tended to wear baggy clothes and baseball caps, and "Femmes," who as the name implies, conformed more closely to the traditional image of women. Each group had its own unique challenges. There seemed to be a cultural prohibition about studs dating studs, for instance. Femmes, on the other hand, could date either a stud or a femme, but faced the challenge of fighting off heterosexual men who refused to believe they were lesbians.

For gay African Americans, choosing which identity to embrace is difficult. Gay blacks often face strong resistance from black friends, family, and church members, who are often unable to acknowledge that African Americans, particularly men, are engaging in same-sex

➲ *For gay African Americans, choosing which **identity** to embrace is difficult.*

relations. There is pressure to start a family, one with solid African-American Christian values. On the other hand, for many African Americans, gay and straight, the face of the gay community is white. Some may encounter discrimination from gay whites, sometimes overt, and sometimes subtle, like being ignored at clubs. Or being snubbed after a night of gallivanting with a partner in the thralls of what Spike Lee called "jungle fever."

## The generational divide

In urban areas, many have embraced the identity of being "homo-thugz" or "gay-thug," which is an alternative to gay culture that has appeal for those who follow the B-boy image, many of whom are on the down low. On weekends in big cities, thousands flock to clubs where they can experience a hip-hop atmosphere, but not expose themselves to the homophobia endemic to that culture. Many homo-thugz adopt tough, streetwise personas, in marked contrast to the images projected by the mainstream gays. Said one promoter of a New York hip-hop club a few years ago in a *Village Voice* interview, "I don't like people that, when I'm walking the streets, say I'm gay. There's still a lot of gay bashing out there. If you dress thug style, nobody's gonna bother you, because thugness and realness is an ultimate man."

The generation gap occurring in the LGBT community was highlighted in a 2007 article in the *Los Angeles Times* which describes conflicts arising in Manhattan's gay mecca, the West Village, between the neighborhood's original gay (and largely white) residents, and a new generation of gays, who hail from neighborhoods in the Bronx, Brooklyn, and Queens, sporting baggy jeans, XXXL t-shirts, do-rags, and Timberland boots. This new generation is also largely black and Latino.

The article quotes David Poster, a 30-year resident of the neighborhood and president of the Christopher Street Patrol, which had been protesting the rowdy behavior occurring in the neighborhood. According to him, it's not about race, but rather peace and quiet. "It's about behavior," he said. "You cannot walk on the street. They force you to walk in the gutter, and if you dare to walk through them or bump into them, that's it. There's a war." But others see it differently. Bob Kohler, an 80-year-old gay rights advocate, compares the neighborhood's outrage to that experienced decades earlier when gays started to move to the West Village in large numbers. Said Kohler, the old generation of gays simply "don't want black faces on Christopher Street."

Clearly, when talking about the LGBT market, it's imperative to know exactly which part of the market you're talking about. So the next time someone asks you where your company stands, tell them you're a "Q": You're questioning which segment to target and how to keep all the other segments from feeling left out.

> *Clearly, when talking about the LGBT market, it's imperative to know exactly which **part** of the market you're talking about.*

## New American pride

I remember an episode of *The Hollywood Squares*. Paul Lynde, the ever-present, ever-flamboyant center square, was asked the question "Why do motorcyclists like to wear leather?" He paused, gave his characteristic grin and cackled mischievously, "Because chiffon wrinkles."

It's hard to know how many watching the show got the veiled reference to the gay leather scene, let alone the comedian's constant double entendres throughout his tenure on the show from 1968 to 1981. But one thing is certain. To have been that edgy, his humor had to stay on the down low.

Times have changed, sort of. Gay culture is mainstream. We have gay networks, gay sitcoms, and gay Westerns. In the realm of corporate America, companies compete for gay customers and face boycotts for *not* standing by the gay community. A Gallup poll conducted in May 2007, found that 89 percent of U.S. citizens believe that gays and lesbians should have protection against workplace discrimination. Still, at press time, employees could be fired simply for being gay in 30 states, although a new federal law adding sexual orientation and gender identification as protected categories against workplace discrimination is working its way through Congress (a similar bill was introduced more than 30 years ago, and was stymied by Republicans). A gay hate crime bill is also winding through Congress. Sadly, the FBI reported that crimes based on sexual orientation accounted for 14.2 percent of reported incidents in 2005.

Today's generation of lesbians and gay men are forging a new consciousness that is based on having the ability to define one's self on one's own terms. As writer Dan Levy noted, "No underground society today, gay life is being transformed by a generation that came of age after Stonewall, a progeny that proudly calls itself 'queer.' For this exuberant set, being gay is more than a struggle for acceptance and equal rights: It is a celebration of American pluralism."

This new generation of gays that is coming of age who do not know who Judy Garland was, other than as a girl in pigtails who went off to see a wizard. They are strangers to police raids, and gay bashers, though still around, are increasingly disparaged as thugs and criminals, rather than heroes. There is no more need for code words or double entendres. Gay clubs are mainstream and fashionable. And, more and more often, young gay men and lesbians don't even feel the need to socialize at gay clubs. In most large cities, twenty-something gays and lesbians feel comfortable socializing in "straight" or "mixed" clubs, where sexual orientation is not a Maginot Line, and less important then club-goers taste in music, ambience, and maybe politics.

The rise in the visibility and acceptance of gays has been precipitous, in absolute terms and relative to the other segments. In 1985, it was fine for an executive to shun a meeting hosted by a transgender person. Today, businesses are clamoring for gay marketing dollars. In Manchester, New Hampshire, the Tudor Café, which had been called Front Runners for a decade, has changed its name back in celebration of its history. It's still on Pine Street near the library, which has an extensive section on gay and lesbian studies.

➲ *The rise in the visibility and acceptance of gays has been **precipitous** relative to the other segments.*

# six

### Post-Ethnic America and People of Mixed Race

In one of my favorite episodes of *Seinfeld*, Elaine is dating a man who looks like he could be either African American or white. Elaine is obsessed with determining his race, and in this scene she asks George for advice.

> George: "Why don't you just ask him?"
>
> Elaine (giving him a "duh" look): "Because if I ask him, then it's like I really want to know."
>
> George: "Maybe he's, um . . . mixed."
>
> Elaine: "Is that the right word?"
>
> George: "I really don't think we're supposed to be talking about this."

➲ *We Americans are **obsessed** by race.*

We Americans are obsessed by race. It has defined our history, and continues to define our future. We ascribe all sorts of traits to people just based on their race. African Americans used to be lazy; now they're cool. Asians used to be sinister; now they're smart. White people used to be ubiquitous. Now, scholars and school kids ponder what it means to be white in today's America.

A few years ago, I did a study on what multiculturalism meant for young white people in their teens and early twenties. I felt like a race detective on a mission to find out what the next generation really thinks about our changing America. I had an arsenal of questions like "How do you really feel about African Americans?" and "How about all these Hispanics?" It was my job to pick and probe and get below the surface. After all, whites are losing the prominence they've held for years. Are they okay with that?

For the first hour or so, I got political correctness of the "some of my best friends are (fill in the ethnic category)" variety. I was starting to fall for it. As we got into the second hour, however, the participants started to get real. One young man started to get rhetorical: "Yeah, I've got a question for you. How come, we can't use the "N" word and yet they call us "white boy?"

It was my job to ask questions and not answer them. "How does that make you feel?"

"F—king angry."

In other interviews, I started to hear similar types of remarks. "How come you have Hispanic or African-American dormitories? Imagine if you had a dorm for just white people." I heard gripes about diversity, affirmative action, and political correctness. I heard sob stories of white guys not being able to get dates because all the girls want Hispanic or black guys. I was told that at the hippest clubs, bouncers would keep white guys waiting at the door while gentlemen of color are shown the red carpet.

It wasn't all griping, however. For every white person whom I interviewed that had problems with the new racial order, there was another who dated interracially or expressed unabashed approbation of the racial tolerance of this new generation. But my hypothesis, that this new generation was in some way *beyond* race, just wasn't playing out. In the end, we were forced to conclude that today's young people relate to race differently, in fact better, than any other generation before them. But race is still a very salient marker of who we are. I advised our client to be as inclusive as possible in its advertising and that the message of racial diversity would resonate well with teen and young adult consumers. We also cautioned them to be careful; that this new generation, while tolerant and accepting, is definitely not colorblind.

We may have a long way to go in this country in realizing true racial equality, but we have certainly made a lot of progress in recent history. Until the mid-twentieth century it was illegal in most states for people of mixed race to marry or even engage in interracial sex. These anti-miscegenation laws, as they have been called since the days of the Civil War, the term being an invention of those who wanted to drum up fear of mulatto babies, were on the books in a majority of states from 1776 (mixing of races was illegal in seven of the thirteen colonies) until the 1950s. From 1913 to 1948, 30 out of the then 48 states had laws prohibiting a union of the races. In 1967, when the United States Supreme Court unanimously ruled in *Loving v. Virginia* that anti-miscegenation laws were unconstitutional, blacks and whites could not legally marry in 16 states. Anti-miscegenation laws focused on Asians as well. As recently as 1960, marriage between whites and Asians was illegal in 14 states; seven of these states explicitly mention Filipinos or "Malays." Three states, Georgia, South Carolina, and Virginia prohibited marriages between whites and "non-whites" until they were struck down by *Loving v. Virginia*.

➲ *Today, **interracial** marriages are commonplace*

Today, interracial marriages are commonplace, and since television's first interracial kiss in 1968 between *Star Trek*'s Captain Kirk and Lieutenant Uhura (an episode which many stations in the south refused to air) people don't bat an eye at an interracial couple. Hispanics, who are largely of *meztiso* or mixed race origin, are the nation's largest and near-fastest growing minority; they will make up 30 percent of the U.S. population by 2050. Golfing great Tiger Woods refers to himself as *Cablinasian*, a mixture of Caucasian, Black, American Indian and Asian (he is actually one-quarter Chinese, one-quarter Thai, one-quarter African American, one-eighth Native

American, and one-eighth Dutch). And let's not forget President Obama who calls himself a "mutt."

Tiger Woods may be a model for the future of racial identity in America—not in his extra-diverse background necessarily, but rather in his refusal to give in to racial absolutism. America is moving behind what historian David Hollinger calls America's "ethno-racial pentagon," the grouping of people into five artificial groups: Caucasians, African Americans, Hispanics, Asians, and Indians or Eskimos. In his view, one that I agree with, we are moving toward a "post-ethnic" America, where Americans will be free to choose which identities, ethnic or otherwise, we pursue. In *Postethnic America: Beyond Multiculturalism* (Basic Books, 1995), Hollinger writes: "Postethnicity prefers voluntary to prescribed affiliations, appreciates multiple identities, pushes for communities of wide scope, recognizes the constructed character of ethno-racial groups, and accepts the formation of new groups as a part of the normal life of a democratic society."

Many marketers suspect that Hollinger may be correct that ethnicity and other traditional marketing markers based on demographics have already become obsolete. One school of thought, for instance, dubbed tribal marketing, focuses on affinity or interest-based "tribes" or groups of consumers. Tribal marketers look at groups like "skateboarders" or "hip-hoppers" that share a similar lifestyle, rather than focusing on traditional demographics—like ethnicity. In the world of tribal marketers, consumers behave as they do in Hollinger's post-ethnic world, actively making choices about how they self-identify, defying the placement of traditional labels.

If traditional racial boundaries are blurring or going away because of intermarriage, if the children of Hispanic and Asian immigrants are assimilating, if African Americans are integrating, if gays are the new straight, if the future of marketing is based on interest and lifestyle rather than ethnicity and race, one could assume that multicultural marketing is heading toward obsolescence.

Not likely. Hollinger's post-ethnic world may be the future, but it's still the future. In today's America, ethnic identity, be it Hispanic, Asian, African American or gay, is still a salient component of how people see themselves. Hispanic and Asian immigration is recent and still expected to continue for years to come. It is these immigrants and their children who will keep the tax coffers full as Baby Boomers continue to age. And shamefully, the days of African-American racism and homophobia are not behind us.

There has been a steady rise in the number of interracial marriages. The 2000 Census counted 3.1 million interracial couples, or about 6 percent of married couples. For the first time, the Census that year allowed respondents to identify themselves as belonging to two or more races, a category that now includes 7.3 million Americans, or about 3 percent of the population. Census experts estimate that the mixed-race population grew by about 25 percent from 2000 to 2006, while the total population grew about 7 percent during the same period. And that trend is likely to continue.

"The multiracial population is much younger than the total population," said Nicholas Jones of the Census Bureau, noting that 70 percent of black/white people are under age 17.

What is certain is that the American mainstream is becoming increasingly multicultural and the prize will go to those companies, those politicians, and those charities that understand what a multi-

> *The prize will go to companies, politicians, and charities that understand what a **multicultural** identity means.*

cultural identity means. The winners will be the ones to see that identity is a dynamic thing, frequently morphing into something else. They'll be the ones to understand what it is morphing towards.

## Mulatto America

In 2000, the popular image of America as a country made up of mostly white people with a sizeable black minority became history.

It was in the 2000 Census that the number of Hispanics, a minority not even characterized by its race, was to surpass the nation's African-American population. Soon afterward, the Census Bureau made news again. It was announced that by 2050, whites would fall to below 50 percent of the population. In 2008, that watershed year was moved up to 2042.

The 2000 census was unique for several reasons. Amazingly, it was the first census that enabled people to indicate that they were of mixed race, allowing them to mark one or more races on their census ballot. The new multi-racial categories gave 126 distinct ways in which Americans could classify themselves. An analysis of 2000 census data by demographer William Frey found that:

- The rise in mixed-race marriages coincides with exploding immigrant populations of Latinos and Asians as a racial category. Nearly three out of 10 marriages involving Latinos or Asians are of mixed-race. Nearly half (1.8 million) of the 3.7 million interracial marriages in the country include a Latino.

- Interracial marriages involving African Americans are much more rare, despite the fact that blacks comprise a similar share of the U.S. population as Latinos. Only about one in eight marriages involving African Americans are of mixed-race. At the other end of the spectrum, nearly three of four marriages involving Native Americans, Eskimos, and Aleuts are interracial.

- One-third of marriages in Hawaii are interracial. In eight other states—Alaska, New Mexico, Oklahoma, Nevada, California, Arizona, Colorado and Washington—at least one out of 10 fit the bill. California is home to one in four of all mixed-race marriages involving Latinos, and nearly one in three involving Asians.

The number of Americans of mixed race can only be expected to increase. Studies conducted by Cara Joyner and Grace Kao find that interracial relationships are more common among younger people, and these numbers are on the rise. In 1990, for example, about 14 percent of 18-to-19-year-olds and 7 percent of 34-to-35-year-olds were involved in interracial relationships. Ten years later, the number of 18-to-19-year-olds in an interracial relationship had risen to 20 percent (information on 34-to-35-year-olds was not available for this period). The latter study also found that within that 18-to-19-year-old group, 45 percent of Hispanics were involved in interracial relationships compared with only 20 percent of African Americans and 16 percent of whites. Interestingly, a 2003 study by Joyner indicated that adolescents involved in interracial relationships were much less likely to tell family members or close friends about those relationships, indicating that we've still got some terrain to cover before race ceases to become an issue.

High and increasing rates of intermarriage lead to a swelling number of interracial offspring, and that will ultimately lead to a new racial order. Some demographers predict that by 2020 almost 20 percent of all Asian Americans will be multiracial and that figure will climb to 36 percent by 2050. Those numbers should be significantly higher for Hispanics, a majority of whom already has a mixed-race identity. Despite the barriers that have been erected in the past to prevent what some have called the "Brazilianization" of America, we are well on our way to becoming a country of *meztisos*, *mulattos*, and *hapas* (the Hawaiian term for persons of mixed descent).

## To Be Young and Multi-Racial

In 2007, New American Dimensions conducted focus groups and in-depth interviews with mixed-race people between the ages of 14 and 28 in Los Angeles. Here's what we found:

- According to our respondents, the number-one advantage of being multi-racial is learning from an early age to be highly adaptable (wearing different hats, code switching, etc). Most have a diverse mix of friends, even beyond their own ethnic mix. Most friends are based on subculture and common interest, rather than ethnicity.

- Most feel they have more latitude to try different things (activities, foods, events, dating other ethnicities) than their full-blood/full-culture counterparts.

- Virtually none viewed being mixed as a liability. Many felt pressured to choose a culture, or to self-classify as one primary ethnicity. This came up often in dating relationships (i.e. "You have to tell my parents you're Puerto Rican!") Some did express never feeling fully accepted and craving a grounded identity. A majority resented always being assumed to be Mexican.

- The number-one complaint was the emphasis that people place on race and on being mixed, and hate being defined by this. Mixed-race people are constantly being asked "what they are." As a result, many reach out to other cultures or subcultures where they feel less attention is given to race.

---

## A black and non-black divide

Despite the proclivity of today's new immigrants to seek out partners of other ethnicities, intermarriage of African Americans has remained low. Part of that is certainly due to pressures within the African-American community to marry within the race, but it is impossible to ignore that extant racism towards African Americans, from whites and today's new immigrants, is also at work. No matter what the cause, low rates of intermarriage between blacks and non-blacks is evidence of what sociologists call a high "social distance," between African Americans and the mainstream. This has prompted many to hypothesize that as new immigrants from Latin America and Asian integrate into the mainstream, the result may be the transformation of America from a country that sees the dichotomy as being white and non-white to one where the real dichotomy is between black and non-black.

There is evidence that supports this. In his book, *Who Is White?: Latinos, Asians, and the New Black/Nonblack Divide* (Lynne Rienner Pub., 2003) sociologist George Yancey reported his research that African Americans are, in fact, very accepting of other races, despite being rejected by all non-black groups. White respondents were more accepting of Latinos and Asian Americans than blacks, and in turn, Latinos and Asian American respondents were much more accepting of each other and whites than they were of African Americans. For example, when he asked respondents to construct an ideal neighborhood, whites, Hispanics, and Asian Americans were okay having each other as neighbors, but their black neighbors were rejected once the number passed a certain threshold.

This would be a troubling shift because it would further perpetuate the divide that currently exists between blacks and whites, extending it well into the 21st century. Others have postulated a different type of divide, with whites, Asians, and lighter skinned Hispanics and people of mixed race on one side of the equation, and African Americans and darker Hispanics and mixed-race Americans on the other. In other words, the new divide would be between people of light skin and people of dark skin. Neither of the scenarios, if realized, would bode well for the coming century.

Barack Obama, America's first black President, technically is half-black, born to a white mother and black (Kenyan) father. Technically speaking, he is mulatto, which was once measured by lineage and percentage of "negro blood line." He's not fully African American, but still, darker than any President we've had. Then there's President Obama's Asian-American half-sister, Maya Soetoro-Ng, who represents yet another aspect of his identity that makes him unique as a President.

Not so long ago it didn't take much "negro" blood to put you on the wrong side of the tracks or bar you from performing in certain movies or lodging in certain parts of town, etc. People of light skin would often pass as white, if they could get away with it. It was called "passing." In the old days of segregation, President Obama would be considered Negro. Now he is considered by some folks to be too white. What does this mean? Is this another facet of racism? And if President Obama is technically mixed race, why is he considered black?

The *San Francisco Chronicle* reported in July 2008, that debate over what to call Obama—and the growing recognition of mixed-race Americans—is also a reminder that race is a very nuanced thing.

## Ethnic identity is fluid

In 1939, Joe DiMaggio was on the cover of *Life* magazine, the first of three seasons in which he would be voted Most Valuable Player in the American league. In the article, the author marvels at the amazing assimilation of the man born Giuseppe Paolo DiMaggio, Jr. in Martinez, California, of immigrant parents. "Although he learned Italian first, Joe, now 24, speaks English without an accent and is otherwise well-adapted to most U.S. mores. Instead of olive oil or smelly bear grease he keeps his hair slick with water. He never reeks of garlic and prefers chicken chow mein to spaghetti."

Americans at the dawn of World War II would not have seen this statement as prejudiced. Rather, they would have been fascinated by the irony of an Italian American on his way to becoming an American icon. DiMaggio was the beneficiary of what today would be called multicultural marketing; he was hired by the Yankees to bolster ticket sales in what was a burgeoning Italian-American market.

In those days, according to Fred Gardaphe, "If the Italian was not seen as a gangster or a knife-wielding, mustachioed foreigner who had taken away American jobs from the earlier immigrants, then he was depicted as 'a restless, roving creature who dislikes the confinement and restraint of mill and factory,' 'very slow to take to American ways,' 'volatile, and incapable of effective team work.'"

> *African Americans, for the first time in America's history, are the open **arbiters** of popular culture.*

Ethnic identity has always been fluid and negotiable, but it has never been more dynamic than it is for today's young people. Since the early twentieth century, immigrants make up a larger share of the population, and African Americans, for the first time in America's history, are the open arbiters of popular culture (the key word being open). Today's younger generation was born and weaned into the world of cyberspace, in which identities are donned and dropped with the rapidity of a theatrical costume change. Avatars, in the online-personality sense (not the Hindu incarnation sense) can be and are adopted in chat rooms, online communities, video games, and personal ads. On the Internet, we can be anyone we want to be, without the visual cues that we unwittingly, involuntarily give off every minute that we present ourselves in person.

In a brilliant paper titled "Cyber-race," UCLA law professor Jerry Kang examines the implications on racial identity of the Internet and its particular brand of social interaction. In a non-cyberspace interaction, we are "mapped" by others into racial categories based on our physical appearance and these racial categories have what he calls "racial meanings," cognitive beliefs we all hold about people who belong to a certain race or ethnicity. In cyberspace, that all goes away. Kang writes: "By making it easier for us to wear a racial veil, cyberspace promotes racial anonymity. This prompts fantasies about realizing Martin Luther King, Jr.'s dream in cyberspace. In the digital remix version, people are judged by the content of their text-characters, not the color of their skin."

The cyber-generation, American youth who have grown up in a

world of possibilities that only the Internet can offer, have come of age in this world of racial potentiality and "cyber-passing," as Kang calls it. With the click of a mouse, we can darken our skin, change our facial features, or for that matter, even our gender. We can interact with people in every corner of the world, people we would never have the opportunity to see in the real world.

In a world of permeable identities, in a world where we can change how we present ourselves so easily, many are finding that the old racial categories are at best an awkward fit. The same applies to sexual orientation. Many, who engage in sexual relationships with members of the same gender, for example, reject the identity of gay, lesbian, or bisexual. There is a substantial population who subscribe to the movement called "Queer," which is considered by its members to be more inclusive of a wider array of identities encompassing sexual orientation and gender. Many who consider themselves Queer reject conventional labels, avoiding the strict boundaries that sometimes accompany them.

Rejection of a gay identity has led to the emergence of an alternative identity to being gay or lesbian; the down low is one such example. There are other designations such as same-gender-loving, and the more clinical MSM, which stands for men who have sex with

> ⊃ Rejection of a gay identity has led to the emergence of an **alternative** identity to being gay or lesbian.

men. In the words of playwright Jennifer Silverman, in the psychology of these men "an act does not (and for their own personal safety and continued status in their community cannot) constitute an identity."

Although they engage in same-sex behavior, they are not gay identified. Novelist James Earl Hardy calls them "homie-sexual," a phenomenon that he points out is about much more than semantics. They are, in his words, "clinically speaking, homosexual. But they very much take on a *machismo* that separates them from associations with words like gay, queer, and most especially fag. I would guess that this has a lot to do with safety, and with a culture that hates you because you're a fag and most definitely hates you because you're black."

➲ As ethnicity and identity become more fluid, multicultural marketing runs the risk of **backfiring**.

As ethnicity and identity become more fluid, multicultural marketing runs the risk of backfiring. For instance Australian advertising executive Martin Lindstrom warns against an approach that is too narrow: "Racial differentiation is subsiding in the hands of the emerging generations. Think of the damage an ethnically focused campaign could cause. Would kids in the upcoming, inclusive generation find it flattering to be singled out in an ad?" Some might. For as we've seen, today's multiculturalism involves a unique blend of inclusiveness and ethnic pride.

## Hip-hop: youth's global culture

For a variety of reasons, many young people reject the labels imposed on them by others, instead selecting their own labels, based on ethnicity, sexual identity or a shared culture and lifestyle. A prime example of a culture that has captured the imagination (and dollars) of today's youth market is hip-hop. Though it traces its roots to young blacks and Puerto Ricans in the urban Northeast, particularly the South Bronx in the 1970s, it has evolved into a culture with its own sense of style, fashion, body language, and worldview. Now hip-hop is an example of what William Eric Perkins has called "Youth's Global Village," a self-identification born out of common lifestyles and shared aesthetics. In the words of Perkins,

➲ Hip-hop is a **self-identification** born out of common lifestyles and shared aesthetics.

"the hip-hop revolution is just that, an uprooting of the old way in style and culture, and the introduction of a taste of black and Latino urban authenticity to every corner of the globe."

What's amazing about hip-hop is that despite its urban appeal and its African-American and Hispanic roots, it has provided an inclusive identity that has managed to transcend race and ethnicity.

In his book, *Why White Kids Love Hip-Hop* (Basic Civitas Books, 2005), Bakari Kitwana writes: "Old ways of thinking about race certainly persist in the younger generation. However, the mainstreaming of hip-hop culture has in part provided a space where American youth, black and white included, can explore these new ideas together, even if the old racial politics are always lurking in the shadows."

Examples of hip-hop transcending ethnic identity abound with today's urban youth. I recently attended a focus group that we conducted with a group of young Asian Americans. About mid-way through, there was an outburst from one of the participants, a 20-year-old Filipino disc jockey and a diehard hip-hop aficionado. "I am sick and tired of people calling Filipinos Asians just because we have slanted eyes." The Philippines do have a unique history compared with other Asian countries; the Spanish colonized it and a majority of its population is Roman Catholic. However, this particular young man, clad in his urban garb, felt most aligned with African Americans, the founders of hip-hop. You could hear it in the cadence of his speech. "You talk to young Filipinos," he said. "We all watch BET, we listen to hip-hop. If it's black, we like it."

Our respondent was deeply immersed in the hip-hop scene in the San Francisco Bay Area, where many Filipinos are at the forefront of setting trends from rap to break dancing. They have developed a particular niche as DJs; some notables of the Pinoy (Filipino for Filipino) record-spinning scene like DJs Apollo, QBert and MixMaster Mike (alias Michael Schwartz, he's half Jewish) have risen to international celebrity. In this scene, Filipino hip-hoppers relish breaking stereotypes, particularly the image of Asians as the model minority.

Another source of hip-hop's power is that it has the marketing muscle of corporate American behind it, and it has helped to drive a consumerism that has become part of the fabric of America. As Kitwana says it, "Hip-hop, as part of the American entertainment industry, is now for sale to all buyers."

Examples of companies that have co-opted hip-hop to add some cool appeal could fill this book. I was privy to one of these at a recent multicultural marketing conference. The presenter was touting that Ford Motor Company had tapped DJ and car designer Funkmaster Flex to design the incredibly hip 2009 Ford Flex. Funkmaster Flex is quoted on the company's website: "I know what this vehicle is going to be in the urban market: "It's going to be killer!" "Whether you're flossin' with your friends, going to the club or riding around with your girl, the Ford Flex is the next urban street vehicle, and Flex2 is my interpretation of the ultimate in street luxury."

## The U.S. Urban Youth Market

A report by MarketResearch.com called "The U.S. Urban Youth Market" estimates that urban youth consumers number nearly 24 million people with a spending power of about $500 billion. The report stresses that "urban" is a mindset, not a geographic place. Its definition of "Urban Youth" is 15-to-29-year-olds who chose hip-hop music as a favorite music type in the Simmons National Consumer Survey of adults and teens. According to the report, one in three hip-hop consumers lives in small cities and towns outside the top 100 metropolitan areas. The study found that:

- The popularity of hip-hop declines with age. Among 15-to-17-year-olds, about half are hip-hop fans. The percentage drops to a little over a third for those aged 25 to 29.

- Females are a strong force in the urban youth population making up nearly six in ten urban consumers.

- Hip-hop consumers are disproportionately black, yet a majority is non-Hispanic white. Although two out of three African Americans in the group aged 15 to 29 were classified as hip-hop consumers, whites make up about 55 percent of the hip-hop population.

- Hip-hoppers are much more likely to say that they live for the moment, are motivated by money, value non-conformity, and that they see themselves as influencers.

- As consumers, they use more personal care products, prefer SUVs and foreign cars, like to snack, try out new drinks, and eat at fast food restaurants. They are more likely to see themselves as spenders and have a positive attitude about advertising.

---

Hip-hoppers are a marketer's dream, having spawned an entire economy going well beyond music that includes products as wide ranging as clothing, footwear, jewelry, soft drinks, cell phones, autos, and credit cards. They pay attention to ads, appreciate them, remember them, and respond to them. And if a brand is really lucky, it might get mentioned in the lyrics of a rapper. To quote Brandchannel.com, "Formerly perceived as a niche strategy, some of today's successful brands realize that the term 'urban marketing' now expands across the entire youth demographic."

> ➲ *If a brand is really **lucky**, it might get mentioned in the lyrics of a rapper.*

Whether a hip-hop attitude represents the future of marketing or if it has played itself out remains to be seen. My generation swore up and down that rock and roll would never die. But if I had to guess, I would say that the trans-cultural sensibility that hip-hop represents will outlive it as a fashion or music genre, at least in advertising. We're already seeing signs of it. We recently tested an advertising campaign loaded with "bling" to some focus groups of African Americans. They hated it. "We're tired of seeing ourselves portrayed this way," was the nearly unanimous response. "This is a stereotype."

There were two big marketing lessons that I learned while working at Levi Strauss. The first is that fashion works in cycles. One year denim is cool, the next it's not; one year people wear knit shirts, the next it's woven. The other lesson is that it is extremely difficult for a mainstream brand (like Levi's) to be really hip. Because after all, trendsetters are the group who determine what is cool, and they are constantly on the lookout for the next thing. That almost always means something niche. Once something becomes mainstream, it loses its cool appeal. Hip-hop's success, its very ubiquity, particularly in the commercial arena, begs the question "How long can it last?" Everything becomes passé after a while.

## Where do we go from here?

It's impossible for us to know, from our unique vantage point at the turn of a new millennium, how the cultural identity of Americans will be different than it is today. In his prophetic book *American Skin: Pop Culture, Big Business, and the End of White America* (Crown Publishers, 2002), Leon Wynter elaborates what I think are five truths about the next generation. Unlike prior generations, they will all grow up with:

- The deeper sense that American is not a synonym for white.

- A cultural mainstream that is fundamentally and unalterably racially and ethnically heterogeneous.

- A world that is more than the United States, Canada and Europe; it's the whole world, and Americans of all colors are obliged to find a place in it, not the other way around.

- The expectation of reaching middle age in an America without a clear white majority.

- The sense that identity is rooted in cultures that can be freely traded in the marketplace, not imposed by race or ethnicity at birth.

Just as ethnic communities have been altered by America's mainstream culture, their swelling ranks enable them to redefine what the mainstream is. Let us remember that today's young Americans have known nothing but a truly multicultural America. It's an America that no longer resists but embraces people of color as its cultural arbiters.

The idea of a white mainstream is fast becoming an anachronism. The newest generation of Americans is developing its own distinctive identity, one that is post-ethnic, as David Hollinger calls it; others have used terms like trans-cultural, trans-ethnic or trans-racial since this new identity, whatever it may be, transcends and antiquates our old categories of race, ethnicity, and sexual orientation. To this new generation, old ideas of race are no longer relevant. To them, a prototypical American is not white but brown. Ethnicity is part of identity, and a source of pride, but there is an inclusiveness that eluded their parents. To connect with them, to skirt total irrelevance, we need a whole new conceptual framework.

> ➲ *The idea of a white **mainstream** is f ast becoming an anachronism.*

In his book, *The Next American Nation*, Michael Lind gives us a glimpse of what the future might hold: "The overwhelming majority of Americans—whatever their arbitrarily defined "race"—belong not just to a single citizenry, but to a single people, a single cultural nation, defined by common language, folkways, memories and mores. Centuries of white supremacy have not prevented the formulation of a transracial American culture blending elements of the cultures of many European, African, American Indian, Latin American and Asian peoples with innovations unique to North America." It is this unique American culture—not race, ethnicity or sexual orientation—that will define who we are as a people.

I don't know all the implications of how this new America will change marketing. However, I am reasonably confident in making two assertions:

1. As long as immigration to the United States continues (and it is expected to do so), there will be a place for multicultural marketing in its current form. That means in-language,

in-culture content created for immigrants by people with the cultural competence to do so. It also implies the continued need for products specifically targeting immigrant groups, appropriately priced and sold in channels where they shop.

2. Multicultural marketing will need to evolve in order to be relevant to native-born Americans. This includes gays and lesbians, African Americans, and the children and grandchildren of today's immigrants who will be English dominant. They will have a strong sense of their own ethnic identity yet they will not consider themselves to be members of a minority. Rather, they will be proud of their strong influence on mainstream American culture, and will connect with brands that engage them in a two-way dialog.

As our national identity evolves to reflect our growing diversity, our relationship to multiculturalism will change. We will no longer need to be reminded that we are a multicultural nation—that will be patently obvious. We will define ourselves less by labels imposed on us by others and focus more on what makes us unique as individuals. As multicultural marketers (something we will all be), we'll need to remove our cultural blinders and understand the symbols and icons, the language and the psyche of a new America. We'll need to understand how our actively chosen identities add to our sense of who we are, as individuals and as a national collective.

# Part II

## The Rules of Multicultural Marketing

# RULE 1

■ ■ ■ ■ ■ ■ ■ ■ ■ ■ ■ ■ ■ ■ ■ ■ ■ ■ ■ ■ ■ ■ ■ ■ ■ ■ ■ ■ ■ ■ ■ ■ ■ ■ ■ ■ ■ ■ ■

## Boost Your MQ

In Daniel Goldman's best selling-book, *Emotional Intelligence: Why It Can Matter More Than IQ* (Bantam, 1995), he argues that it is emotional intelligence—factors such as self-awareness, altruism, personal motivation, empathy, and the ability to love and be loved—that determines success in life. I would propose that in the New America, another type of intelligence, multicultural intelligence, or MQ, is what will separate the winners from the losers.

We've found that companies, like people, have an MQ, and we've developed a battery of questions to measure it:

- What percentage of your employees owns a passport and has visited a foreign country in the last three years?

- What percentage of your management team is non-white or gay?

- How many speak a language in addition to English?

- Does your company offer diversity training?

- Do you have a multicultural advertising agency?

In the New America, the most successful businesses are the ones who do their homework and have a clearly articulated multicultural strategy. They identify a multicultural segment—be it Hispanic, African American, LGBT, or Asian—as a strategic priority and get the people in their organization to rally around the cause.

A few years ago, I had the opportunity to be involved in a project sponsored by the Coca-Cola Retailing Research Council, a group of supermarket executives who commission a study each year to benefit the supermarket industry. My company was hired to identify best practices: What the most successful supermarkets were doing to attract and retain Hispanic, African-American, and Asian-American customers. In collaboration with Terry Soto, of About Marketing Solutions, our partner on this project, we came up with six. I recall that the first—"Think like your ethnic consumers so you can serve them better"—was the most powerful and far reaching, applicable to any marketer in any field.

> ➲ *The best retailers went to stores that **specialize** in ethnic consumers to see what they were doing right.*

We found that the best retailers were the ones who shopped the market. They went to stores that specialize in ethnic consumers to see what they were doing right. They got a feel for the stores—how they were laid out, what products and brands they carried, and how those were priced. When it came to gathering information, they were like sponges. They interviewed distributors, wholesalers, and manufacturers, most of whom are normally generous when it comes to sharing information; it is vested self-interest.

The best retailers had a simple approach to information gathering. They obsessively talked to consumers—on the street, in their stores and, in focus groups. They endeavored to answer such questions as:

- What is important and unimportant to this consumer?
- What needs do they have that are not being met?
- Where are they currently shopping? If they're not shopping at my store, why not?
- Where do they get information when it comes to making purchase decisions?
- What brands are they currently using? Why these brands? Why not others?

- How do they feel about my store? Does it deliver on things that are important to this consumer? Where am I missing the boat?
- Are my products at the right price point for this consumer?
- What would it take for them to shop at my store?

### The Six Best Practices in Ethnic Marketing and Merchandising

1. Think like your ethnic consumers so you can serve them better.
2. Define your ethnic merchandising "look" and organize to execute it.
3. Tailor your offering to appeal to your ethnic customers.
4. Create a culture that enhances the store experience and "connects" with the community.
5. Recruit and retain a diverse staff to help you successfully serve your target customers.
6. Develop a marketing plan to communicate value at all points of customer contact.

Ultimately, the most successful retailers are those who realize that developing a relationship with multicultural consumers requires a commitment of time, money, and other resources. But the real key to marketing success with any consumer group is to have a genuine interest in the customers, what their needs are, and how your company might fill those needs. Multicultural consumers are no different.

Good market research can do so much more than prevent costly mistakes. It can help you identify needs that your consumers have; unmet needs that your company might be able to meet. And good research does not always mean telephone surveys or using focus group facilities. We've done research in bars and barbershops, on buses and basketball courts, and inside people's bathrooms and bedrooms. For the latter, we pay high incentives. The reason is basic. The better you understand someone, the better you can market to him or her. And if they're different than you, the more likely you are to make mistakes and to have your communications misread.

## Teens say the darnedest things

Some of the most interesting stuff I've heard in focus groups has come from teens. A few years ago, I observed a focus group in New York conducted with about ten African-American male teens. The objective was to understand the role that African-American identity played in their lives and how our client, a well-known consumer products company, might tailor its marketing communications to better reach them. Since it's hard for many of us, particularly teens, to express our feelings about race and ethnicity in today's world of political correctness, it's often effective to get at this information in a roundabout way. The African American moderator asked the question: "How are we blacks different from white folks?" Muffled snickers could be heard throughout the focus group room.

"What planet have you been on?" asked a heavyset 17-year-old African-American man clad in a size XXXL Enyce t-shirt, a gold chain as thick as my index finger around his neck, and a Yankee baseball cap turned backwards.

"No, I'm serious," said the moderator. "What makes us unique?"

"We have better values."

"How so?" the moderator probed.

"White people. They're crazy. You take a black guy. He might go out and shoot one person, maybe two. You'll never see a brutha blowing up a whole building. That's what white people do."

My white clients laughed, comfortably seated behind the two-way mirror, but this was a shocking revelation to them. The unspoken reality was that they had always associated crime with blacks. Yet with a few exceptions, like the Atlanta serial killer Wayne Williams and the Washington, D.C., freeway sniper John Muhammad, most serial killers have been white. The remark by a 17-year-old opened up my clients' eyes to a new way of seeing the world, and perhaps a new way of speaking to African Americans—emphasizing what many blacks call the Afro-centric values of church, family, and hard work.

## Do it yourself

I have a big bias. I conduct market research for a living, and I do believe that hiring a firm like mine—notice I didn't say *my* firm—can be an important step toward fully understanding your multicultural consumers. Since I have a lot to gain, I'll be the last person to tell you not to do it. But there are caveats: Hire a marketing research company only if you can afford it, and only for work you can't do on your own.

Now, I'll probably get in big trouble with my staff for saying this, but since you've invested the time and money to buy and read this book, I'd like to let you in on a little secret. There's a ton of information out there that's free. Some resources include:

U.S. Census: *www.census.gov*

Consumer Expenditure Survey: *www.bls.gov/cex*

Current Population Survey: *www.bls.census.gov/cps*

Pew Hispanic Center: *http://pewhispanic.org*

Lewis Mumford Center for Comparative Urban & Regional Research: *www.albany.edu/mumford*

Selig Center for Economic Growth: *www.selig.uga.edu*

Let's start with the U.S. Census. It's mandated by the United States Constitution, has been going on since 1790, and is conducted every ten years (the next Census will be 2010). Unlike surveys, which are based on statistical samples, the Census is an actual count-ing of everyone in the country, including citizens, non-citizen legal residents, long-term visitors, and illegal aliens. It has even begun to include estimates of people who might not normally be counted, such as homeless and migratory people.

The Census tracks race, Hispanic origin, country of birth, income, educational levels, language use, and a slew of other variables down to very small geographical groupings called census blocks (there were eight million census blocks in the 2000 census).

In addition to offering a number of relevant publications, some other marketing uses of census data are to:

- Measure the size of ethnic markets from national to local and sub-local.

- Identify top markets for a given ethnic group.

- Understand what percentage of a multicultural market, say Hispanics, is foreign born.

- Determine which areas of a city or state might represent opportunities, based on the demographics of residents.

- Develop weighted sampling plans for market research studies.

- Explore how your target group has changed over time.

- See projections of the U.S. population, by ethnicity, through the year 2100.

The Census tracks race and Hispanic origin separately, since in the eyes of the Census, Hispanics are not a race. The Census does not track religion or sexual orientation because the Constitutional mandate for a Census does not include these categories.

However, if you are interested in the LGBT market, the Census does track unmarried partners; and if they happen to be of the same sex, then it can be safely assumed that the couple is gay or lesbian. The 2000 Census showed that nearly a million people fell into this category. It's a flawed, gross under representation of the gay population since not all gays are in partnered relationships. In fact, some studies have shown that it severely undercounts the number of gays who are partners, despite the efforts of LGBT activists to get them to check the box—but it does give a good proxy and is useful for understanding areas with a high concentration of gays.

A couple of other useful governmental sources of information are the Consumer Expenditure Survey and the Current Population Survey. The Consumer Expenditure Survey is conducted by the United States Department of Labor and administered by the Census Bureau. It consists of two surveys, an Interview and a Diary survey, which provide in-depth information on how Americans of different ethnic groups spend their money. (See page 157 for an example.)

The Current Population Survey is a national, monthly survey of 60,000 households, conducted by the Census Bureau for the Bureau of Labor Statistics, which uses the report to estimate the number of unemployed people in the United States. I like it because it's an easy tool to query, and is the only governmental source I know of that provides visibility to the third-generation, since it asks the birth country of one's father and mother. If you're interested in what percentage of, for instance, the Asian population is first-, second-, or third-generation, this is the place to look.

A great source of free information on the Hispanic population is the Pew Hispanic Center, a non-partisan research organization that conducts frequent studies on a range of topics including demography, economics, education, identity, immigration, labor, remittances, and politics. Additionally, The Center regularly conducts public opinion surveys on social and public policy issues relating to Latinos. Its 2002 National Survey of Latinos is one of the best Hispanic studies I've seen, ever, and it's available online for downloading.

In addition to professional journals, many of which can be found online, we can all benefit from the writings of academics that are under the yoke of the adage, "publish or perish." There's a ton of research coming out of America's universities on the subject of multicultural marketing. For instance, the Lewis Mumford Center for Comparative Urban and Regional Research is a good source for information on assimilation and the emerging second generation. The University of Georgia's Selig Center for Economic Growth is the definitive resource for information about purchasing power and the multicultural economy.

Once you've exhausted the free information available, you might want to consider subscribing to syndicated stud-

> ➲ *Once you've exhausted the free information available, consider **subscribing** to syndicated studies.*

ies. Both ACNielsen (*www.acnielsen.com*) and Information Resources Inc. (*www.infores.com*) have consumer panels of African-American and Hispanic consumers. These are invaluable sources to obtain detailed information on what consumers are buying, where they buy it, and how much they're paying. They also have data that provide details of what gets scanned at the checkout counter in stores located in heavily Hispanic or African-American neighborhoods. In terms of top-notch survey data, both Simmons Market Research (*www.smrb.com*) and Scarborough Research (*www.scarborough.com*) offer a Hispanic study, a gay and lesbian study, as well as significant reads of African Americans in their general market survey.

Data is harder to come by for Asian-American consumers. The fact that they skew foreign-born and speak myriad languages has, unfortunately, been an obstacle for researchers. New America Media (*www.newamericamedia.org*) does do a study with a substantial in-language sample for Asians and a focus on media. In 2004, Arbitron (*www.arbitron.com*) began to survey Chinese radio listeners in New York and Los Angeles. As the Asian-American population continues to grow, and as marketers get increasingly savvy about this burgeoning market, the amount of available information will grow as well.

*Average annual food expenditures by race, 2007*

| | WHITES | ASIANS | BLACKS |
|---|---|---|---|
| **Average annual expenditure** | $51,120 | $60,402 | $36,067 |
| **Food** | 6,312 | 7,139 | 4,601 |
| **Food at home** | 3,539 | 3,890 | 2,831 |
| Cereals & bakery products | 473 | 469 | 365 |
| Cereals and cereal products | 143 | 195 | 127 |
| Bakery products | 330 | 275 | 237 |
| **Meats, poultry, fish & eggs** | 760 | 1,026 | 834 |
| Beef | 220 | 221 | 185 |
| Pork | 144 | 160 | 185 |
| Other meats | 106 | 106 | 95 |
| Poultry | 135 | 158 | 189 |
| Fish & Seafood | 132 | 321 | 138 |
| Eggs | 42 | 60 | 41 |
| **Dairy products** | 407 | 349 | 259 |
| Fresh milk & cream | 160 | 154 | 111 |
| Other dairy products | 247 | 196 | 147 |
| **Fruits and vegetables** | 610 | 887 | 455 |
| Fresh fruits | 208 | 309 | 131 |
| Fresh vegetables | 192 | 369 | 133 |
| Processed fruits | 113 | 116 | 107 |
| Processed vegetables | 97 | 93 | 83 |
| **Other food at home** | 1,290 | 1,159 | 919 |
| Sugars and other sweets | 129 | 133 | 88 |
| Fats & Oils | 93 | 93 | 81 |
| Miscellaneous foods | 680 | 549 | 456 |
| Nonalcoholic beverages | 340 | 343 | 279 |
| **Food away from home** | 2,773 | 3,249 | 1,771 |

*Source*: 2007 Consumer Expenditure Survey

## Do diversity training—don't drop the ball

To many white Americans, the very word "diversity" is enough to conjure up images of quotas, time-wasting training programs, and a tyrannical political correctness. When I worked at Levi Strauss &

Co., where diversity training was mandatory, most people dreaded the three days away from the office, painfully picking at each other's racial wounds, only to return to a pile of work that would take twenty days to get rid of.

There were horror stories of cathartic breakdowns, temper tantrums, and altercations bordering on the physical. I once casually remarked to a colleague about some homophobic jibes that the husband of another colleague had unwittingly made to me at the company Christmas party. The next week, the entire Levi "campus" was plastered with letters from the company's president saying that anyone caught making homophobic remarks would be terminated. Without my knowing about it, the "incident" had been a *cause célèbre* at the gay and lesbian employee organization and had escalated to the top of the organization. I loved the fact that the company took its diversity policy so seriously. Still, a part of me thought the whole thing had gone too far and I wished I'd kept my mouth shut.

➲ *That diversity training can go too far does not detract from the reality that it's **sorely** needed.*

That diversity training can go too far does not detract from the reality that it is sorely needed in today's business world. The problem, in my opinion, is that too many people put it into the category of being the right thing to do, and ignore the fact that it is also the smart thing to do.

Examples of costly corporate mishaps, due to a lack of diversity awareness, multiply like weeds on the grassy knoll of corporate America. In 2005, Macy's East agreed to pay New York State $600,000 to settle a racial profiling suit. According to the complaint, African-American and Latino shoppers were routinely followed, questioned, and searched by security guards. Suits against JCPenney and Dillard's were also filed that year. That June, retailer Abercrombie & Fitch agreed to pay $40 million for focusing its employee recruitment on white fraternities and sororities, relegating minority applicants to back-of-the store jobs.

In 2007, *Time* did a story called "Employee Diversity Training Doesn't Work." In it, the magazine cited a study by Frank Dobbin of Harvard, Alexandra Kalev of the University of California, Berkeley, and Erin Kelly of the University of Minnesota, who found no real change in the number of minority managers after companies began diversity training. In the words of Dobbin, "Companies have spent millions of dollars a year on these programs without actually knowing 'Are these efforts worth it?' In the case of diversity training, the answer is no."

What the study found was that when diversity programs had teeth, when people were held accountable for results, the results were more substantial. The article cited an example from General Electric under former CEO Jack Welch, the ultimate no-nonsense manager, who implemented a diversity strategy that included appointing a chief diversity officer, Deborah Elam. The results were impressive, and by 2005, the percentage of women and minorities making up the ranks of senior management increased dramatically. According to Elam, "Training just to train is not enough. You've got to have accountability at the top."

One company that found significant value from diversity training was Denny's. It hired a diversity guru and spent millions on its diversity initiative. Unfortunately, this was a result of a PR fiasco in 1994 after one of its restaurants asked a group of African-American Secret Service agents to pay for their meal in advance. Denny's paid $54 million after being hit with two class-action lawsuits filed by more than 250,000 customers.

According to *Essence* magazine, within a year, all but one of the senior executives was gone, and the mostly white, male board of directors was overhauled. The company began diversity training and an analysis every three months of who was hired, fired, and promoted to ensure that discrimination was not rearing its ugly head. Results of the study were presented to the board of directors and the NAACP. Importantly, the diversity initiative is tied to Denny's rewards-and-recognition program.

In consumer studies, African Americans tend to rank "respect" as second only to price in terms of importance. Given the reality of race in the marketplace, it's easy to see why. Denny's is proof that good intentions coupled with effective action can lead to results. In 1996, a third of African Americans gave Denny's a positive rating for respectful service; today, they estimate that number to be around 80 percent.

Diversity training can be extremely effective in helping companies uncover discrimination of a more subtle variety that might be handicapping their best efforts.

A large financial institution asked my company to run some focus groups among its Asian-American employees to find out why so many of them were leaving, despite the fact that they represented an inordinately high number of new hires. When we interviewed some Asian Americans who had not left the company, they resoundingly expressed what Jane Hyun calls "The Bamboo Ceiling," the fact that Asian Americans are pathetically underrepresented in the ranks of management. When we interviewed white members of the company's management, several expressed their conception that Asians were much better "number crunchers" than managers. Clearly, this attitude was being conveyed, if not verbally, then in terms of the low promotion rate.

In cases like this, it's usually not a case of intentional discrimination. Rather, it's a misreading of cultural cues. Asian Americans are often taught from the time they are young to keep their noses to the grindstone, be humble, and not blow their own horns. Non-Asians, by contrast, learn to be aggressive, to speak up on their own behalf, and that the squeaky wheel gets the grease.

Unlike IQ, MQ can be improved. Conducting market research, walking stores, talking to customers, absorbing what academics and other researchers have to offer, and diversity training are all means to acquire the knowledge and wisdom that will equip you for the new America. It's a skill that has never been a high priority for Americans. Rather, the image of the "ugly American" doing business abroad with limited cultural sensitivity and even less language ability has been the norm. That will all change soon. For in the new America, MQ will not only be required of those engaged in international affairs, it will be required of all of us.

# RULE 2

■ ■ ■ ■ ■ ■ ■ ■ ■ ■ ■ ■ ■ ■ ■ ■ ■ ■ ■ ■ ■ ■ ■ ■ ■ ■ ■ ■ ■ ■ ■ ■ ■ ■ ■ ■ ■ ■ ■

## Divide and Conquer

The original title of this chapter was going to be "Don't Trust the Argentineans." But they are already the butt of so many jokes in Latin America, I'll let them be. Argentineans do get around. They make up a large share of the creative people who work for U.S. Hispanic advertising agencies, a phenomenal fact given that they make up less than one-half of one percent of the U.S. Hispanic population. As we've seen, Mexicans make up two-thirds of U.S. Hispanics and a majority of them were born in the United States. So, what do people from a South American country that borders the South Pole know about Mexicans living in East Los Angeles? And what do they know about the Puerto Rican or Dominican kid who lives in the South Bronx? Or perhaps the granddaddy of all these questions: To what extent does the Latino market or the Asian (or black or LGBT) market even exist?

The reality is that no consumer group, no group of human beings is nearly as homogenous as multicultural marketers would like them to be. Argentineans are as different from Mexicans as Anglo Americans are from Scots or New Zealanders. Asians speak scores of languages and dialects, and worship in all of the world's major religions. The 37 million or so African Americans run the gamut in terms of age, socioeconomic status, product preference, shopping habits, and even skin color.

If you're American, and someone tells you that Americans are patriotic or religious, you'd think that is ridiculous and you'd think of all the Americans you know who are not. If you're white and someone tells you that white people are not family orientated, you'd go through the roof. Yet, when it comes to multicultural segments, we buy the stereotypes, maybe because it just seems easier to believe the clichés.

To be successful with multicultural consumers, to be successful marketing to any group of people, the secret is to segment. You need to divide and conquer.

## The rise and fall of the generic Hispanic

In her book, *Latinos Inc.: The Marketing and Making of a People* (UC Press, 2001), author Arlene Dávila recounts how a small group of charming, charismatic, and wonderfully Latin entrepreneurs succeeded in creating and selling the Hispanic consumer to Corporate America: A "family-oriented, Catholic, traditional, conservative, and immigrant Spanish-speaking individual." And let's not forget intensely brand loyal.

One obstacle that the early agencies frequently encountered from their corporate clients was that Hispanics from different countries look differently, speak with different accents, and use different words. These differences made it challenging for companies to create a simple, one size fits all, Hispanic marketing strategy.

Enter the Generic Hispanic Person.

The Generic Hispanic speaks a kind of unaccented, non-specific Spanish devoid of any regional slang. He or she lacks any physical distinctions that might identity him or her as coming from any particular country, thereby turning off other Hispanics.

The Generic Hispanic should be dark enough to not be labeled as a *gringo* (an interesting contrast to the Nordic types that appear on Mexican television), but not too dark either. The Generic Hispanic Person started out as a marketing ploy, a cultural shorthand, but became a real image that Hispanic consumers bought into, and continue to buy into today.

I've observed scores of focus group respondents as they watched a dark haired, olive skinned Anglo actor appear in a commercial. "What do you like about the ad?" asks the moderator.

"I like that they're showing Latinos."

"If I see a Latino using the product, I know it must be for me."

"They're taking us into account."

I've seen the opposite happen too—good commercials being tested in Los Angeles with a black actor who is, for example, Dominican. "We don't look like that," is often the reply. Similarly, "Mexican looking" actors don't tend to test well in markets like New York or Miami. I've heard lots of sarcastic remarks like, "Where is the sombrero and burro?" Hispanic focus groups are not the domain of political correctness.

> ➲ In multicultural marketing circles, the **stereotype** with the most staying power seems to be that of the brand loyal Hispanic.

In multicultural marketing circles, the stereotype with the most staying power seems to be that of the brand loyal Hispanic. After years of hearing the message, it seems to have become an incontrovertible marketing truth. A few years back, my company partnered with the Food Marketing Institute and ADVO to put the idea to the test. It didn't hold water.

Our study, a Hispanic market segmentation in which we divided consumers into different segments or clusters, was called El Mercado 2005 and uncovered four distinct segments, only one of which, "Loyalists," is *brand* loyal. They make up 20 percent of Hispanics. Another segment, "Budgeters," makes up 25 percent of Hispanics and is *store* loyal. The other two segments, "Impulsives" (30 percent) and "Inquirers" (25 percent), shop around and are driven mostly by price. Our conclusion: Slightly less than half of Hispanics are loyal. Of these, about half are loyal to brands and the other half are loyal to stores.

The *raison d'être* of a segmentation study is to understand what

makes each segment tick, and clearly each of the El Mercado segments is driven by different factors. Each segment uses a different
strategy for economizing. Impulsives and Inquirers buy cheap. Budgeters save money by sticking to their list.

Even Loyalists are not brand loyal, at least not in the way marketers want to believe. Based on qualitative research we've done,
what drives them is not loyalty to a brand, in the sense of fidelity
or allegiance. It's more about risk aversion. There's an expression
in Spanish, *lo barato sale caro*—that which is cheap ends up being
expensive. In other words, you end up throwing it out or having to
replace it. If you stick to a familiar brand, you've eliminated the risk
that you're not going to like something.

## Acculturated or U.S. Born?

When it comes to Hispanic and Asian-American groups, the issue
of assimilation, or its counterpart, acculturation baffles even the
most seasoned marketers. They are baffled because it is still an
unknown as to how the children of today's immigrants will melt
into the proverbial pot, or if any melting will occur at all. Adding
to the confusion is the lack of standard measures of acculturation
among multicultural marketing companies. Each company has its
own point of view, its own algorithm, its own way of segmenting
the market.

Sociologists tend to look at generation as the defining variable, in the sense of how many generations someone has been
in the United States (for example, immigrants are first-generation,
the children of immigrants are second-generation, etc.). I like this
approach. It's intuitive, unlike a black box algorithm, which many
companies use, an amalgamation of questions designed to impress
and confuse clients. It's also objective and measurable since the
U.S. Census and the Current Population Survey provide generational
numbers. Other traditional measures such as language preference

are subjective, and as researcher Ed Rincon has shown, can vary even with the same people from one interview to another.

> ⮑ *A good logical rule is to* **target** *people in their native language.*

In terms of language, a good logical rule is to target people in their native language. In the case of immigrants, the language of their native country is the best bet. English is highly recommended for Asian Indians (English is one of the official languages of India) and Taglish (a mixture of Tagalog and English) for Filipinos. And despite what you may have been told, for those born in the United States or those who came at an early age, English almost always works best.

## Dead Spanish?

One 1996 study, "Linguistic Life Expectancies: Immigrant Language Retention in Southern California," shows that, at least in the realm of language, the children of recent immigrants are learning English, much to the detriment of their parents' native tongue. The study draws from the merging of two large surveys, the "Immigration and Intergenerational Mobility in Metropolitan Los Angeles" (IIMMLA) survey and the third wave of the "Children of Immigrants Longitudinal Study" (CILS), resulting in a sample size of 5,703 respondents.

According to the authors' definition, a language is considered "born" in the United States with the arrival of first-generation immigrants. A language is considered "dead" when the percentage of immigrant descendents that either speak the language "very well" or prefer to speak that language at home declines to below 5 percent.

The study found that Hispanics *did* retain Spanish longer than other groups. For instance, in generation 2.5 (U.S. born, one parent born in U.S. and one abroad), 35 percent of Mexicans, 29 percent of Salvadorans and Guatemalans, and 13 percent of other Hispanics still spoke Spanish very well. In contrast, the proportion of all other ethnicities speaking their mother tongue in generation 2.5 never exceeded 6 percent. Despite the staying power of Spanish, by the third generation (both parents born in the U.S.) only 17 percent of third-generation Mexicans spoke Spanish fluently; the number dropped to 5 percent by the fourth generation.

The study found that life expectancies for a language were even lower when language life was defined in terms of having a preference for using that language at home. According to the authors, "Spanish can be expected to die out after 2 generations among Mexicans, 2.1 generations among Guatemalans and Salvadorans, and 1.7 generations for other Latin Americans." Similarly, the average Asian language "can be expected to die out at or near the second generation."

---

So what is the take-away here for marketers? My advice is that if you are targeting a recent immigrant group like Hispanics or Asians, understand how their relationship to your product changes with the acculturation process. Some questions you might ask are:

- How will use or consumption change with acculturation? Will it increase, decrease, or remain unchanged?

- Does your product or brand mean different things to the recent immigrant and the more acculturated consumer? Do they aspire to different things? Do their needs change with acculturation?

- Should you target consumers at different levels of acculturation? Does it make more sense to focus on one acculturation segment or another? Language aside, should the message be the same or does it need to change?

- Does your consumer prefer to speak English or another language? How does acculturation affect media preferences?

How does it impact the need for more non-traditional marketing, be it grass roots, experiential, online, or others?

And the advice I give all my clients—solicited or otherwise—forget the black box algorithms and look at acculturation in terms of generations.

## Segmenting African Americans: The Three Gs

Acculturation as a segmentation variable hardly makes sense with African-American consumers, except in the case of immigrants. For nine in ten African Americans, the issue is irrelevant, since most have relatives who have been in America for hundreds of years.

One interesting exception is a fascinating study of race by Harvard sociologist Mary Waters who documents the lives of U.S.-born West Indians living in New York City. In her book, *Black Identities: West Indian Immigrant Dreams and American Realities* (Harvard, 1999), she writes that black West Indian immigrants often fare better economically than their U.S.-born children, a factor she attributes to losing their connection to their West Indian culture, which helps keep their parents a degree or two detached from the institutional racism they encounter in the United States. The U.S.-born West Indians, because they are black, will often identify with African-American culture and develop an underclass mentality that is less conducive to economic success in the mainstream culture. It's what sociologists Alejandro Portes and Ruben Rumbaut call "segmented" or "selective" assimilation, in which the children of many lower income immigrants, after becoming exposed to the crime, drugs, and gangs that are often endemic where they live, develop an adversarial relationship with the society at large.

➲ *A common mistake is to assume that the African-American market is **homogenous**.*

A common mistake is to assume that the African-American market is homogenous. When targeting African Americans, marketers should take note of personality characteristics, buying behavior, and most certainly socio-economic factors such as income and education. And then there is what I like to call the three great dividers of the African-American market, the three G's: gender, geography and generation.

Gender takes on special significance in the African-American market where strong gender roles exacerbated by currents of misogyny in hip-hop culture and its lyrics, have led to a rift between African-American men and women. In terms of geography, a second divide is found between African Americans living in rural areas and in urban areas. And in terms of generation, there is a big difference between older African Americans, who grew up in or before the Civil Rights movement and listened to jazz and soul, versus those who grew up post-Civil Rights and listen to hip-hop.

And within each of these groups, further segmentation is possible. For instance, in his book *The Hip Hop Generation: Young Blacks and the Crisis in African American Culture*, author Bakari Kitwana divides that group into three subgroups: Those at the beginning who listen to rappers like LL Cool J, those in the middle who may be defined by the Wu-Tang Clan, and those at the end (his book was written in 2002) who find themselves into the Hot Boys or Lil' Bow Wow. He further delineates what he calls the "bridge generation," people like Russell Simmons and Nelson George, who were too young to be defined by civil rights but too old to hang out at hip-hop clubs.

## Say goodbye to Judy Garland

LGBT consumers constitute a market that, through a powerful sense of pride, a shared sense of history, a vision of unity, and the strength of political activism, often manages to speak as a single voice. But as we've seen in this chapter, from a marketing perspective, the idea of a homogenous, monolithic market can be at best misleading, at worst, disastrous. I have yet to meet a monolith that couldn't be slain with a small dose of reality.

I know of no large companies that are marketing to either bisexual or transgender people, or for that matter, the Queer or Questioning communities. So let's focus on the L and the G, lesbians and gays, two very disparate groups that need to be looked at separately. Similar to African Americans, there is a large generational divide—between older gays weaned on Judy Garland who grew up in a world of homophobia and few or no gay rights, and younger gays, who grew up with *Will and Grace*, Ellen, and Rosie, and who take their right to drink a beer at a gay bar as a given, rather than an opportunity to be harassed by cops.

## L vs G Choices

A 2007 study by New American Dimensions of gay and lesbian consumers found numerous differences among gays in terms of their attitudes, lifestyle, and media choices:

- Compared with gay men, lesbians are more inclined to live with a partner in a relationship, and are more likely to be raising kids at home. Gay men make greater use of gay-oriented media than do lesbians, and visit gay bars more frequently.

- Older gays and lesbians are more likely than the younger group to believe they are "completely out and fine with that." Their media use also differs from that of their younger counterparts: Older gays and lesbians report more frequent readership of gay-oriented magazines and newspapers, while the younger group more often uses community websites.

- Relative to gay/lesbian Hispanics and African Americans, a higher percent of Caucasians say they have "come out." African Americans are much more likely to identify with their race/ethnicity as opposed to their sexual orientation than Hispanics or whites. Perhaps as a result, Caucasians have a greater likelihood of living with a partner in a relationship.

- The study identified five distinct segments of the gay/lesbian community:
  - *Super Gays:* Highest in "outness," perceived discrimination against gays, and activism in the gay community.
  - *Party People:* Cutting edge, youthful, risk-taking party-goers who typically live in metro areas of big cities. Although being gay is a big part of their identity, few think "coming out" had a big impact on their lives.
  - *Gay Mainstream:* Consider themselves complex yet average. Full-time workers who acknowledge the great impact of "coming out," and consume a mix of mainstream and gay media.
  - *Habitaters:* Serious, responsible, down-to-earth, and older. Homebodies who have stable relationships.
  - *Closeted:* Almost completely in the closet and deny the influence of gay identity. Older, traditional, and introverted sideliners.

---

## Any way you slice it . . .

Don't buy the fiction of an amalgamated Latin (or gay or Asian or African-American) market. Question assumptions, and by all means, segment when you can. Rather than believing what the pundits have to say, identify which consumer groups make the most sense for you and your brand, product, or service. Learn what turns these groups on and why they buy what they do.

If there is one fundamental rule for how to best divide and conquer a consumer segment it is the following: Target the entire group in a big way with the advertising bucks while at the same time taking a more grassroots approach to reach the subgroups. In other words, depth does not need to be sacrificed for breadth, nor vice versa. The further you segment, the smaller the market gets. At the same time, the smaller the segment, the more opportunity there is for making a truly deep connection.

How finely do you segment? That depends on your goals and your budget. There may be cases, of course, when it makes sense to stop slicing and dicing.

# RULE 3

■ ■ ■ ■ ■ ■ ■ ■ ■ ■ ■ ■ ■ ■ ■ ■ ■ ■ ■ ■ ■ ■ ■ ■ ■ ■ ■ ■ ■ ■ ■ ■ ■

## Don't Trust the Experts

There are lots of consultants and research companies that specialize in particular segments of the population. Unfortunately, sometimes they are so obsessed by the need to sell their particular segment that they lose their sense of proportion and find a way to either ignore statistics that don't present their group in the best light, or manipulate research so that the segment always looks the way they think it should.

Employing people, either on your staff or as consultants, who live the culture of the group to which you're hoping to market, is invaluable. If you don't get their input, you're bound to make mistakes. But never assume that they speak for the entire group that you want to reach. And always be alert to what might be their blind spots, their prejudices.

My personal litmus test for separating the pundits from the parrots is to ask them to tell me about the Chevy Nova. It's an urban legend, but one I've heard told many times by self-proclaimed marketing gurus. The story goes that when Chevrolet launched the Nova in Latin America it was a disaster, because it never occurred to anyone that the words "no va" mean "it doesn't go" in Spanish. The point of the Nova story is that ethnic marketing is tricky and you need to hire experts to avoid serious blunders. It's the right point, but the story is completely false. To begin with, Pemex, Mexico's government controlled oil company used the name "Nova" for years at all its gas stations for premium gas—apparently in the Mexican mind, the name evokes images of stars or newness, not a lack of mobility. Second, between 1972 and 1978, the NOVA did well in Latin America and exceeded all expectations. Third, it is absurd to assume that the world's largest corporation (at that time), with its extensive network of factories, subsidiaries, and dealerships in Latin America might have just let this one slip through the cracks. In fact, according to marketing analyst Cecelia Bouleau, GM marketers discussed the possibility that the name would be confused but they decided to keep it, given the frequency of the word nova in Spanish as in "bossa nova." So much for the so-called experts.

### Some persistent, and incorrect, urban legends . . .

**Legend:** Mitsubishi had to rename its Pajero automobile because the word is a vulgar term for a masturbating man.

**Comment:** There was no blunder involved because the car was marketed under a different name from the beginning. In Spanish-speaking countries, this model has been sold as the Montero.

**Legend:** A major airline (some accounts say American, others say Braniff) literally translated its "fly in leather" slogan as *vuela en cuero,* which means "fly naked."

**Comment:** The idiom for "buck naked" is *en cueros,* not *en cuero.*

**Legend:** Parker Pen intended to use the slogan "it won't stain your pocket and embarrass you," to emphasize how its pens wouldn't leak, translating it as *no manchará tu bolsillo, ni te embarazará.* But *embarazar* usually means "to be pregnant" rather than "to embarrass." So the slogan was understood as "it won't stain your pocket and get you pregnant."

**Comment:** Anyone who learns much about Spanish learns quickly about such common mistakes as confusing *embarazada* ("pregnant") for "embarrassed." For a professional to make this translating mistake seems highly unlikely.

**Legend:** A Spanish version of the "Got Milk?" campaign used *¿Tienes leche?*, which can be understood as "Are you lactating?"

**Comment:** This might have happened, but no verification has been found. Many such promotional campaigns are locally run, making it more likely this understandable mistake could have been made.

**Legend:** Coors translated the slogan "turn it loose" in such a way that it was understood as slang for "suffer from diarrhea."

**Comment:** Reports differ on whether Coors used the phrase *suéltalo con Coors* (literally, "loosen it with Coors") or *suéltate con Coors* (literally, "set yourself free with Coors").

**Legend:** Nestlé was unable to sell Nescafé instant coffee in Latin America because the name is understood as *No es café* or "It isn't coffee."

**Comment:** This story is demonstrably false. Nestlé not only sells instant coffee under that name in Spain and Latin America, it is common in Latin American coffee shops to display a sign in the window proudly proclaiming "Si, tenemos Nescafé" (Yes, we have Nescafé). Also, while consonants are often softened in Spanish, vowels are usually distinct, so *nes* is unlikely to be confused for *no es*.

**Legend:** A slogan for Frank Perdue chicken, "it takes a strong man to make a tender chicken," was translated as the equivalent of "it takes a sexually aroused man to make a chicken affectionate."

**Comment:** Like "tender," *tierno* can mean either "soft" or "affectionate." The accounts differ on the phrase used to translate "a strong man." One account uses the phrase *un tipo duro* (literally, "a hard chap"), which seems extremely unlikely.

Translation problems are ubiquitous, though many are greatly exaggerated and like the Chevy Nova, become the stuff of urban legends. Other communication mistakes are made because a message lacks what many have called "cultural competence;" in other words, the message works linguistically but misses the mark culturally. Usually the most egregious mistakes result from misreading how an ad or communication is going to be read.

## Turf wars and silos

In its early days, advertising used to be about reaching a mass-market audience with as broad a swath as a marketer could. Today, it's all about niche marketing, and there are specialized advertising agencies to help you reach Hispanics, African Americans, Asian Americans, gays, teens, kids, seniors, people with disabilities, affluent people, trendsetters and just about any other segment you could dream up. Some big companies have multicultural marketing departments; others have specialists in certain areas like Hispanic or African-American marketing. Sometimes these functions live within a brand management organization; other times they are autonomous, having their own budgets and revenue objectives. In other companies they are housed within a human resources function where they are often given a name like "diversity marketing."

Specialization can be a good thing. It promotes focus and ensures that a category receives the attention that it merits. It enables people to develop expertise. And in the case of large companies, a specialized person or department often means that multicultural marketing initiatives get adequate funding.

But being the territorial species that we are, specialization can often lead to balkanization, with specialists bustling to protect their own turfs, their own budgets, their own jobs. The creation of multicultural silos in a company can lead to a jealous and ugly defense of self-interest that prevents the creation of an integrated strategy.

For years, I've been coaxing Hispanic advertising agencies to admit that Hispanics born in the United States prefer English. It's a logical and intuitive conclusion, but at the beginning of the decade, it was heresy to imply that Hispanics spoke anything but Spanish.

In 2002, I was president of the multicultural market research company Cultural Access Group. We conducted a survey of Latino teens and young adults, most of whom are second-generation. We found English was preferred by 57 percent of respondents in Los Angeles; the number increased to 90 percent in New York and Miami.

Before we released the results, my COO and second-in-command, a cautious and conservative Cuban American, Raul Lopez, with tons of experience in the industry, told me he wanted to "go on record" against releasing the results (Raul is now president of Phoenix Multicultural, the renamed Cultural Access Group). A longtime Hispanic marketing veteran, he knew that to say that Hispanics might prefer English to Spanish was heresy and an affront to the deeply embedded party line. He argued that we would lose a lot of friends and a lot of business by going public with the study. He was right.

I decided to move forward anyway. The day we published our findings, I received a phone call form a senior executive at Univision, telling me that the network was not happy with our results. (I later was told that the network prepared an internal memo instructing its sales force on how to respond to inquiries about our study). Weeks later, I presented the results to one of the large Hispanic advertising agencies in Los Angeles. "Be careful with this study," I was told by the agency's founder, a kindly, wise and debonair gentleman. "What do you mean?" I asked. "Just be careful." Now I was getting paranoid.

Some in the industry embraced the study. Guy Garcia quotes it in his book, *The New Mainstream* (Rayo, 2004). Others looked for holes. "They just say they prefer English because they're teenagers," someone countered. "They're just rebelling against their parents.

They'll come back to Spanish." A former Miami mayoral candidate and Univision anchor, Jose Cancela, still argues that he and (apparently all) other Hispanics might speak English, but make love in Spanish. I can assure you, he's wrong.

I'm not sure if I had the last laugh. As Raul feared, I did alienate people and probably lost some business. But many in the industry are coming around to accepting a growing body of research that demonstrates unequivocally that Hispanics, though holding on to Spanish longer than any other ethnic group, lose their Spanish by about the third-generation.

## Thinking outside the language box

The problem with English-speaking Hispanics, or English-speaking anyone for that matter, is that it turns the existing multicultural marketing infrastructure on its head. That all or most Hispanics prefer Spanish was an unquestioned assumption of the early Hispanic advertising agencies that sprung up in the 1980s. And it made sense in those days, with the huge influx of Hispanic immigration that occurred. But that generation of immigrants has spawned a U.S.-born, English-fluent second-generation, raised on MTV and video games, educated in the American public school system.

The result is many Hispanic advertising agencies would more aptly be called Spanish-language agencies since they don't get how to market to English-speaking Hispanics and they have their heads buried in the sand, hiding from changing demographics. It's enlightened, though misguided self-interest. If clients catch on that many Hispanics prefer English, the playing field is now up for grabs. There's nothing to prevent their general market or even African-American agency from getting the business. At least, that's their fear.

I've seen the politics rage just as fierce within a client's own organization. A company's multicultural marketing department might control the budget for Hispanic marketing dollars in Spanish. Change to English, though, and the dollars move to the general marketing budget. Or they simply disappear. If Hispanics speak English, then they will be reached with a mainstream campaign, or so the argument often goes. The idea that Hispanics must be marketed to in Spanish has some absurd manifestations. Take the case of *Tu Ciudad*, the former bimonthly magazine in Los Angeles that targeted acculturated Hispanics. All the articles were written in English and the magazine catered to the tastes of an English-speaking Hispanic audience. But most of the ads appearing in its pages were in Spanish. *Tu Ciudad* publisher Jaime Gamboa, tried, often unsuccessfully, to persuade his clients to advertise in English. It's very often a case of a company's Hispanic advertising agency insisting that Spanish is more effective than English.

Despite what multicultural advertising agencies might tell you, you will reach many multicultural consumers with an English language, general market campaign. Multicultural media, be it Univision for Hispanics, BET for African Americans, ImaginAsian TV for Asian Americans, or MTV's Logo for LGBT viewers, provide an additional vehicle for you to connect with them. But don't overspend on them, because these same multicultural viewers, unless they speak no English, are watching mainstream networks as well.

While Hispanic ad agencies have focused on the differences between Hispanics and the general market, with language being a fundamental ingredient, the African-American multicultural marketing infrastructure, especially in the old days, used a formula for selling companies on African-American consumers that was one part economic, three parts political. In his book, *How to Succeed in Business Without Being White*, Earl Graves, founder of *Black Enterprise* magazine, recounts one of his earliest successes, a sales call to a vice president at Hertz. He brought with him two black political heavy hitters, both Georgia legislators: Julian Bond, a founding member of the Student Nonviolent Coordinating Committee (SNCC), and John Lewis, a civil rights activist and ex-leader of the SNCC. After Bond and Lewis made their arguments for the minority market, Graves followed with statistics on the economics of Hertz's minority customers. Graves then "demanded that [the Hertz VP] show his appreciation and awareness of his loyal African-American customers by purchasing full-page color ads in several issues of Black Enterprise during the next several months." Hertz bought the ad space.

Since the civil rights days, politics and multicultural marketing have been intimately linked. My former colleague Susanna Whitmore once sold advertising for The Wave, a Los Angeles–based "urban" newspaper with a largely African-American focus and following. According to Susanna, "Many of the old-school sales people used to threaten potential customers with a boycott if they refused to advertise. It was normal; it was common; it was the mindset, especially when selling to grocery stores, banks, and other large retailers in African-American communities. Management would go in and strong-arm them into buying ads. The racial politics model was deeply ingrained in the organization."

## Get the biggest bang for your buck

I often get calls from executives at Hispanic advertising agencies, who want to target some so-called underserved market segment, say wealthy South Americans. Chances are that the person calling me is South American herself, most definitely from money, white, and has a client in the luxury goods business. For argument's sake, let's say the client is Porsche. I say Porsche to keep things completely hypothetical; they have never called me to do Hispanic research, and probably never will.

The logic usually goes something like this. We are a luxury brand and 75 percent of our sales are to whites, 10 percent to Asians, 10 percent to African Americans and 5 percent to Hispanics. "Something is wrong here," they think. "There are 48 million Hispanics. They make up 15 percent of the population. Why are they not buying my product?" They then hire a Hispanic advertising agency or consultancy firm (a good move) that recommends targeting South Americans since their per capita income is higher than other Hispanics in the U.S. They then call me or one of my competitors to do a market research study.

The problem here is that the logic is flawed. The most compelling reason to target Hispanics is the size of the market—48 million in 2008 and growing. But now let's do the math. Of these, 5.5 percent are South Americans. Of South Americans, 75 percent are adults. Now we're down to about two million. Of those, half have a household income under $45,000 a year. If we take the percentage of those making over $45,000 who can afford a Porsche, we've gone from a very large market to a very small market. You get my point.

We always want to put our money where we'll get the biggest bang for the buck, but in multicultural marketing as it is often practiced by the experts, the logic gets screwy. Here are some statements that I hear all the time:

- "We're not targeting African Americans because they speak English." The same can be said for Asian Indians, Filipinos, Canadians, or English-speaking Hispanics. The fact is that each of these groups possesses a unique culture that rarely is targeted in advertising.

- "Muslim Americans are considered white, so they are part of the general market. The same with Jews, disabled people, seniors, etc." The fact is that the racial construct used by the Census has everything to do with politics and little to do with identity. It may make sense for the government. It may be nonsense for your brand.

- "There's no way to reach these other groups because they don't have their own television networks or media." The fact is that non-traditional advertising, be it on the Internet, grass-roots event sponsorship, or viral marketing can be extremely effective and often much less expensive than an advertising campaign.

- "Hispanics and African Americans have been singled out as a top priority for our company; my objectives are based on my successfully increasing sales to these consumers." The fact is that it probably does make sense that these two groups should be a priority for your brand. Just be smart.

- "Our general market advertising agency figures all this stuff out." The problem is, they may be clueless when it comes to multicultural marketing. Also, let's be honest. Any advertising agency has its own interests at heart. If they don't have experience in a certain segment, or if they feel that someone else can do it better than they can, they're not likely to admit it.

The bottom line is, if you don't look out for yourself, no one else will. Educate yourself and your employees about the market. Don't make the mistake I've seen so many companies make of entrusting your business to an advertising agency or a consultant. And when you hear someone tell the story of the Chevy Nova, run away as fast as you can.

# RULE 4

■ ■ ■ ■ ■ ■ ■ ■ ■ ■ ■ ■ ■ ■ ■ ■ ■ ■ ■ ■ ■ ■ ■ ■ ■ ■ ■ ■ ■ ■ ■ ■ ■ ■ ■ ■ ■ ■ ■

## Don't Let the Joke Be on You

When the Indianapolis Colts beat the Chicago Bears in Super Bowl XLI in 2007, two ads aired that made the marketing news. The first, a Bud Light ad featuring Honduran-born comedian Carlos Mencia, was praised for its innovation and comic flair. The second, a Snickers commercial, which featured two macho men panicked after accidentally kissing each other while sharing a candy bar, caused outrage in the gay community.

Both ads tapped into cultural stereotypes for their humor. In the Bud Light commercial, Mencia played an ESL instructor teaching a classroom of immigrants how to order a Bud Light. He teaches them to order in the South with a southern drawl and in New York with an exaggerated "youz guyz" Brooklyn accent. When in L.A., "Give me a Bud Light, Holmes," he says, sounding like Cheech Marin in an old Cheech and Chong routine. It's funny because the students, largely South Asian, try to imitate his speech with stereotypical Indian accents.

In the Snickers ad, two manly mechanics lock lips after one is unable to resist taking a bite of the Snickers bar that his buddy has sticking out of his mouth. After the "kiss," the two he-men are so mortified that they each pull out a handful of their own chest hair to reaffirm their manliness, i.e., their heterosexuality. Snickers' company, Mars, had been planning to build a whole campaign around the ad, which included an invitation to visit a website and vote on three alternative endings. One ending showed a third mechanic joining them and asking, "Is there room for three on this love boat?"

Unlike the Bud Light campaign that was heaped with accolades from critics and viewers alike, the Mars ad was quickly pulled, after vociferous protests from gay watchdogs like the Human Rights Campaign (HRC) and The Gay and Lesbian Alliance Against Defamation (GLAAD). "That Snickers, Mars, and the NFL would promote and endorse this kind of prejudice is simply inexcusable," GLAAD president Neil Giuliani said in a press statement. "Mars needs to apologize for the deplorable actions of its Snickers brand," he said.

If the Snickers commercial's only offence had been to hit on a worn stereotype, the backlash would have been minimal. What put it over the edge, what incurred the wrath of the LGBT community, was the violence and homo-hatred the ads portrayed. In one web ad, after the guys kiss, they decide to "do something manly," and proceed to drink motor oil and anti-freeze; they guzzle it down, screaming at the top of their lungs, making them sick to their stomachs. The ad suggests that it's better to die than be gay.

In the most offensive Snickers web ad, entitled "Wrench," after the two guys accidentally kiss, one guy proceeds to pick up a huge oversized wrench and violently attack the other guy, while the second takes the first and throws him under the hood of the car, slamming it down on his head. Message: the appropriate reaction to a guy kissing you is to beat him to within an inch of his life.

Anti-gay hate crimes are rampant in the United States, the most famous example having been the brutal murder of Matthew Shepard, the gay college student who was beaten to death in Laramie, Wyoming, in 1998. In fact, Shepard's mother, Judy Shepard, who is now Executive Director of the Matthew Shepard Foundation, came down hard on Mars. In a press statement she said that the campaign "encourages the same type of hate that led to the death of my son Matthew. It essentially gives 'permission' to our society to verbally or physically harass individuals who are gay, lesbian or bisexual."

So what went wrong? Mars wanted an edgy, humorous campaign that would get America talking. Instead, they used a tired stereotype to evoke the memory of a brutal murder. "It was never our intent to offend anyone," said a spokesperson from Masterfoods USA, Mars' parent company. "We know that humor is highly subjective and understand that some people may have found the ad offensive."

Too bad Mars didn't learn its lesson. Over a year later, in 2008, the company again used gender stereotyping and violence for laughs. In this ad, Mr. T—yes, *that* Mr. T—bursts out of a home in a truck, follows a slightly effete power-walker, and yells at him to "get some nuts" and "be a man" and then shoots him with an old fashioned gatling gun. Hmmmm.

One might say that speed walking is not a gay thing. True. But the power-walker was clearly anything but macho, and the effeminate stereotype has been so often used for gays in the past. *Advertising Age* said the "get some nuts" ad was Mars' attempt to once again drink from the homophobic well, and a popular blogger at TheCriticalCondition.com said, "Um . . . can Snickers please stop hating gay people? We like nougat too."

The usual gay rights groups pressured Mars to cancel the Mr. T campaign, and the company relented. The furor was just another reminder of how easily a blowup can occur, and how repeatedly boneheaded a company can be. My advice to Mars: do some research on gays and lesbians next time. And having a few open gays or lesbians on your marketing staff might help you avoid embarrassing your company again.

## Don't assume humor translates

In 2002, an English professor at the University of Hertfordshire, Richard Wiseman, best known as a buster of parapsychology claims, set out to test the adage that humor doesn't travel well. For his experiment, he solicited people around the world to contribute jokes and judge them. In the end, he evaluated over 40,000 jokes and tallied nearly 2 million votes using his "Giggleometer," a five-point laugh scale ranging from "not very funny" to "very funny."

Wiseman found that humor is, indeed, different around the world. For instance, people from France, Denmark, and Belgium preferred offbeat, surreal types of jokes. People from the UK, Australia, and New Zealand liked jokes with word play. Americans and Canadians preferred jokes where there was a strong sense of superiority—where a character was made to look stupid. Germans, who are not particularly known for their sense of humor, found just about everything funny.

- The favorite joke in Germany was: Why is television called a "medium"? Answer: It is neither rare nor well done.

- Here's the winner in Sweden: A guy phones the local hospital and yells: "You've gotta send help! My wife is in labor!" The nurse says: "Calm down. Is this her first child?" He replies: "No! This is her husband!"

- The favorite joke overall, the one with the most universal appeal, also happened to be the favorite in the United States: Two hunters are out in the woods when one of them collapses. He doesn't seem to be breathing and his eyes are glazed. The other hunter takes out his phone and calls 911. He gasps: "My friend is dead! What can I do?" The operator says: "Calm down, I can help. First, let's make sure he's dead." There is silence, then a gunshot. Back on the phone, the man says: "OK, now what?"

One type of humor that has pervasive international appeal is the pun, the word play, though they don't work as well in some languages like Russian. In Japanese, there is a word play answer to that time-honored question: "Which came first the chicken or the egg?" The answer is "Niwa Tori." It has two meanings, depending on how you say it. "Ni wa tori" means "the bird is second," in other words the egg is first. "Niwatori" means "it's the chicken," in other words the chicken is first. It gets a laugh every time, at least from a foreigner. Mexicans have a special word for the double entendre, the *albur*; to be a good *alburero* is considered to be a master of a time honored art form, albeit a raunchy one, whereby the objective is to stick it (no pun intended) to your adversary with a dose of sexual innuendo.

In terms of commercials, humor as a medium has been oft studied because of its universality—a humorous message that works across cultures and languages offers global brands the double advantage of having a consistent branding message as well as the economy of scale of producing a single campaign. But like everything else in international (and multicultural) marketing, it's not that simple. Humor doesn't always translate, and even when it appears to on the surface, it might not come across in the way it was intended.

One of the more publicized examples of a very funny campaign for an American mainstream audience that simply did not work in the Hispanic market is the California Milk Processor Board (CMPB)'s "Got Milk?" (of "are you lactating?" fame) campaign. The general market ads, created by Goodby, Siverstein & Partners, attempt to humorously show what life would be like in a world without milk. The first ad featured a history buff whose apartment is a shrine to the dual between Alexander Hamilton and Aaron Burr. As he eats a peanut butter sandwich, he receives a call from a radio station to answer its $10,000 trivia question, "Who shot Alexander Hamilton in that famous duel?" His mouth is full of peanut butter and he can't get the words out so he tries to pour himself a glass of milk, only to find that the carton is empty. Despite being a fanatical expert on the duel, he loses the contest because he doesn't have milk.

The ad was extremely successful. In 1998, the slogan "Got Milk?" was licensed to the National Milk Processor Board which features a slew of celebrities including fictional characters like Superman, Batman, and Bart Simpson, all mustachioed with milk. In 2002, it was named one of the ten best commercials of all time by a USA Today poll.

Despite its success with the campaign, when the CMPB wanted to take the campaign to Hispanic consumers, they found out it didn't translate. It wasn't a translation problem, as I pointed out in the previous chapter. It was the message—running out of milk—that Hispanics didn't find funny. In fact, they found the idea of not having enough to eat or drink rather scary. Today, CMPB's Hispanic advertising firm, Grupo Gallegos, uses the tagline "Toma Leche" or "Drink Milk" in a very funny campaign which features ads showing a universe of people performing all kinds of amazing feats with their teeth and contortions with their bodies, the result of having drunk their milk.

The difficulty of translating humor transcends language and enters the realm of culture, as is evidenced by the fact that African-American and white humor can be very different. According to Bob Peete, a black writer who worked on The Cosby Show and Good Times for several years:

> "There is a real difference between black humor and white humor. White humor is structured to a straight-line, punchline format. And television has become a medium of one-liners. One of the problems for a lot of black writers, at least in the scripts I read while working with Good Times, was that they could not effectively write one-liners. They could write lines that, in their heads, they could imagine the performer delivering with a certain attitude. But on paper it doesn't translate, especially to somebody white who is expecting the one-liners. They simply don't see the humor."

He uses the examples of Redd Foxx and Richard Prior, comedians who don't tell jokes per se, but who can convey an attitude with a simple line like "come in" that cracks the audience up every time. It reminds me of an episode from *The Family Guy*, a show that doesn't balk at spoofing anything. In one of the show's numerous "plays within a play," the family is watching an African-American sitcom. In the spoof, one black character lets loose attitude with a big "hmm-mm" followed by hysterical "canned" laughter; the other character counters with an even bigger "hmm-mm" as the imaginary African-American audience roars with laughter.

## The difficulty with satire and parody

Dame Edna is a drag queen/comedian played by Australian Barry Humphries, who is well known (in some circles) for irreverent and scathing humor. To Aussies, he, or rather she, is a national icon. Those who aren't in on the jokes, however, can take her comments quite literally, as Hispanics in the U.S. did, after *Vanity Fair* magazine published this exchange in the satirical "Ask Dame Edna" column in 2003.

Dear Dame Edna,

I would very much like to learn a foreign language, preferably French or Italian, but every time I mention this, people tell me to learn Spanish instead. They say, "Everyone is going to be speaking Spanish in 10 years. George W. Bush speaks Spanish." Could this be true? Are we all going to have to speak Spanish?

*Torn Romantic, Palm Beach*

Dear Torn:

Forget Spanish. There's nothing in that language worth reading except *Don Quixote*, and a quick listen to the CD of *Man of La Mancha* will take care of that.

There was a poet named Garcia Lorca, but I'd leave him on the intellectual back burner if I were you. As for everyone's speaking it, what twaddle! Who speaks it that you are really desperate to talk to? The help? Your leaf blower? Study French or German, where there are at least a few books worth reading, or, if you're American, try English.

*Dame Edna*

*Vanity Fair* counted on its readers knowing that Edna is a caricature of a certain type of small-minded, socially ambitious, pretentious, pseudo upper-class person. Those familiar with Dame Edna's performances understand that her politically incorrect and often insulting utterances are meant as a parody of backward attitudes.

But they miscalculated. The next day, I was inundated by "Can you believe this?" e-mails from colleagues who had no idea that Dame Edna was a fictitious character whose doses of advice were satirical. The magazine was hit with scathing criticism from the National Association of Hispanic Journalists and other Hispanic groups, who said Dame Edna's response was offensive. The editors of *Vanity Fair* issued several public apologies, to the offended groups, and in print in their next issue.

So, where did the magazine screw up? By hiring Dame Edna in the first place? Or by not reviewing this particular column, as opposed to other columns where she takes pot shots at other targets? Should the magazine run a disclaimer in the column: "Beware, this is only satire?" Should they have considered the fact that, while their intended audience was likely to get the joke, other audiences would hear about it soon in today's media world where the Internet can reduce the interval from publication to scandal to about the time it takes to hard boil an egg?

I suspect the editors must have realized that they didn't give the column enough consideration before running it. Satire and parody are hard to pull off; everyone must be in on the joke. When they're not, the joke not only falls flat, it can offend. Does this mean that all companies should stay away from satire? I hope they don't. But I think they do need to ask some questions first: Who else might see this? Who might not get the joke? What kind of damage could the aggrieved parties do to us if they don't get it? Do we have a damage control policy in case it gets out of hand?

For those of us who are fans of satire, it's kind of a shame, since companies might decide that in today's multicultural society with its diverse perspectives, satire might be too much of a risk. I have to say, responsible marketers might do themselves a favor by going for the "safe" humor. One must wonder, though, what would have been the fate of the great Irish satirist Jonathan Swift if there had been an Internet in the eighteenth century. In all likelihood, *Gulliver's Travels* would have been condemned for offending little people.

## R.E.S.P.E.C.T.

Most minorities in America have encountered some form of discrimination or prejudice. While discrimination is generally condemned in the larger society, stereotyping seems to sometimes elicit a chuckle and a nod; except, of course, from the group being stereotyped.

African Americans grow up with a legacy of racism and knowing that their chances of success are far less than those of whites. Hispanics and Asian immigrants may have seen their parents struggling to adapt to a new country and getting put down. They may have had their own "American-ness" or ability to speak English questioned, even if they were born here. Gays and lesbians, unless they're very young, grew up never seeing themselves on television and went through the likely painful ordeal of coming out of the closet.

The result is that minorities have developed a hypersensitivity to when they are not liked, wanted, or accepted. And this translates into an acute awareness about how they are portrayed in the media. Even the youngest members of minorities have had a sense of their group's historical portrayal handed down to them. Some inherited it from their parents. Others, gays or the children of immigrants, for instance, may not have gotten a sense of past wrongs until attending Asian, Chicano, or gay and lesbian studies classes. But at some point they get it.

Nowadays, African-American consumers are coveted and targeted, and marketers make great efforts to appeal to their sense of humor. But it's amazing how often companies get it wrong. A major car manufacturer asked my company to test a series of TV spots recently. The commercials were clever, using knock offs of well-known nursery rhymes, with a "black" twist. So, Jack and Jill became Jill "jacking" a house (robbing it); Rapunzel was a black woman with hair extensions (she threw her extension in the back seat as the car sped away from the scene of a crime). The company and its ad agency thought the spots were hilarious, but they decided to test it out to make sure.

Good move. Our focus group included many African Americans who asked, "Why are we being shown over and over as criminals?" It simply hadn't occurred to the company and the ad creators; or if it had, they dismissed the conflict too quickly. But to African Americans, who are sensitive to the very real statistic that black men are more likely to end up in jail, showing a black character robbing a house was nothing to laugh at. In this case, research saved the client from going on the air with something offensive, and having to face the wrath of watchdog groups (and the ire of consumers).

Earlier in this book, I mentioned how the Frito Bandito image stirred up controversy from image-sensitive Latinos. Beyond that, the stereotype of the Mexican revolutionary and the lazy Mexican peasant was commonplace in commercials in the late sixties and early seventies, and was used for "comic" effect. A Liggett & Myers cigarette ad introduced "Paco" who never "feenishes" anything, not even the revolution. An Arrid underarm deodorant ad showed a gang of banditos on horseback when their leader stops to give himself a spray as the voice over says "If it works for him, it'll work for you." A Granny Goose potato chip ad showed a fat Mexican toting guns and ammunition.

Stereotyping of gays has been around for millennia, and though America is becoming more aware of the "political incorrectness" of deriding gays, it's still commonplace in many circles, and advertisements are no exception. A common depiction is the swishy, histrionic, effeminate queen who is loaded with attitude. An example is the flamboyant designer featured in a 1996 T.J. Maxx commercial who has a hissy fit when- he reads a newspaper ad saying that the discounter is selling designer clothing for up to 60 percent off department store prices. "It's official. I have a migraine," he snivels after playing three notes on a piano: F, A and G.

## When in doubt, try it out

One of the best parts of being the president of a market research company is that I get to do my own research. It helps keep me grounded in reality and ensures that, as much as possible, I keep my finger on the pulse of the market.

In 2008, NBC Universal's Mun2, an English language network that targets young, bilingual Hispanics, came out with a much hyped ad campaign dubbed as "edgy" and "irreverent." The campaign included three commercials that ask its target audience the question "Are you becoming too *gringo*?" One Mun2 spot featured two young Latino men who are unable to jump a fence while running after two girls who have stolen the giant ice cream cone from their truck. A voice-over asks: "Is your *gringo* diet killing your Latin skills?" In another spot, a Latino teen in a classroom daydreams that he is president of the U.S. and facing an impending missile attack. A voiceover says, "Instead of dreaming about war, dream about nice things." He then sees himself as a gardener trimming hedges. In a third spot, a young Latino who is a contestant on a game show, guesses that France is in Minnesota and that Rio de Janeiro is near Kansas as a voice-over asks: "Are you becoming too *gringo*? Does the rest of the world not exist for you?"

When I saw the commercials, my gut told me that they missed the mark. At first, I thought that the depiction of *"gringos"* as war mongering, ethnocentric imbeciles might cause some backlash. At the very least, I thought it raised an interesting question: In today's world of political correctness, are white people fair game for mockery? More relevant to Mun2's target viewer, I thought that the ads crossed the line; implying that Hispanics are suited to be gardeners but not presidents seemed to go too far. Also, in all the focus groups we've done with acculturated Hispanics of that age, the idea of "becoming too gringo" never came up. Rather, even the most assimilated spoke with pride about retaining their Hispanic heritage. Mostly I was annoyed by Mun2's hubris. For all of the hype about being cutting edge, I thought the ads were just flat out not funny.

We decided to take the campaign to the people. We showed Hispanics and non-Hispanics the three commercials, and as a control, we showed them the Bud Light commercial with Carlos Mencia. The research, which was both quantitative and qualitative, showed that my instincts were right. Well, at least partially right. Four in ten Hispanics found the "White House" and "Fences" ads as "inappropriate." All the Mun2 ads received a much lower rating than the Bud Light commercial, and significantly fewer thought they were funny.

In this case, Mun2 was it's own worst enemy. The press releases boasted that the network was run by Latinos, and as Latinos, they were going to take the liberty of being edgy. Obviously, the Latino consumers that they purported to represent weren't having it. Luckily for them, a scandal was averted since the ads were limited to their own network and website.

Given the treatment that minorities have been afforded by corporate America in the past, it's no wonder that they're sensitive to how they're portrayed. Thankfully for conscientious marketers, it works the other way. Non-mainstream Americans notice and appreciate a respectful portrayal. Since being absent from the media has for so long been the norm, being included—in a respectful way—is so much more meaningful. Since the wounds of the past were so recently inflicted, companies today have a real opportunity to forge a lasting, intimate bond with multicultural consumers.

# RULE 5

■ ■ ■ ■ ■ ■ ■ ■ ■ ■ ■ ■ ■ ■ ■ ■ ■ ■ ■ ■ ■ ■ ■ ■ ■ ■ ■ ■ ■ ■ ■ ■ ■ ■ ■ ■ ■ ■ ■

## Don't Get Lost in Translation

In the first crisis of George W. Bush's presidency, a carefully worded
apology ended a major international incident. That was no mean
feat for a President who raised malapropism to an art form. The
tense standoff between the U.S. and China began April 1, 2002, when
an American surveillance plane and a Chinese fighter jet collided off
the coast of China. The Chinese jet crashed into the sea, and the
pilot was presumed dead. The American crew made an emergency
landing on China's Hainan Island. The 24 crew members were well
cared for, but not permitted to leave the country until the United
States issued a formal apology to "bear all responsibilities for the
consequences of the incident" and cease all surveillance activities
along the Chinese coastline.

President Bush refused to apologize, stating that the plane was
over international waters. For days after the crash, U.S. officials
insisted they had nothing to apologize for, although they did say
they "regretted" the death of the Chinese pilot. But this was not
enough for Chinese President Jiang Zemin and the Chinese people,
who remained outraged at the "arrogant" Americans.

A deal was struck eleven days later, when the U.S. ambassador to
China said in a letter that the U.S. was "very sorry" the Chinese pilot
died and apologized for landing on Chinese soil without permission.
The statement did not say that the accident was the American's fault,

but this didn't matter. Whereas "regret" was arrogant, "very sorry" was a serious statement. It is important to note that "sorry" was not good enough for China. Only "very sorry" was enough for Chinese leaders to save face and allow the U.S. to bring its pilots home. Although this linguistic hair-splitting was a puzzle to the average American, it was of paramount importance to the Chinese. It has to do with culture; the place that an apology has in Chinese culture is more exulted, and is taken more seriously, than in America. In the Chinese translation of "sorry," there is no indication that the speaker has acknowledged wrongdoing, whereas by adding the syllable "quian," transforming the term into "very sorry," the apology then becomes an expression of contrition and admission of guilt.

Why was an apology so important? Again, it's the culture. Unlike in the United States, where racist celebrities, philandering politicians, and careless corporations routinely say they're sorry, apologies have become ubiquitous and perfunctory. Apologies in Chinese and Asian cultures are more rare and take on greater significance. In China, offering an apology means admitting you are wrong; it is rarely uttered and highly symbolic. In many cases, the moral victory of receiving an apology takes the place of lawsuits or trials.

On the 50th anniversary of the bombing of Pearl Harbor, for example, Japan issued what was translated into English as an expression of deep remorse for the attack, and for its occupation of Asian countries during the war. The U.S. reacted positively to the statement. Leaders in China, South Korea, and countries in Southeast Asia interpreted the wording of the apology as a mere expression of "deep reflection, a far milder form of regret," and thus spurned the statement.

As diplomats have known for millennia, translating from one language into another isn't easy. Language is more than a mere currency of everyday, rational exchange, for there is organic, vital reciprocity between those who speak a language and their felt reality. Not only are a culture's value system and historical experience semantically embodied in its conventions of speech, but also its entire repertoire of consciousness.

To translate from and into the languages of two peoples, sometimes all you can hope to attain are rough or approximate results. Often, however, the task, even in the hands of translators with the most penetrative grasp of both languages, is daunting. The issue is that to translate a language is to translate the culture of the people who speak it. Your company may not be in the throes of an international conflagration. But understanding language—including not just correct syntax but also cultural meanings and nuances—may save you from some costly mistakes.

## You say either, I say *cualquiera*

One widely used technique to catch any potential translation gaffes, although it's not 100 percent flawless, and may not work in every case, is to back-translate. In other words, once you've translated your document into the language of choice, you back-translate it into English to see if it still says what you want it to.

I see translation mistakes in Spanish constantly. Sometimes, they're made by *gringos* dangerously armed with a Spanish-English dictionary. Other times, they're made by a second-generation Hispanic who never really learned to speak Spanish outside of a household environment. And I've seen atrocious spelling mistakes made by native speakers. In Spanish, if you see the letter "b" get confused with "v," that's your clue it was a native speaker. On the other hand, if a man tells you he's pregnant—*estoy embarasado*—when he wants to say embarrassed, you're most likely dealing with a *gringo*; I've made that mistake, as well as announcing to a client that I was "standing in his urine," rather than expressing my enthusiasm.

Another trick is to check the translated text against cultural sensitivities. Particularly if you're dealing with Spanish, it's a good idea to test your translation on people representing different countries of origin, to make sure you're not saying anything you don't want to. I once found a copy of Kafka's *Metamorphosis* translated into Spanish. The first line would have been read by a Puerto Rican as, "He found himself transformed into a monstrous penis." Hershey's took some heat when it launched a product, Elegancita, in *People en Español*, with the message that the candy bar has *sabor a chocolate blanco con cajeta* (the flavor of white chocolate with *cajeta*). *Cajeta* is delicious caramelized milk, similar to *dulce de leche*, but made with goat milk; using it was a smart decision given that Mexicans make up about two-thirds of the U.S. Hispanic population. But *cajeta* sounds offensive in other parts of Latin America. In a few countries including Argentina, it can refer to part of the female anatomy (then again, living in Mexico I found out that a lot of words can refer to parts of the male or female anatomy). I'm not saying they made a wrong decision; just that you need to be careful.

## Mistranslations

- *In a Belgrade elevator:* To move the cabin, push button for the wishing floor. If the cabin should enter more persons, each one should press a number of wishing floor. Driving is then going alphabetically by national order.

- *In a doctor's office in Rome:* Specialist in women and other diseases.

- *On a menu of a Polish hotel:* Salad a firm's own make; limpid red beer soup with cheesy dumplings in the form of a finger; roasted duck let loose; beef rashers beaten up in the country people's fashion.

- *A Finnish hotel's instructions in case of fire:* If you are unable to leave your room, expose yourself in the window.

- *Ad for donkey rides in Thailand:* Would you like to ride your own ass?

- *In a Czech tourist agency:* Take one of our horse driven tours—we guarantee no miscarriages.

- *Car rental brochure in Tokyo:* When passenger of foot heave in sight, tootle the horn. Trumpet him melodiously at first, but if he still obstacles your passage then tootle him with vigor.

- *A temple in Bangkok:* It is forbidden to enter a woman even a foreigner if dressed like a man.

- *In a Paris hotel elevator:* Please leave your values at the front desk.

---

## English-to-English translation

Different words can mean different things, even in English. In the 1990s, General Foods discovered that African Americans (as well as many Southerners) referred to stuffing as "dressing," posing somewhat of a problem for its Stove Top stuffing brand. Additionally, it found out that traditional African-American dressing was made with cornbread, not breadcrumbs. With the help of its African-American advertising agency, Burrell Communications, it developed a cornbread recipe and a tagline that said, "The box says stuffing, but the taste says dressing." According to Pepper Miller, author of *What's Black About It?*, awareness and sales among African Americans went through the roof.

In 1999, David Howard, a white aide to Washington, D.C., mayor Anthony Williams, an African American, resigned after a complaint was filed after he used the word "niggardly" as a racial slur. "Niggardly" means "miserly" or "stingy" and has a long history. It is believed to be derived from the Old Norse word *hnøgger*, meaning "stingy" and has nothing to do with the word "nigger," which ultimately comes from the Latin *niger*, meaning "black." Williams accepted Howard's resignation, saying that the latter had used poor judgment in using the word. And although Williams later recanted, the whole thing really makes you wonder if we are all speaking the same language.

Translation goes beyond language; it's about culture. And if you get the cultural context wrong, you'll wind up with a miscommunication. Take the word "healthy." It translates easily enough into Spanish, *"saludable"* (when people toast in Spanish, they say *"salud,"* toasting to each other's health). But the word "healthy" means different things to different people. To us, "healthy" can mean low in fat, sugar, cholesterol, or calories. To a recent Latin American immigrant, "healthy" can mean anything freshly made, traditional, or not containing preservatives. A Healthy Choice baked chicken dinner with wild rice is "unhealthy." Freshly fried pork rinds served with beans refried in lard are "healthy" if they are fresh and made with mother's love. So if you're doing a study on the health habits of Hispanic immigrants, and you ask the question "How important to you is it to serve healthy food to your family?" don't assume your respondent is serving fresh vegetables at every meal when she tells you it's "extremely important."

## Many ways of getting lost in translation

It's not just advertisements that you need to watch; if you're doing market research you need to be careful with your questionnaires. We once conducted a study on Internet usage among Hispanics and African Americans to see how each group related to the medium. One of the questions was an agree/disagree five-point scale to the statement "The Internet is colorblind." When I got the results back, nearly all of the 300 or so Spanish-language respondents either disagreed or didn't answer the question at all. For a second, I thought I was on to some great insight. But then, prudence got the better of me. I realized there must be a mistake in the data.

I started going through my retinue of tricks that I employ whenever results seem strange. Did the coding get inverted, making the "strongly agrees" into "strongly disagrees"? No. Did a question get added along the way, turning question ten into question eleven? No. And then it hit me. How did we translate the term "color-blind?" Sure enough, the translator used the word *"daltónico"* which means "color-blind;" in the sense of blue-green color-blindness, not "does not discriminate by color." So we blew it (luckily the study was for ourselves and not a client), and unless another researcher has asked that same question correctly, the world may never know if Spanish-speaking Hispanics feel that the Internet discriminates based on color.

Native speakers are sometimes stymied when language pertains to a particular subculture. If you don't believe me, try talking to a teenager. We were working on a study for a governmental agency that wanted to test the results of its "safe sex" campaign to prevent the spread of HIV. The questionnaire, focused on MSM's (men who have sex with men) was quite explicit, and though I'm embarrassed to admit it, seemed to cause quite a bit of giggling with some of our newer interviewers. It was quite a challenge to translate. One of the questions was "Are you generally a top or a bottom?" Our field director, an Argentinean was stumped; she had no idea how to translate it. She asked me and I knew the answer, which if not technically correct, would certainly get the message across—one of those things you kind of pick up along the way.

> ➲ *Focus groups are a great source of information, **if** they're done right.*

Focus groups are a great source of information, if they're done right. Don't assume, however, that a skillful moderator is all you need to elicit good responses from your participants. Consider the many Asian cultures. In mixed-gender groups, women often don't speak, and will defer to men. Also, when there's a wide gap in ages, the respondent will defer to a person who is older. The moderator needs to be aware of those dynamics, to prevent skewing the results.

Bill Imada, whose company IW Group does advertising, marketing and PR for Fortune 500 companies, is one of the founding fathers of Asian-American marketing and has had a great deal of experience with Asian focus groups. He has seen them handled well, and handled poorly.

> "My company came in after a pizza company badly handled their focus group. They wanted to know whether Cambodian women in their 40s and 50s liked pizza, and what kind they liked. But they used a white moderator who had no experience with Asian Americans, and a translator who wasn't aware of the verbal cues and nuances. Behind them sat pizza company executives who were really hoping that the women would like pizza, and like *their* pizza. But through a series of missed cues, and a moderator eager to give the company what it wanted to hear, the data became seriously skewed. When the moderator asked, 'Are you familiar with pizza?' the translator said, 'All of you are familiar with pizza, right?' All the women said, yes, because if they had said 'no' it would have been viewed as a challenge to the moderator, and to the pizza executives sitting behind him. Right after that, the women all agreed that they liked pizza, when in fact—my company learned later—they really hated it, thought it was disgusting, and stunk up the house."

The fundamental problem with the pizza focus group, the one that leads to cultural gaffes again and again, is a lack of cultural understanding. Asians, for example, are more visually oriented, not verbal. One needs to look closer for body cues. "Yes," doesn't necessarily mean "yes, I agree with that statement." It could mean "yes, I understand what you're trying to tell me." Japanese will rarely say no; rather a "maybe," "we will look into it" or what a friend of mine calls "sucking air" is often a cloaked refusal. Asian Indians bob their head in a unique way that can mean no. Asking for clarification may elicit a "yes" answer, to avoid challenging the perceived authority of the person doing the asking, but body language, often a subtle fidget or head scratch, will tell a different story. Only a sensitive and experienced moderator (and translator) will pick up on those cues.

Unless you or someone in your company knows the language and the culture of a group inside out, hire someone who does. Don't show an ad for a Chinese bank to an executive assistant just because his last name is Chang. Don't rely on feedback for you Spanish-language commercial from your IT person whose mother came from Colombia. They might just say, "it looks fine to me." But that doesn't mean it's really fine. Using an outside translator—one who understands not only the language, but also the idioms and the visual cultural cues—will help you minimize the possibility of miscommunication. But don't just leave it there. Test your communications with a diverse group of consumers. And, if your company does a lot of work with a particular segment, it wouldn't be a bad idea to hire someone who knows the language and the culture very well; that is, if you can find him.

I should underscore the importance of the visual as well as the verbal. This is especially important in ads. A common complaint of Asians is that Americans can't tell the difference between a Cambodian, a Laotian, a Korean, or a Thai. But their intended audience surely can tell the difference. Try putting in a photo of a Japanese family in an ad targeting Korean customers. You'll risk not only missing the mark, but also making an enemy for life.

As with the plane crash standoff in China, understanding context and meaning and significance of words—and visual cues—is crucial. A true expert (the kind you can trust) will not only know the language, he or she will understand the culture. The closer your marketing campaign reflects the cultural standards of the group you're speaking to, the less chance you'll need to later say you're sorry; or, in some cases "very sorry."

# RULE 6

■ ■ ■ ■ ■ ■ ■ ■ ■ ■ ■ ■ ■ ■ ■ ■ ■ ■ ■ ■ ■ ■ ■ ■ ■ ■ ■ ■ ■ ■ ■ ■ ■ ■ ■ ■ ■

## Push Their Buttons

The secret of pushing multicultural buttons—hitting the proverbial sweet spot—is to understand what moves people, all within the context of culture. Like any successful marketing campaign, a successful multicultural campaign makes an emotional connection with the target audience. How do you make that emotional connection? Find out how they see themselves. Or better yet, find out how they want to see themselves.

In one study, my company asked U.S.-born Hispanics the question: "Who do you identify with more: an actor who is Hispanic and speaks Spanish, an actor who is Hispanic and speaks English, or a non-Hispanic actor?" In a second study, we asked the corresponding question to U.S.-born Asians. The top answer in both groups was a Hispanic or Asian actor speaking English. Hispanics were twice as likely to prefer a Spanish-speaking actor than Asians preferring an actor speaking an Asian language. Interestingly, Asians were twice as likely as Hispanics to want to see an actor who was not of their ethnicity (24 percent vs. 12 percent).

Though both U.S.-born groups demonstrated a preference for someone of their own ethnicity speaking English, the relative preference of Asians for a commercial with non-Asian actors is deeply rooted in culture and the response of each ethnicity's second generation to life in the United States.

The first difference relates to language. In focus groups and

quantitative research that I've seen and conducted, Hispanics over-
whelmingly hope to pass Spanish on to their children. That the
language becomes virtually lost by the third generation is beside
the point. Passing on the mother tongue is much less important for
Asian immigrants, many more of whom come to the United States
already speaking English. Maintaining traditional Asian values, be
they Confucian or Ayurvedic, are important. But apart from after-
school Chinese or Korean classes, language is not.

The second difference, as to why Asians are relatively less open
than Hispanics to a commercial featuring someone of their ethnicity
is a little more subtle and requires some speculation. Stereotyping
is tricky, but it's safe to say that Hispanics love to stand out. Many
are overtly proud of their expanding influence in the U.S. They're
proud of their growing numbers, the explosion of Latin culture and
music, and the proliferation of Spanish (even if they may not speak
it fluently). In traditional Asian culture, standing out is often a negative. What does resonate, however, is a genuine inclusiveness that
represents them as part of the group, that is, part of the *mainstream*.
An example occurs in a Tim Hortons' commercial that I describe.

African Americans, as well as LGBT Americans, both have a long
history of being either stereotyped or excluded from mainstream
media, so sometimes the mere fact of inclusion can be enough to
push buttons. But mere inclusion packs less of a punch than it once
did. Plus, be aware that years of exclusion (and negative portrayals) have also made both groups very sensitive to their image in
the media.

A lot of it comes down to simple numbers. Because straight
whites make up the overwhelming majority of images that we see in
the media, a few negative portrayals are just a drop in the bucket.
If you're a minority member, the few images that reflect you are
rare, and thus carry a lot of weight; they can actually influence how
you are seen by a lot of people who might not really know you. So

this sensitivity comes from being a member of a group that has a history of being kept down, vilified, or stereotyped, and women of all colors belong in this category, straight or gay.

To a group that's been excluded, a realistic, sensitive portrayal in a commercial can be worth its weight in gold.

## Ads That Worked

An ad by Kenneth Cole shows two hands, both men's, holding each other. The caption reads: "Fifty-two percent of Americans think same-sex marriages don't deserve a good reception. Are you putting us on?" In a tearjerker ad from Hallmark, a father and mother are putting on their coats and saying goodbye to their son. As they get to the door, the son tells his father that though they don't always see eye to eye, he'll always love him. They embrace. At that moment the son's male lover appears. "So does this mean you'll be staying for dinner?" he asks in a matter of fact way.

Super Bowl XVI featured two commercials acknowledging Black History Month, one for Coke and the other from Frito-Lay, part of the PepsiCo family. The Coke ad paired key moments in black history with a Coke bottle from the same era—from Robert Peary's exploration of the North Pole in 1909 through the march on Washington, D.C., in 1963. The Frito-Lay ad showed African Americans watching the historic Super Bowl itself, which featured the first and second African-American coaches ever to lead their teams to football's biggest event, Lovie Smith of the Chicago Bears and Tony Dungy of the Indianapolis Colts. The ad asks the question "Who's Winning?" and responds, "We all are."

## Home away from home

Button pushing doesn't stop with advertising; a company must keep doing it until the sale is made. That means doing what's necessary to draw in customers, and making them feel comfortable in a store. What makes a buyer comfortable differs depending on the ethnicity and business. Top retailers are as good at doing a painstaking self-analysis as a Freudian psychoanalyst. Important questions they ask are: To whom does my store cater? Do my customers feel uncomfortable with the layout of my store, and why? Don't adopt the old adage from the movie, *Field of Dreams*: "If you build it, they will come." I've found that, in the retail environment, it isn't necessarily so.

I once did a focus group with Hispanic immigrant mothers to understand why they picked one supermarket as their main shopping destination over another. All the women ranked cleanliness and neatness as traits important to a grocery store. Yet when asked about their favorite store, they named Superior, a small Mexican chain in Los Angeles, that all participants described as disorganized.

With more probing, we discovered that Superior, aptly named, created a familiarity that the American chains lacked, familiar store layout, familiar brands, familiar cuts of meat, familiar types of produce, and such.

As the discussion continued, a common denominator became apparent to all present including the women themselves. They enjoyed shopping and looked forward to it. They were good at it and took pride in being able to keep their families happy, healthy, and well fed, on very limited budgets. Shopping enabled them to recapture the feeling of self-confidence and competence that they felt they had lost when coming to a new country. While shopping there, they felt in control of their lives. In a nutshell, they felt comfortable.

Superior offered a general "warm and fuzzy" feeling that customers couldn't find in the highly sanitized, orderly aisles of mainstream mega-grocery stores. And though the focus was on supermarkets, we could have been talking about apparel stores, restaurants, or automobile dealerships. In fact, we could be talking about Asians, African Americans, or gays.

My company often gets hired to do "mystery shopping" whereby we'll visit stores, call customer service numbers, or go to companies' websites to see how positive a shopping experience is. We'll look to see if a store has those things that are going to make customers feel comfortable. If they are targeting immigrants, do they have point of sale material that is in-language? And do they have the right languages, the ones that represent the people in the local community? If they are targeting African Americans, do they have African Americans working in the store? Or do they have security guards that follow African American shoppers around the store? If they are targeting gays, do they have gay employees, or at least employees that are comfortable with gays? Or do they have employees who visibly wince when an obviously gay couple walks into the store?

I recently worked on a gay and lesbian study for a large, well-known bank that was looking to increase its presence in the gay community. I was amazed at the number of respondents who reported having banking experiences that they described as being homophobic or outright discriminatory. One lesbian woman said that her partner, who was much more "butch" than she, was getting sneers from a bank teller until the two reported him to the branch manager. Many, both male and female, related having similar experiences.

A common theme that comes up in gay and lesbian research is what many call "the assumption of heterosexuality." Sometimes called heterocentrism, it means that naïve straight people will often assume, in the absence of patent homosexuality, that someone is straight. It manifests itself in questions like "Will your wife be joining you?" and the ultimate look of shock when the wife, well, isn't quite what was expected. The same, of course, can be said of husbands. This theme is a frequent one in research we've done with financial or medical companies because gay men or women acting on behalf of their partners are often treated like pariahs by well meaning personnel who refuse to deal with a "spouse" of the same sex.

There are often legal issues at stake and companies are very often prohibited from giving out information to anyone who is not a lawfully wedded spouse. My point is that when companies are sensitive to gay and lesbians and the type of difficulties they encounter, they are in a much better position to forge a relationship.

## Give the people what they want

Customization to consumer needs is crucial. Smart supermarket retailers know this. Ethnic consumers, particularly immigrants are big on fresh produce, and the type of produce they buy is often different from that of mainstream shoppers. A large mainstream supermarket may, for instance, have multiple kinds of apples: Red Delicious, Golden Delicious, McIntosh, Fuji, Granny Smith, etc. Hispanics are large consumers of fresh apples, but to many immigrants, a *manzana* is a *manzana*. So a supermarket with a percentage of Mexican shoppers may want to stock a smaller variety of apples, and a larger variety of, say chili peppers. Smart supermarkets know their consumers and stock accordingly. Let's stay with the analogy of the chili pepper, that Mexican and Central American favorite. Notice I say Mexican and Central American, not Caribbean or South American, which do not feature the hot and spicy as part of their traditional diets. For Mexicans and Central Americans, however, chili peppers are a staple. And depending on where your shoppers come from and what their tastes might be on a given day, they might be looking for jalapeños, chipotles, serranos, chiltecpins, or anchos, to name a few. The savvy retailers price some of the more exotic chiles as staples since that's what they are to Hispanic shoppers.

Customization is also crucial for any multicultural marketer, retailer or otherwise. Successful marketers have the flexibility to build, buy, or bake any product that their consumers want, provided they can do so and make a decent profit.

Without a doubt, the most important factor for any multicultural effort to be successful is that it be authentic; that it reflects the lives of consumers as they live them. I remember a commercial for Prince Spaghetti when I was growing up. It took place in Boston's Italian North End and featured a character, Anthony, whose mother's voice calling him to dinner emerged above all the street noise in the neighborhood. Anthony was already running, however, the point of the ad being that in the North End, Wednesday was Prince Spaghetti day, so Anthony didn't need to be called twice. I remember the ad to this day and I'm not Italian. I would wager that any Italian kid, whether he lived in Boston or not, had his buttons pushed with that commercial. To him, it was a wink—but I'll save that for the next section.

# RULE 7

■ ■ ■ ■ ■ ■ ■ ■ ■ ■ ■ ■ ■ ■ ■ ■ ■ ■ ■ ■ ■ ■ ■ ■ ■ ■ ■ ■ ■ ■ ■ ■ ■ ■ ■

## Market on a Wink and a Prayer

In the old days, multicultural marketing was easy. There were two secrets. First, since African Americans rarely if ever appeared in ads as anything but distorted stereotypes, the trick was to include them, and don't make them look too silly. Second, since Latin American and Asian immigrants were arriving in the United States in vast numbers, give them a commercial in their native language with a cultural reference or two and they'll love you forever.

Today, things are different. Advertisers use ethnic actors, particularly African Americans, to add an urban edge or "street cred" to a product. But when they do, authentic African-American culture is often sacrificed. Asian Americans rarely show up in commercials, and when they do, they are often in stereotypical roles, usually nerdy characters, often with foreign accents. Hispanics rarely appear in ads, Spanish television aside. And since Hispanics do not represent a race, it's hard to depict a Hispanic presence in a commercial without casting dark-skinned actors or oft-used cultural stereotypes like salsa music, piñatas, or corny accents. Gays rarely if ever show up in mainstream ads, except as bitchy designers or foppish "best girlfriends."

The most successful marketers are beginning to discover that the secret to advertising to multicultural consumers is with a mainstream ad with an embedded culturally relevant message, a private communication of camaraderie and recognition—a "wink." To understand how powerful a wink is, imagine if someone you didn't know winked at you. Depending on the context and how it's done, you'll either feel complimented or offended. English language ethnic marketing walks this high wire act; pump up the ethnic or cultural references too high and the audience may reject it as stereotyping; marginalize these attributes too much and the efficacy of the wink is lost. Get it just right and the audience is impressed—"Did you see that ad?"—and willing to patronize the businesses that made the effort to do so. Mastering the wink in advertising or communications is an art.

## Seven Characteristics of the Wink

1. It's a mainstream ad; in others words, it's not in the "ethnic" media.

2. It's subtle; it doesn't hit you over the head.

3. It's devoid of stereotypes.

4. It challenges preconceptions.

5. It has an insider reference that an outsider would miss.

6. It appeals to a mainstream audience, hitting the target consumer's sweet spot.

7. It elicits a "That was for us!" response from multicultural viewers.

I've seen the wink executed really well only a few times. In a 2003 Coke ad titled "Care Package" by Berlin Cameron Red Cell/New York, a Hispanic looking young man returns to his dorm room and finds a plate of *empanadas* and a coke in the fridge, which he proceeds to devour. His roommate, who is black, comes home and is furious when he finds a mother's note that reads: "Tito, I've left you some *empanadas* in the refrigerator. Tito is the black character with the doting Hispanic mother. The commercial executes the wink perfectly because it shows Hispanic characters as they really are: regular guys with Hispanic moms that spoil them. It tricks us into seeing our own stereotypes—that Hispanics are always brown, never black. The wink says, "We get you. We see you in all your diversity."

Another successful ad features a Hispanic family sitting around the breakfast table eating Cheerios; the kids speak English, the parents speak Spanish. It looks like hundreds of Hispanic families I've seen during in-home research. What's so amazing is that this was a general market ad, showing a "typical" American family eating breakfast together. But by making that American family Hispanic and bilingual, every Hispanic person watching that ad got the wink.

One of the best executions of the wink I've seen was developed in 2002 for the California Milk Processor Board's "Got Milk?" campaign by four Hispanic students of the Art Center College of Design in Pasadena. The ad features *la Llorona*, the weeper, a mythical Latina ghost, and the stuff that every Hispanic kid's nightmare is made of. Though the story has many variations, typically it goes that *la Llorona* drowned her children and then herself in a river, henceforth being condemned to wander the earth while crying for her children. In the commercial, *la Llorona* wanders through a house and makes her way to the refrigerator. She sees a *concha*, a Mexican pastry, which she proceeds to devour. Grabbing a milk carton to wash it down, she discovers that the carton is empty. True to her name, she lets out a wail to make your hair stand on end. To non-Hispanics watching the ad, she's a ghost. To Hispanics, it's *la Llorona*.

An effective use of the wink with LGBT consumers is using what Michael Wilke, Commercial Closet's founder, has called "gay vague." It's a kind of covert communication from gays to other gays, a wink that often goes right over the heads of straight people. It can be intentional, unintentional, or probably intentional but denied (like Abercrombie & Fitch ads of nearly naked young men in sensuous poses).

A 1999 Suburu print ad, though clearly gay as opposed to gay vague, is a great example of the wink. The tag line is "Different drivers. Different Roads. One car." It features three cars outfitted with license plates that read "Xena Lvr," "P-Town," and "Camp Out." The TV show *Xena, Warrior Princess* is a cult classic among lesbians; "P-Town" is short for Provincetown, a very gay resort; and "Camp Out" is a reference to the word "camp" which refers to gay sensibility, gay humor.

One ad for the Canadian coffee, doughnut, and fast-food chain, Tim Hortons, successfully winked at Chinese Canadians. Timmy's (as it's affectionately called by Canadians), is a Canadian institution—part what Dunkin' Donuts is to New England, part what the Statue of Liberty used to be to immigrants. Tim Horton who started the chain in 1964 was a defenseman for the hockey team the Toronto Maple Leafs; ten years later, he was tragically killed in an automobile accident. Today, he is a national icon, as is the chain, which bears his name.

Even though the chain was taken over by Wendy's in 1995, its marketing is developed to tug at Canadian heartstrings with commercials that play on national, very Canadian themes: hockey, curling, and Canada's identity as a multicultural nation. In one commercial, "Proud Fathers," a father and son drink a cup of Tim Hortons coffee while watching their respective grandson and son playing hockey. When the father tells his son that he used to watch him when he was younger, unbeknownst to the son, it's impossible to keep your eyes from misting. Interestingly, the company chose to use actors who are ethnically Chinese in this Canadian folk tale. Canadians are proud of their country's diversity, something that was not lost on the commercial's developers. I haven't seen data, but I'd say it's a risk-free wager that Timmy's scored a "hat trick" with any Chinese Canadian watching the ad—for showing them, for showing them as regular people, and for showing them as regular Tim Hortons coffee-drinking, hockey-playing Canadians.

## Five Reasons to Use the Wink

1. Multicultural consumers rarely see themselves portrayed in mainstream ads.

2. When they do, they are stereotyped or watered down.

3. It's a way to really connect.

4. It sends a message you are talking to them.

5. It shows you "get them."

---

Our research consistently shows that the inclusion of multicultural actors in mainstream advertising seldom goes unappreciated by, or is seldom lost on multicultural members of that group. With African Americans, they expect it, and if a commercial contains a multi-character cast that doesn't include an African American, it is absolutely noticed. What is often missing, however, is an authentic taste of African-American culture that goes beyond just casting. A cultural reference, a piece of artwork on the wall, or a gesture can go a long way to connecting with consumers.

One of the pioneers of multicultural marketing research was Paul K. Edwards. His book, *The Southern Urban Negro as a Consumer* (Prentice-Hall, 1932), is a compilation of census data and his own research into African-American consumption habits, with a particular focus on brand loyalty. Edwards took a particular interest in how blacks responded to seeing themselves in advertising. No surprise, he found that when the representation was not negative, African Americans responded well to seeing themselves depicted in ads. Subjects clearly preferred an ad for Rinso laundry soap featuring a black laundress to one that featured only whites. Aunt Jemima ads, on the other hand, fared poorly. Edwards concluded that respondents disliked the "use of Negro mammy and the log cabin plus the reference to Aunt Jemima's master—all of which savored too much of slavery days."

In the case of Hispanics and Asians, when they do appear, it is on in-language television, which is most often imported from Latin America or Asia. In the realm of English-language television, despite some notable exceptions like the now defunct *George Lopez Show* and *Ugly Betty*, Hispanics represent about 5 percent of all television characters, often being typecast as servants or gangsters. Asians, too, are few and far between, and are often shown in background roles, again with exceptions like Lucy Liu or Sandra Oh.

For the less represented multicultural folks, the inclusion of a character can go a long way. This is particularly true with gay and lesbian consumers, whose lifestyle for so long has been ignored or portrayed as deviant. Advertising in the gay press is a good thing, but the power of including a gay couple in a mainstream ad goes so much further. It's appreciated because it demonstrates real commitment. Gays know that companies take a risk by publicly expressing support for the gay community and attacks from the Christian Right are not infrequent. Perhaps more importantly, a gay person or couple depicted as normal, with no stereotypes and no clichés, because it is so infrequently done, is an enormously meaningful gesture to the gay community.

## The language of the wink

For Hispanics born in the United States, even English dominant ones, Spanish has a symbolic importance that is as much about culture as it is linguistics. As a fourth-generation Jew, I can relate. When I hear Yiddish words spoken, it warms me up inside. It reminds me of my grandmother. When English didn't seem to do a situation justice, she would start a sentence with "As my mother used to say," and then launch into a sentence like "*Ich zol azoy vissen fun tsores*"—"I should know as little about troubles as I know about what you are talking about," and my great-aunts and -uncles would explode with laughter I would laugh along with them, though I would understand nothing. Hearing Yiddish takes me back to those days.

Okay, so maybe Yiddish isn't the best example. It was the language of the *shtetl*, the ghettos of Eastern Europe and later America's cities, a dying language. Spanish is alive; it breathes; it evolves. The fruit of its linguistic loins—"Spanglish"—is a mixture of Spanish and English spoken by millions of second generation Hispanics. It's an example of what linguists call "code switching," where a bi- or multi-lingual person speaks in two or more languages. Spanglish speakers blend Spanish and English as effortlessly as DJ Danger Mouse combined the vocals from rapper Jay-Z's *The Black Album* and the Beatles' *White Album* to produce *The Gray Album*.

But maybe Yiddish isn't such a far-fetched analogy as it first appears.

I didn't realize it at the time, but when I was a kid watching syndicated runs of *The Three Stooges*, words I thought were gibberish were often Yiddish puns. In one episode, as Moe is heading to a hockshop, Larry tells him, "While you're there, hock me a *tshaynik*." A *tshaynik* in Yiddish is a teakettle and the word *hak*, pronounced something like "hock," means "to knock." A popular expression in Yiddish is, "*Hak mir nisht ken tshaynik*," which literally means, "Don't knock me a teakettle." It refers to the increasingly loud knocking noise made by a teakettle as the steam escapes. Don't knock me a teakettle is a polite way of asking someone to shut-up.

Spanglish, like the Yiddish of the Stooges, is an insider's language, since you have to be able to speak both languages in order to get what the heck is being said. When Puerto Rican comedian Bill Santiago, in his standup routine *Spanglish* 101, jokes that his mother is fond of calling his father *"el hijo de la gran puta,"*—you have to speak Spanish to know exactly what she thinks of him (or her mother-in-law).

Depending on who you talk to, Spanglish gets mixed reviews. Santiago jokes that it is a language with "double the vocabulary, half the grammar." Nobel Prize–winning Mexican author Octavio Paz called it "neither good nor bad, but abominable." In his book *Living in Spanglish: The Search for Latino Identity in America* (St. Martin's Press, 2002), Ed Morales writes that it "describes a feeling, an attitude that is quintessentially American, but it is both older and newer. It is a culture with one foot in the medieval and the other in the next century." Good or bad, Spanglish is likely to stick around for awhile, as reflected in the comedy of George Lopez; *La Cucaracha*, a Spanglish comic strip by Lalo Alcaraz; or the *Spy Kids* movies by Robert Rodriguez, where Spanish words are tossed out with the nonchalance of Ricky Ricardo shouting at Lucy.

As America grows more diverse and as the boundaries between multicultural consumers and the so-called general market become more blurry, it is likely that the wink will become more prevalent—and subtle. A targeted ad is a great way to say, "I'm talking to you." An ad with a wink is a more powerful connection. It says, "I'm talking to you and only you." Perhaps what is most powerful about the wink is that in a multicultural country, the rest of the country should connect to the commercial as well, and that means that using targeted multicultural media will become less necessary—and that's good for budgets.

# RULE 8

................................

## Make Up, Don't Cover Up

You've done your market research. You've tested your campaign in focus groups and your target consumers love it. You and the ad agency are high-fiving in the back room, gloating over your collective brilliance. But the unexpected happens: A gay group declares your "gay dad" ad offensive because it deems the humor stereotypical. Or a right wing Christian group threatens a boycott because you're doing ads in the gay media. A prominent anti-gay black preacher is mad that you used a pro-gay hip-hop star in your ad and a black organization thinks that same star isn't "black enough." A group of Puerto Rican bloggers is angered at being excluded from an ad that seems to reach out only to Mexicans—and their protests are getting the attention of the mainstream press.

You started with the best of intentions: to gain the affection, respect (and dollars) of a multicultural group. Now, not only has your campaign missed the mark, it may even cause your target group to hate you.

Cultural watchdogs are quick to anger and their wrath can be without mercy. They will spin your attempts at creativity into egregious sins committed against the innocent. Sometimes they are right. Other times, their goal is simply to make you jump or to make a bigger name for themselves. Obviously it's important to avoid angering any of these groups in the first place. When that fails—and some of the smartest and best companies have failed at one time or another—you'll need a sophisticated and rapid response strategy.

The first step in developing a strategy is knowing whether you have a true crisis. Howard Bragman, founder of the Los Angeles PR firm FifteenMinutes, believes that much of the time, watchdog groups are more bark than bite. "Many of these groups thrive on controversy, be they religious, cultural, or ethnic or race-based. Threatening a protest is how they raise money. A company isn't going to stop these groups, so you have to be prepared for their attacks and demands. But in most cases the protests they threaten you with go nowhere."

The worst thing a company can do, Bragman says, is run for cover and shut down (a marketing campaign) at the first sign of anger from one of these groups. "You have to be smart about it and take a step back; otherwise you might just get backlash from an opposing group for capitulating to the first group."

## Watching the watchdogs

The term "watchdog" is a bit broad, and encompasses some large, established organizations that, in addition to wanting to raise money, genuinely do have an interest in improving the image of their constituent groups in the media. Many pride themselves on holding the media and advertising worlds accountable for overt and subtle negative stereotypes and messages. There are other watchdogs that simply want to stir up controversy. And today, with the ubiquity of the Internet and the rise of blogging, there are citizen watchdogs that can attract the attention of the media as well. Some of them are well-meaning, some are flakes, and some really can cause a PR nightmare if they play their cards right, and if you mistakenly play into their hands. It's important for any marketer to know who the players are, what they want, what they can do, and how to respond appropriately in order to avoid a true crisis.

The Gay and Lesbian Alliance Against Defamation (GLAAD) will be the first to tell you that they have been instrumental in turning around public perceptions of gay, lesbian, and transgender people, and there is ample evidence for this. Other prominent and established LGBT groups include the Human Rights Campaign (HRC), and National Gay and Lesbian Task Force (NGLTF). These latter two groups operate primarily in the political sphere, promoting legislation favorable to LGBTs, but they also weigh in on media issues, and have a good deal of clout.

The Media Action Network for Asian Americans (MANAA) is the first, and the most influential watchdog group that monitors the media for inaccurate portrayals of Asian Americans. It was founded to "address the negative stereotypes long perpetuated by the media, which detrimentally affect all Asian Americans, hurting not only their self image but also how non-Asians treat them." Its founder, Guy Aoki was angered by the news media's negligent portrayals of Japanese Americans in their coverage of the 50th anniversary of the Pearl Harbor bombing, which, he said, led to hate crimes against Asian Americans including the desecration of a Japanese-American community center.

While there is no single clearinghouse for negative portrayals of Hispanics in the media, such issues may be taken on by the left-leaning Fairness and Accuracy in Reporting, or the National Council of La Raza (NCLR), the largest national Hispanic civil rights and advocacy organization in the United States, or hundreds of community based organizations.

In 1999 the NAACP began a campaign to promote diversity within the media industry infrastructure and to improve African-American representations. The group called for viewer boycott of the major television networks, thereby, boycotting the commercials that support programming. The NAACP demanded that the media hire more people of color and begin to rid television of the stereotypes so frequently assigned to blacks. Today, viewers can link with the NAACP and a variety of other organizations or begin their own grassroots boycott by recruiting friends, family, and co-workers to tune out the negative and tune into shows that represent African Americans well. And when the Reverends Al Sharpton and Jesse Jackson take up an issue, you know you've got a problem with the African-American community. If the matter reaches Oprah, be it a perceived disparagement of blacks, women, gays, or any group, you'll need some heavy-duty damage control. Never underestimate the power of Oprah.

More and more, smaller watchdogs feed bigger ones, including bloggers, who can develop a loyal following of activists. Some bloggers, especially those targeting a specific niche (for example, gay African Americans, liberal, politically aware voters, or consumer-rights watchers) are becoming the modern electronic equivalent of print journalism's muckrakers of a century ago. Issues that go unreported by mainstream media, and even established watchdog groups, get noticed by bloggers. Some of the most influential blogs have caused enough furor around specific issues to make the established news outlets reluctantly take notice. Whether every grievance is legitimate is a matter for debate, but several bloggers' demonstrated ability to inspire grassroots activism has taken mainstream media by surprise, and caused some of the largest U.S. companies to change their marketing strategies, issue apologies, and, in some cases, go into "duck and cover" mode.

As Howard Bragman suggested, making nice with one watchdog may land you in trouble with another. Gays and ultra-conservative Christian groups have been in a tug of war for years. As I mentioned in the LGBT chapter, anti-gay, religious right organizations such as Focus on the Family and the American Family Association have been especially aggressive in promising to punish companies that are too friendly to gays (whether in their marketing, or in their employment and non-discrimination policies). Groups like this, so far, have made a lot of noise, but there is little evidence that their tactics (usually centering around petition campaigns and promised boycotts) have damaged the bottom line of their targeted companies. But boy, have they made some companies dance.

One mini-firestorm that could have been handled better, involved the Chrysler Corporation and the introduction of a Dodge product, the Caliber, in 2006. Their 30-second ad, entitled "Anything but Cute," involves a fluttery fairy who zaps buildings and trains into cute-looking gingerbread houses and toy trains, but is unable to transform a black Dodge Caliber. When a macho male passerby snarls, "Silly little fairy," the fairy retaliates by turning the man's button-down shirt and jeans into white shorts and pastel polo shirt draped with a sweater. With the flick of a wand, the fairy also transforms the man's tough dog into four Pomeranians with pink leashes. The formerly macho man then shrieks in horror. Several gay groups claimed the ad agency was out of line for coaxing laughs from gay stereotypes. Many, including the Triangle Foundation, a Michigan LGBT rights organization, insisted that the ad really did drive home a gay stereotype by having the man expel a "feminine gasp" when he finds himself girly looking. But no group actually called the ad blatantly homophobic, and nobody called for a retraction. It was simply an outdated gay joke, and the groups wanted parent company DaimlerChrysler to recognize that their joke was hackneyed and stereotypical and that they would be wise to get with the program.

Instead of responding with, "Thank you for your insight; we'll be more careful in the future." DaimlerChrysler took a surprising approach. They blamed the watchdogs. "We're kind of surprised that people are making a conclusion about someone's sexual orientation based on the type of clothes you wear and the type of dog you're walking," a company spokeswoman told the Associated Press. The spokesperson went on to suggest that it was gay men who were the ones doing the stereotyping, calling the commercial's hapless dog walker gay based on what he was wearing.

"It's kind of a disingenuous answer, because it's not just about the clothes, but the man's shriek and affectation in the ad," according to Mike Wilke of Commercial Closet. "Turning around and suggesting that gays are to blame was not the best response." In addition to "blaming the victim," DaimlerChrysler made a mistake in the beginning by likely not consulting with watchdog groups or LGBT advocacy groups to find out whether the ad might touch a nerve. Wilke asserts that it's important to educate companies on ways of avoiding comedy malfunction stemming from stereotypes before a watchdog has to step in and bring it to their attention.

DaimlerChrysler did not pull the ad, and did not suffer from any boycott. Did it leave a bad impression among potential Dodge shoppers who happen to be gay? Maybe. Will it hurt their bottom line? Not likely. An interesting footnote: as part of our LGBT study, my company tested the Dodge Fairy ad among the different segments. Surprisingly, it tested pretty well; a majority thought it was funny. So it goes to show that the watchdogs are not always in tune with the constituents that they supposedly represent.

## Know when to hold 'em, and when to fold 'em

Major companies are learning an important lesson: when the watchdog barks, you don't have to jump right away. However, when you do need to jump, do so gracefully. PepsiCo learned the hard way. In 2002, the company pulled a commercial created by African-American agency UniWorld featuring rapper Ludacris, after Fox News commentator Bill O'Reilly called for a Pepsi boycott because of the rapper's edgy lyrics. Hip-hop icon Russell Simmons threatened a Pepsi boycott for applying a double standard by pulling Ludacris, an African American, while continuing to air spots by foul-mouthed, bat-decapitating, English rocker Ozzy Osbourne. Ultimately, PepsiCo agreed to pay $5 million to the Ludacris Foundation and to continue working with Simmons' Hip-Hop Summit Action Network. Good intentions, bad result.

In 2001, Jesse Jackson called for a boycott of Toyota, after the company issued postcard ads featuring a smiling African-American man with the image of a gold RAV4 on his tooth. Toyota called the ad a form of tooth art, aimed at a "young and very trendy audience." Jackson's response: "The only thing missing is the watermelon."

When pulling the ad failed to satisfy Jackson, Toyota announced that it would spend $8 billion over ten years on a diversity plan that included hiring more minority ad agencies. Toyota should have known better. In 1999, they had run an ad in *Jet Magazine* with the caption "Unlike your last boyfriend, the Corolla goes to work every morning."

One example of a watchdog that didn't back down was the fight over *The War*, a high-profile documentary about WWII, and filmmaker Ken Burn's inadvertent omission of Latinos from the 14-hour documentary. In an unprecedented move, the demands of activists tried to preempt artistic vision, forcing Burns to go back into the editing room months before the public saw his documentary.

The fuss started when a project manager from a University of Texas sponsored project, U.S. *Latinos and Latinas and World War II*, asked Ken Burns if Latino veterans were included among the more than 40 men and women who were interviewed for the documentary. When Burns replied that there were none, the project's boss, Maggie Rivas-Rodriguez spearheaded the Defend the Honor Campaign to force PBS to add a Hispanic perspective. PBS resisted, citing the special consideration given to Japanese Americans and African Americans, and that they couldn't include every group's experience. In a statement, Burns and co-producer Lynn Novick wrote, "We are dismayed and saddened by any assumption that we intentionally excluded anyone from our series on the Second World War. Nothing could be further from the truth. For thirty years we have made films that have tried to tell many of the stories that haven't been told in American history. In this latest project, we have attempted to show the universal human experience of war by focusing on the testimonies of just a handful of people—mostly from four American towns. As a result, millions of stories are not explored in our film."

Rivas-Rodriguez was unrelenting and her grass roots initiative enlisted the support of groups such as the National Hispanic Media Coalition, the National Institute for Latino Policy, and even the House Hispanic Caucus. "Our people weren't valued," she said. "Not only were they not valued then, they are not being valued today."

PBS CEO Paula Kerger met with a group of Hispanic leaders including Rivas-Rodriguez on March 6, but the network dug in its heels. In a letter to the attendees a few weeks later, Kerger touted PBS' commitment to reflect the Hispanic population in programs such as *Maya and Miguel*, *Los Niños en Su Casa*, and its "V-me" national Spanish-language network that features the best of public television. The battle finally ended when PBS announced that it would add material about the contributions of Hispanics to the war effort. They also said that a Hispanic producer would be hired to help with the content.

## Hispanics and World War II

By most accounts, there were between 250,000 and 500,000 Hispanics who served in the armed forces during World War II. This represents a range of 2.5 to 5 percent of all people who served during the war. Hispanics during that time were officially classified as "white" so no numbers were kept. To be precise, the census tracked "Mexicans" as a distinct race in 1930 for the first time, but this was abolished in 1940 when the census eliminated Mexicans as a racial category and began counting people of "Spanish Mother Tongue." There were 1.9 million that year. It wasn't until 1970 that the Census Bureau made any serious attempt to estimate the number of Hispanics.

During World War Two, Hispanics were allowed to hold U.S. citizenship, marry non-Hispanic whites (unlike blacks and Asians), and serve in all-white units. Japanese-American men fought while their families were in internment camps; African Americans fought in segregated units like the Tuskeegee Airmen; Navajo "Wind Talkers" gave the U.S. a code that was unbreakable. All these groups including Hispanics returned to face discrimination at home.

---

A three-day firestorm that erupted after two antigay reggae artists were invited to appear at an AIDS concert shows the power of bloggers to mobilize quickly and effectively. And it shows how blogs can further segment a market in a way that a bigger watchdog group cannot. In the summer of 2006, LIFEbeat, the music industry's AIDS organization, planned a Reggae Gold Live concert at New York's Webster Hall. But when word got out that performers included reggae artists Beenie Man and TOK—whose lyrics call for beating and killing gays—African American and Caribbean LGBT bloggers were outraged. LIFEbeat's executive director, told Associated Press that the performers' presence would "create dialogue around AIDS and the Caribbean-American community" and an "opportunity for groundbreaking change and good to come from it." Protesters were insulted that an organization whose mission is to educate youth about the dangers of HIV/AIDS invited musicians who celebrate brutality against gay men and lesbians. The promoters were taken aback. They didn't know how many LGBT bloggers of color there were, how many readers they had, and that they had the ability to mobilize so quickly. Their tone deaf, patronizing responses added fuel to the fire. Instead of canceling the offending artists, the promoters pulled the plug on the whole concert.

Even then, the promoters continued to face the wrath of bloggers, who were stunned that the group didn't get it. Bloggers spearheading the effort called LIFEbeat's stated rationale for canceling the concert—promoters said they feared "violence" if the concert were to go on—to be a cop out. Bloggers emphasized that no threats of violence were ever made against LIFEbeat's staff or board of directors, or the concert. Jasmyne Cannick, activist and blogger, said the campaign was simply to "educate LIFEbeat about the history of the performers that they choose and to make them aware of the recent murders of gay people in the Caribbean."

"Everything in their statement was an attempt to deflect from the real issue, which is homophobia and its connection to the spread of HIV/AIDS," author, TV personality Keith Boykin said. "Their statement is insulting and made it sound like the bloggers were inciting violence, and tried to make it sound like we don't care about the Caribbean AIDS crisis. The people making decisions at LIFEbeat have been totally clueless," Boykin said.

### Yo quiero Taco Bell

Sometimes, controversy can be turned into PR gold. The famous case of watchdog fever was in 1998 when "Dinky," a talking Chihuahua with a stereotypical Mexican accent, made his debut and immortalized the words "Yo quiero Taco Bell." Gabriel Cazares, a former mayor of Clearwater, Florida, and president of the Tampa chapter of the League of United Latin American Citizens (LULAC), got national attention when he called for a national Hispanic boycott of Taco Bell for its alleged stereotypical depiction of Mexicans, calling the ad "immigrant bashing," "insensitive," and "criminal." Another LULAC member charged that the ad sent the message that "Spanish is OK—for dogs." A result of the protests, Taco Bell received an outpouring of support from those who liked the Dinky character including LULAC headquarters in Washington, D.C., which said in an official statement that it was a "non-issue" and the organization had "more important substantive things to worry about."

Taco Bell did not pull the ads, did not issue an apology, and to this day the ad is well remembered. Because marketing strategies are held close to the vest in companies, we can't know what lesson

Taco Bell took from the ad. But if I had to guess, they became even less inclined to jump when a watchdog told them to do so.

Earlier in the book, I suggested doing some research on your own (when your time and budget allows). Damage control is one thing I don't advocate doing yourself, especially when your company is large, and it appears that a small flap could ignite into a huge controversy. There are simply too many pitfalls. In those cases, a good PR agency —one that clearly understands multicultural groups and their media outlets—can turn a potential loss into a win.

A simple "we're sorry," is sometimes the best response to quell the anger produced by a boneheaded marketing decision. In other circumstances, a more aggressive damage control strategy is needed. Other times, the watchdog's threats may amount to nothing, or, as in the case of Taco Bell, work in your favor. When it comes to watchdogs, the old adage "an ounce of prevention is worth a pound of cure" could not be truer. A good multicultural ad agency or strategy company, ideally with extensive experience with your target consumer, is always the best medicine.

A diverse staff also helps. Diversity means having people from a variety of backgrounds (ethnic and otherwise) who see things from a vantage point that is different from that of the white Anglo-Saxon heterosexual males who often are decision makers. Do your research. And work with a good multicultural public relations company to develop good disaster planning, just in case despite your best intentions, a watchdog starts chomping on your foot.

# Conclusion

When it comes to marketing to race, ethnicity and sexual orientation, Americans are in a bizarre place, somewhere between culturally
astute and clueless. Gone from advertising are the images of banjo-
eyed, slave-in-a-box Stepin Fetchits and pickaninnies, the greedy,
greasy Frito Banditos, the Fu Manchus, the Charlie Chans. Thanks
to the vigilance of watchdog groups like GLAAD and the Human
Rights Campaign, the shrieking queen, bull-dyke, "don't get too
close, gay boy"–laden humor of years past and present is on its way
to being an anachronism. Still, it seems like every week some commentator has been fired, some company is forced to pay millions
to the charity of the Reverend Sharpton's choosing, or some actor
is pressured by his studio to apologize for being racially insensitive. In most cases, regardless of whether or not the perpetrator
is truly a racist or homophobe, and precluding the possibility of
some kind of closet masochism at work, incidents are the results
of communication mistakes with a single cause: someone made
the assumption that everyone else was going to interpret what he
said in the same way that he himself understood it. "I didn't think
anyone would be offended," and "I was only trying to be funny," are
no longer acceptable excuses.

Effective communication and compelling marketing in today's
multicultural America is the converse of this. It stems from the
recognition that in a country as diverse as ours, we all interpret

messages through the lens of culture. Good multicultural marketers understand the important role that an identity based on race, ethnicity, or sexual orientation plays in the lives of those who are in the minority. They understand the need to make a special connection and they are good at doing so. They understand how to communicate to often misunderstood and ignored people that they are valued customers.

Things aren't likely to get any easier. The seven years from 2000 to 2007 brought 10.3 million immigrants to the United States, the largest seven year gain in U.S. history. Once we think we've figured things out, something changes. The immigrants acculturate. A new immigrant group arrives in large numbers. There's an addition to the triad of race, ethnicity, and sexual orientation such as religion or the haves and the have-nots. Or maybe the old distinctions just dissolve, as is happening in the case of people of mixed race.

For society, coming to grips with who we are in this fluid and quickly changing nation will remain challenging. For marketers, understanding race, ethnicity and sexual orientation is a bit easier. Do your market research. Use common sense. Do what you can to tune into the pulse of a rapidly changing population. Show a genuine interest in people from other cultures. Respect them. Like them. And they will likely reciprocate the gesture.

# Bibliography

Alba, Richard & Victor Nee, *Remaking the American Mainstream: Assimilation and Contemporary Immigration*, Cambridge: Harvard University Press, 2003.

Barone, Michael, *The New Americans: How the Melting Pot Can Work Again*, Washington D.C.: Regnery Publishing, Inc., 2006.

Bogle, Donald, *Prime Time Blues: African Americans on Network Television*, New York: Farrar, Straus and Giroux, 2001

————, *Toms, Coons, Mulattoes, Mammies, & Bucks*, New York: Continuum International Publishing Group, 2003.

Boykin, Keith, *Beyond the Down Low: Sex, Lies, and Denial in Black America*, New York: Carroll & Graf Publishers, 2005.

Buchanan, Patrick J., *The Death of the West: How Dying Populations and Immigrant Invasions Imperil Our Country and Civilization*, New York: St. Martin Press, 2002.

Correspondents of The New York Times, *How Race Is Lived in America: Pulling Together, Pulling Apart*, New York: Times Books, 2001.

Davila, Arlene, *Latinos Inc.: The Marketing and Making of a People*, Berkeley: University of California Press, 1965.

Edwards, Paul K., *The Southern Urban Negro as a Consumer*, New York: Prentice-Hall, 1932.

Garcia, Guy, *The New Mainstream: How the Multicultural Consumer Is Transforming American Business*, New York: Rayo-HarperCollins Publishers, Inc., 2004.

Goldman, Daniel, *Emotional Intelligence: Why It Can Matter More Than IQ*, New York: Bantam, 1995.

Graves, Earl G., *How to Succeed in Business Without Being White: Straight Talk on Making It in America*, New York: Collins Business, 1998.

Halter, Marilyn, *Shopping for Identity: The Marketing of Ethnicity*, New York: Schocken Books, 2000.

Hamamoto, Darrell Y., *Monitored Peril: Asian Americans and the Politics of TV Representation*, Minneapolis: University of Minnesota Press, 1994.

Hollinger, David A., *Postethnic America: Beyond Multiculturalism*, New York: Basic Books, 1995.

Hyun, Jane, *Breaking the Bamboo Ceiling: Career Strategies for Asians*, New York: Collins Business, 2006.

Jacoby, Tamar, *Reinventing the Melting Pot: The New Immigrants and What It Means To Be American*, New York: Basic Books, 2004.

Jhally, Sut and Justin M. Lewis, *Enlightened Racism: The Cosby Show, Audiences, and the Myth of the American Dream*, Boulder: Westview Press, 1992.

Kelts, Roland, *Japanamerica: How Japanese Pop Culture Has Invaded the U.S.*, New York: Palgrave MacMillian, 2006.

Kern-Forxworth, Marilyn, *Aunt Jemima, Uncle Ben, and Rastus: Blacks in Advertising, Yesterday, Today, and Tomorrow*, (Westport: Praeger, 1994.

Kibria, Nazli, *Becoming Asian American: Second Generation Chinese and Korean American Identities*, Baltimore: The Johns Hopkins University Press, 2002.

Kitwana, Bakari, *The Hip Hop Generation: The Crisis in African American Culture*, New York: Basic Civitas Books, 2002.

————, *Why White Kids Love Hip Hop: Wankstas, Wiggers, Wannabes, and the New Reality of Race in America*, New York: Basic Civitas Books, 2006.

Korzenny, Felipe and Betty Ann Korzenny, *Hispanic Marketing: A Cultural Perspective*, Burlington, MA: Elsevier Butterworth Heinemann, 2005.

Lee, Jennifer and Min Zhou, *Asian American Youth: Culture, Identity and Ethnicity*, New York: Routledge, 2004.

Lee, Robert G., *Orientals: Asian Americans in Popular Culture*, Philadelphia: Temple University Press, 1999.

Lee, Stacey J., *Unraveling the "Model Minority" Stereotype: Listening to Asian American Youth*, New York, NY: Teachers College Columbia University, 1996.

Lind, Michael, *The Next American Nation: The New Nationalism and the Fourth American Revolution*, New York: Free Press Paperbacks, 1995.

MacDonald, J. Fred, *Blacks and White TV: African Americans in Television Since 1948*, Chicago: Nelson-Hall, Inc. Publishers, 1992.

Manring, M. M., *Slave in a Box: The Strange Career of Aunt Jemima*, Charlottesville, VA: University of Virginia Press, 1995.

Miller, Pepper and Herb Kemp, *What's Black About It? Insights to Increase Your Share of a Changing African-American Market*, Ithaca, NY: Paramount Market Publishing, Inc., 2005.

Min, Pyong Gap, *Asian Americans: Contemporary Trends and Issues*, Thousand Oaks, CA: SAGE Publications, Inc., 1995.

Morales, Ed, *Living in Spanglish: The Search for Latino Identity in America*, New York: St. Martin's Press, 2002.

Perkins, William Eric, *Droppin' Science: Critical Essays on Rap Music and Hip Hop Culture*, (Philadelphia: Temple University Press, 1995.

Portes, Alejandro, *The New Second Generation*, New York: Russell Sage Foundation, 1996.

Portes, Alejandro and Ruben G. Rumbaut, *Immigrant America: A Portrait*, Berkeley: University of California Press, 1996.

————, *Legacies: The Story of the Immigrant Second Generation*, Berkeley: University of California Press, 2001.

————, *Ethnicities: Children of Immigrants in America*, Berkeley and Los Angeles: University of California Press, 2001.

Ramos, Jorge, *The Latino Wave: How Hispanics Will Elect the Next American President*, New York: Rayo, 2005.

Shorris, Earl, *Latinos: A Biography of the People*, New York: W.W.Norton & Company, Inc., 1992.

Takaki, Ronald, *Strangers from a Different Shore: A History of Asian Americans*, New York: A Back Bay Books, 1989.

*A Different Mirror: A History of Multicultural America*, New York: A Back Bay Books, 1993.

Talty, Stephan, *Mulatto America: At the Crossroads of Black and White Culture: A Social History*, New York: Perennial-HarperCollins Publishers, Inc., 2003.

Tatum, Beverly Daniel, *Why Are All the Black Kids Sitting Together in the Cafeteria? A Psychologist Explains the Development of Racial Identity*, New York: Basic Books, 1997.

Thernstrom, Stephan and Abigail Thernstrom, *America in Black and White: One Nation, Indivisible*, New York: Touchstone, 1997.

Tuan, Mia, *Forever Foreigners or Honorary Whites? The Asian Ethnic Experience Today*, New Bruswick, NJ: Rutgers University Press, 1968.

Tung, May Paomay, Ph.D., *Chinese Americans and Their Immigrant Parents: Conflict, Identity, and Values*, Binghamton, NY: The Haworth Clinical Practice Press, 2000.

Valdes, M. Isabel and Marta H. Seoane, *Hispanic Market Handbook*, New York: Gale Research Inc., 1995.

Valdes, M. Isabel, *Marketing to American Latinos: A Guide to the In-Culture Approach*, Ithaca, NY: Paramount Market Publishing, Inc., 2000.

Walters, Suzanna Danuta, *All the Rage: The Story of Gay Visibility in America*, Chicago: The University of Chicago Press, 2001.

Waters, Mary C., *Black Identities: West Indian Immigrant Dreams and American Realities*, New York: Russell Sage Foundation, 1999.

Waters, Mary C., and Reed Ueda with Marrow, Helen B., *The New Americans: A Guide to Immigration since 1965*, Cambridge: Harvard University Press, 2007.

West, Cornel, *Race Matters*, New York: Vintage Books, 1994.

Wilson II, Clint and Felix Gutierrez, *Minorities and Media: Diversity and the End of Mass Communication*, (Newbury Park: SAGE Publications, Inc., 1985.

Witeck, Robert and Combs, Wesley. *Business Inside Out: Capturing Millions of Brand Loyal Gay Consumers*, New York: Kaplan Business, 2006.

Wu, Frank H., *Yellow: Race in America Beyond Black and White*, New York: Basic Books, 2002.

Wynter, Leon E., *American Skin: Pop Culture, Big Business, and the End of White America*, New York: Crown Publishers, 2000.

Yancey, George, *Who is White?: Latinos, Asians, and the New Black/Nonblack Divide*, Boulder: Lynne Rienner Publishers, Inc., 2004.

Zia, Helen, *Asian American Dreams: The Emergence of an American People*, New York, NY: Farrar, Straus and Giroux, 2000.

# Index

# About the Author

**David Morse** is the President and CEO of New American Dimensions, the nation's leading multicultural market research and consulting firm specializing in analysis and intelligence on the "hyphenated American." The company has pioneered in-depth research techniques that incorporate regional, generational, acculturation, and lifestyle factors to identify and articulate the complex consumer landscape to its clients. David and his colleagues have advised clients that include Fortune 100 executives, marketers, and key business leaders on strategizing and executing million dollar campaigns.

Mr. Morse is uniquely positioned to identify the complex and changing attitudes of hyphenated Americans; he regularly travels the country conducting field research as a focus group moderator. His 25 years of experience includes senior marketing and market research positions in the U.S. and abroad at Levi Strauss & Co, Gillette de Mexico, Southern Pacific Transportation Company, and American Honda Motor Company.

Frequently quoted by the media such as *The New York Times, The New York Post, The Christian Science Monitor, La Opinión, the Dallas Morning News*, and the Associated Press, Mr. Morse often speaks to national companies, research groups, and marketing industry conferences about current and future consumer trends in the U.S., especially as it relates to how ethnic Americans are rewriting the rules of the marketplace.

He is a discussion moderator and panelist for the Multicultural Marketplace column on RetailWire.com, an online retail industry news analysis and discussion forum. He also publishes a blog titled "Morse's Code" on NewAmericanDimensions.com. Most recently, his article "America in Black and White" was a featured chapter in the Cabletelevision Advertising Bureau's 1997 book *Race, Relevance, Revenue*.

David holds a Master of International Management degree from Thunderbird, The American Graduate School of International Management. There he specialized in Consumer Marketing with a special emphasis on Latin America. His Bachelor of Arts in Psychology and Japanese Studies is from the University of New Hampshire. He also speaks Japanese and is fluent in Spanish.